GRETZKY TO LEMIEUX

GRETZKY TO LEMIEUX

THE STORY OF THE
1987 CANADA CUP

ED WILLES

McCLELLAND & STEWART

Library and Archives Canada Cataloguing in Publication

Willes, Ed
   Gretzky to Lemieux : the story of the 1987 Canada Cup / Ed Willes.

ISBN 978-0-7710-8942-8

   1. Canada Cup (Hockey) – History.   2. Gretzky, Wayne, 1961-.
3. Lemieux, Mario, 1965-.   4. Hockey – History.   I. Title.

GV847.7.W54 2007   796.962´66   C2007-901045-8

We acknowledge the financial support of the Government of Canada through the Book Publishing Industry Development Program and that of the Government of Ontario through the Ontario Media Development Corporation's Ontario Book Initiative. We further acknowledge the support of the Canada Council for the Arts and the Ontario Arts Council for our publishing program.

Typeset in Bembo by M&S, Toronto
Printed and bound in Canada

This book is printed on acid-free paper that is 100% recycled, ancient-forest friendly (100% post-consumer recycled).

McClelland & Stewart Ltd.
75 Sherbourne Street
Toronto, Ontario
M5A 2P9
www.mcclelland.com

1 2 3 4 5   11 10 09 08 07

This book is dedicated to Joe Carveth,
his teammate Gordie Howe, and a generation of players
who gave more to the game than they took out of it.

CONTENTS

ACKNOWLEDGEMENTS

Prying history out of hockey people is sometimes a difficult exercise. Thankfully, that was not the case with this project. The author would like to thank all the parties interviewed and extend special thanks to Mike Keenan, Dale Hawerchuk, Igor Larionov, Kelly Hrudey, Wayne Gretzky, and Jean Perron for their time and their candour; Jay Greenberg for providing valuable resource material; Mike Armstrong for being a great hockey fan; and Igor Kuperman for his pro bono fact checking.

I t is the final minute of the second period in Game 2 of the 1987 Canada Cup final and the Canadians and Soviets have been battling like Carthage and Rome for two hours. This game, the greatest hockey game ever played, will continue for two more hours, ending midway through the second overtime period when Wayne Gretzky sets up Mario Lemieux for his third goal of the game, giving Canada a 6–5 win and tying the series at one game apiece. Gretzky records five assists this night. Canada has forty-five scoring chances, the Soviets thirty-eight. Four times the Soviets fall behind and claw back to tie, but they can never get the go-ahead goal behind the unflappable Grant Fuhr in the Canadian net. Canada also plays the game with ten forwards, and head coach Mike Keenan will use twenty-nine different line combinations.

Gretzky calls the 1987 Canada Cup the greatest hockey of his career and this shift is a tiny, perfect microcosm of those glorious three nights in September. Gretzky has been sprung on a three-on-two rush courtesy of a surgical breakout pass from Paul Coffey. Lemieux is on his right. Michel Goulet is on his left. Defending for the Russians are Viacheslav Fetisov and Alexei Kasatonov, the best blue line pairing in the world. As he gains the Russian zone, Gretzky, a left-handed shot, veers to his right, taking Fetisov with him, and everyone at Copps Coliseum is expecting a pass to Lemieux, including Lemieux, who's scored on a textbook two-on-one with Gretzky just three minutes before. But, as Fetisov overplays to Lemieux's side, Gretzky lays a no-look, backhand saucer pass to Goulet, who is all alone in front of Russian goalie Evgeny Belosheikin. The pass, made while Gretzky is moving at top speed, is so soft and delicate it almost melts into the ice. It also puts Goulet a shade too tight to the Russian goalie and Belosheikin, who will die by his own hand twelve years later, has no trouble making the save.

But the play is not over. The puck is scrambled out near the Russian blue line, where Russian star Vladimir Krutov is trying to gain clear possession. Gretzky re-materializes in front of him, steals the puck, then chips it past Kasatonov, who is about to head up-ice. Again, Gretzky is on the attack, with Lemieux on his right. Again, he drives toward Lemieux, taking the Russian defence and Belosheikin with him.

With all eyes on Gretzky, however, a whipped Goulet has limped to the Team Canada bench, where twenty-four-year-old Doug Gilmour leaps over the boards and charges into the play. This time Gretzky is on his forehand before he executes a slight pivot and leaves the puck for Gilmour, who is unchecked and looking at three-quarters of an empty net. The crowd is on its feet again. Gilmour fires, and, out of nowhere, Krutov frantically slides into Gilmour's shooting lane and deflects the puck over the glass.

The whole sequence, from the moment Coffey starts the rush from behind the Team Canada net, takes twenty-five seconds in real time. At its conclusion, Gretzky hobbles to the Team Canada bench and leans over, spent. Lemieux slumps by the far post next to Belosheikin. The crowd at Copps is on its feet. To this point, they've already been up and down twenty times, saluting each highlight with a standing ovation. They will be on their feet twenty more times before the game finally ends at about one in the morning, after an exhausted Gretzky wets himself on the Team Canada bench, after Fuhr keeps Canada in the game and the series with an epic performance, after Gretzky sets up

Lemieux for the game-winner and finally they float out of Copps only to return two nights later to a game that isn't quite as artistic but is every bit as dramatic.

It's now almost twenty years after the fact but this hockey still throbs with an energy so great it takes your breath away. Rick Tocchet, the Team Canada forward who will announce his presence to the game during the tournament, still has tapes of those final three games that he watches when his confidence needs boosting. "It still gives me tingles," he says.

In Detroit, Igor Larionov, the magical Russian centreman who played on the greatest five-man unit the game has ever seen, still marvels at this tournament. "You can talk about the '72 series," Larionov says. "That was the first page of the history. But '87 was like pure hockey. There were no systems. There were no traps. We just played wide-open, instinctive hockey. You can't really say the Canadians won and the Russians lost. Hockey won in that series."

Keenan, of course, isn't quite as philosophical about the final outcome but even the veteran coach, who's never been confused for the sensitive type, turns poetic as he recalls the series. "If Gary Bettman wants to change the face of hockey, someone should show him that series and tell him, 'This is what we're trying to achieve.'" Keenan says. "The speed, the cadence of what was happening at ice level was unbelievable. You didn't have the time to be reflective while it's going on. You had to be in the moment and even a little ahead of the moment. But sitting here in my office now I can say, 'Wow, that was incredible.'"

So can every hockey fan who witnessed those three games; who saw hockey played at its highest purpose; who saw two teams explore the sport's endless possibilities. The final series also represents a remarkable moment of convergence for the feature players, all of whom are at the peak of their Hall-of-Fame careers. Gretzky, at twenty-six, is at the apex of his powers. His teammates Mark Messier and Coffey are the same age and at the same stage in their careers. Lemieux, the twenty-one-year-old acolyte, learns the secrets of greatness from the Oilers. Brian Propp is the oldest player on the Team Canada roster. He's twenty-eight.

It's a similar story on the Soviet side. Fetisov and the brilliant Sergei Makarov are both twenty-nine, which makes them old men in this series. The other three members of the Green Unit – Larionov, Krutov, and Kasatonov – are all twenty-seven. Breakout Russian star Valeri Kamensky is twenty-one. And for all that, perhaps the most extraordinary thing about this series is the whole is greater than the sum of these matchless parts. "I don't know why anyone ever asks me about the '81 Canada Cup," Kasatonov says with a laugh, referring to the Russian win six years earlier. "It's always '84 and '87. I guess '87 was more dramatic, but in Russia we always want to talk about the '81 Canada Cup."

So let's savour this moment. Let's remember those three nights in September 1987 when things were as they'd always been between Russia and Canada but never would be again. The Russians, who are hearing about this new idea, perestroika, will never be the same. The Edmonton Oilers, who've built a dynasty in northern Alberta, are hearing about a new world that offers new riches and will never be the same. Alan Eagleson, the show's impresario, is hearing the first rumbles of discontent from his constituents and his empire is also starting to crumble. But all this will happen soon enough. Right now, it's about the hockey, the best hockey ever played.

"Hockey like this?" said Team Canada assistant Jean Perron. "I've never seen hockey like this. No one has ever seen hockey like this."

CHAPTER I

The Making of a Team

For the first time in his life, Wayne Gretzky was tired of hockey.

He was tired after another marathon season with the Edmonton Oilers. He was tired of GM Glen Sather's constant needling and mind games. He was tired of being ground by Peter Pocklington, the Oilers' doofus owner who'd lucked into the most talented team in hockey history. Gretzky had started with the Oilers as a scrawny seventeen-year-old in a league that no longer existed and over the next nine seasons, he and an incredible group of players had conquered the NHL. But no matter what he did – 215 points in one season, ninety-six goals in another, eight Hart Trophies, four Stanley Cups; things, in short, no one had done before or has done since – it never seemed to be enough for the team's management or hockey fans who expected the impossible from him every night. Between the pre-season, regular season, playoffs, and various All-Star Games and international tournaments, he'd averaged well over 100 games a year over the previous five campaigns and that fearsome workload had taken its toll. Few people outside of his inner circle seemed to understand, but the Great One was burnt to a crisp. And now Alan Eagleson was calling with the same sales pitch Gretzky had been hearing since he was sixteen. Eagleson was staging his fourth Canada Cup and he needed the game's greatest star to pull it off. The Eagle didn't present it that way, of course. Instead, he appealed to Gretzky as a hockey player and a Canadian. The game needs you. Your country needs you. The Players' Association needs you. It wasn't easy saying no to Alan Eagleson, and Gretzky, whose preternatural sense of anticipation wasn't limited to the ice, could see it all coming. Back in February, during Rendez-Vous '87, he had even sounded off on the subject, suggesting, politely of course, that maybe the tournament should be pushed back to '89.

He also knew he should have saved his breath.

"I think we should have waited until 1989," Gretzky said at the time. "The players have no objections to playing in these series, but maybe somewhere along the line the owners have to step in and say well, maybe it's physically and mentally too much. . . . I think the owners should sit down with Mr. Eagleson and talk to him and say maybe we should play in '89 and give the players a little rest."

It didn't dawn on Gretzky, or anyone else in hockey for that matter, that it was a trifle odd that he was asking NHL owners to speak to the head of the Players' Association on behalf of the players, but others would take note of Eagleson's methods soon enough. "It just seemed like hockey was going from June 15 to the end of July every year," Gretzky says. "I was just fatigued mentally and physically."

There were other things on Gretzky's mind as the Canada Cup approached. The previous year, the Oilers had won their third Stanley Cup in four seasons, celebrating their Game-7 triumph over Mike Keenan's Philadelphia Flyers on May 31, and Gretzky was trying to renegotiate his convoluted personal-services contract with Pocklington. He wanted a deal that would make him an Oiler for the rest of his career before he assumed a management position with the franchise, because that's the way he always thought it would go. But that idea, which once seemed like a foregone conclusion, had become more complicated with each passing year and now he was beginning to wonder about Pocklington's motives and his own future with the team.

If that wasn't enough, Gretzky also had a new woman in his life, the actress Janet Jones. They'd first met in 1981, when he was a celebrity judge on the TV show *Dance Fever* and she, a sixteen-year-old contestant. Six years later they met again by chance at a basketball game in Los Angeles, about the time Jones was making an appearance in *Playboy*, and the sparks flew. Both had just ended long-term relationships, Gretzky with the singer Vicky Moss and Jones with tennis star Vitus Gerulaitis, and they were from different worlds – Brampton and St. Louis? Hockey and Hollywood? But there was something about this one that felt very real and very permanent from the beginning.

Add it all up and it was clear the last thing Gretzky wanted to do was cut his summer in half to begin the arduous process of preparing for a Canada Cup. In the end, he knew he didn't have a great deal of choice in the matter, but, in a rare display of militancy, he made Eagleson sweat before he committed to Team Canada.

As far back as June, stories were appearing in the popular press about the Great One's reticence and that precipitated a shitstorm across the country. A story ran in the *Globe and Mail* on July 9, less than a month before the Team Canada camp was set to open, which said Sather was begging off Team Canada duty this time and was instructing his players to follow suit.

That story caught people's attention and had Eagleson on the defensive. "It's the players who will make the final decision," the Eagle sniffed in response. "If a Wayne Gretzky wants to play, there's nothing Glen Sather can do about it."

Sather, for his part, backpedalled furiously, saying he hadn't talked to Eagleson about his participation. As for his players, Sather said: "I haven't got any control over the players in the summertime. Everyone is over twenty-one. How can I tell Canadian players they can't play for Canada?"

Three days later, a subdued Sather, who was in charge in 1984, appeared at a press conference hosted by Eagleson that announced the four-man conglomerate that would select the players and coaches for Team Canada. Sather joined Flyers GM Bobby Clarke, Montreal GM Serge Savard, and Rangers GM Phil Esposito on the selection committee, but it was clear from the start his heart wasn't in it this time. Clarke and Savard would eventually run the show and that suited Sather just fine. His biggest contribution to the effort would consist of hosting a couple of Team Canada gatherings at his mansion in Banff. "I told [Eagleson] I wasn't that keen on running things again," Sather said at the presser. "But I never considered not taking part in some fashion. I just want it structured so I get some free time."

The Gretzky soap opera, meanwhile, would take a little longer to play out. Shortly after Sather announced he was on board, sort of, Eagleson told a couple of reporters in Detroit that Gretzky was delaying his decision because of negotiations with Sather and Pocklington over a new deal. That suggestion generated a swift response from the Gretzky camp. "Alan Eagleson should mind his own business," said Mike Barnett, then Gretzky's business manager. "I know he wears a lot of hats in hockey but this is one he doesn't wear."

And even the normally placid Gretzky was irked at Eagleson's presumption. "I hope Alan isn't trying to embarrass me into playing," he said. "He's not going to influence me."

But Gretzky was conflicted over the matter. His preference was to opt out and he was being encouraged in that direction by Sather and the Edmonton media. He made no attempt to hide his feelings. "We've got to stop playing summer hockey," he said, before adding, "I think the ideal would be to play [the Canada Cup] every six years. That way, every great player would be asked, once in his career, to dedicate one summer of his life to playing in the Canada Cup."

The same day those quotes appeared in the *Edmonton Journal*, another story ran in the paper under the headline: "Gretzky agrees to a new deal." That story reported that Gretzky's personal-services contract with Pocklington, which was set to run to 2002, was rewritten to end in 1992. Gretzky's contract had been the subject of considerable conjecture over the years. He was said to be making about CAD$1 million, annually, a figure that, even by the standards of the time, would have made him sinfully under-paid. But no one in Edmonton seemed to know what exactly were the terms of his singular agreement with Pocklington. "To be honest I can't remember if I ever signed that deal," Gretzky says. "It was all handshakes. There wasn't a lot on paper. It was ridiculous in those days."

Still, people in Edmonton took great comfort in Gretzky's pronouncement he was happy in Edmonton, and the general perception was he would sign one more contract with the Oilers before retiring. True, there were disturbing reports that the New York Rangers were offering Pocklington $15 million for his prize jewel, but, in the summer of 1987, players didn't leave their teams for money and free agency wasn't an option. "People making comments about that forgot to ask Wayne Gretzky if he'd like to play [in New York]," said Gretzky. "I wouldn't. The grass isn't always greener elsewhere. I like the city and the people here. I enjoy playing in Edmonton. Under no circumstances do I want to leave."

A year later, some unforeseen circumstances must have arisen.

As for the matter of Team Canada, Gretzky travelled to Brampton in late July to consult with his father, and, in the end, it was Walter Gretzky who would remind his son of the reality of his situation. At the family home, Walter laid out his son's choices to him. You can skip the tournament, he said, in which case you'll be branded a traitor. You can also show up and go through the motions, in which case they'll call you a quitter. Maybe it's not fair but, in the end, the only choice you have is to play and play well, which, come to think of it, is the only choice Gretzky ever had in his career.

"I was twenty-six," Gretzky says with a shrug. "What else was I going to do?"

Following his heart-to-heart with his dad, Gretzky revealed to an Edmonton radio station that he'd decided to play for Team Canada with the understanding he'd get a few days off from the Oilers after the tournament. He also said his father had "suggested" this was the wisest course of action. Gretzky then returned to Edmonton, where New York Islanders goalie Kelly Hrudey was spending the summer. Hrudey, who'd earned an invitation to the Team Canada camp following his breakout performance against the Washington Capitals in the 1987 playoffs, was about to begin training when, out of the blue, he got a call from Gretzky. I've rented this rink in Edmonton, Gretzky said, you want to start working out? Hrudey, who'd just finished his fourth season in the NHL, was understandably thrilled and presented himself at the appointed hour and began donning his equipment in a deserted locker room.

"I was thinking it was going to be a bunch of guys," says Hrudey. "I'm sitting in the dressing room getting ready and wondering if I had the right time or if everyone was late. Then Wayne walks in with Janet. He goes, Do you mind if Janet skates with us?" And his assessment of the future Mrs. Great One as a hockey player? "Honestly, she wasn't bad," says Hrudey.

"I always wanted a defenceman to move around and a goalie to shoot at," says Gretzky. "So Janet was the defenceman and Kelly was the goalie. My wife's a pretty good athlete."

Gretzky would be Eagleson's last holdout. His Oiler buddies were already on board. Mark Messier? Are you kidding? Another shot at the Russians? Mess wouldn't miss that for the world. Grant Fuhr? Just tell him where the game was and what time they dropped the puck. Paul Coffey? Cripes, he might have been the most competitive guy in the whole group. Glenn Anderson? Who knew what he was thinking, but he always showed up and he always played his ass off. They were an unusual confederacy, five incandescent talents, five disparate personalities, but they lived for challenges like this. They also subscribed to the Oilers' ethic that, loosely stated, demanded you play like hell on the ice and, if you were of a mind, play like hell off it. This would meet with some resistance from Keenan, but, in time, that ethic would come to define Team Canada. "You think about it," says Messier. "From '84 to '90, we won five Stanley Cups and we played an amazing amount of hockey, but we were young and it never seemed like too much. We were into it."

The rest of the players didn't have to be asked twice. They regarded it as an honour and a privilege when Eagleson came calling and there was no question that they would play. Nor was there much of a question about the training camp. The players were polled informally and asked if they wanted the GMs and coaches to simply select the team or if they would prefer the gruelling three-week camp that offered no guarantees. They wanted the camp. They wanted the competition.

"After calling all the players I could reach, I was surprised because I had read so many times in the newspapers that many players wouldn't attend," Savard said as the stars filed into the camp. "But it took two seconds for them to say they'd be honoured to play for Canada."

Many of them had been through it before. There were the veterans of the '84 Canada Cup – Brent Sutter, Ray Bourque, Mike Gartner, Michel Goulet. There were the young, emerging stars – Mario Lemieux, Doug Gilmour, Rick Tocchet, and Larry Murphy. And there was still another group who had something to prove – Dale Hawerchuk, Brian Propp, Craig Hartsburg, and

Doug Crossman. Hawerchuk, especially, longed to be included on this team, longed to be recognized as something other than a Gretzky poseur who piled up points in Winnipeg but had little substance to his game. He was a long shot to make the team that year, especially as a centreman where he was competing against Gretzky, Lemieux, and Messier. But over the next two months, the hockey world would change its opinion of Hawerchuk. "I wasn't invited in '84 and I'm not sure if they saw me making the team in '87," he says. "Sometimes I just think it was Sather and he didn't want me to see too much or learn too much. I just wanted the opportunity. Just give me the shot, that's all I asked for. And Keenan gave me the shot."

Thirty-seven players would be invited to the Team Canada camp in Montreal and, despite the presence of so many familiar faces, it was apparent there would be changes this time around. Larry Robinson, the patriarch of the Canadian defence for so many years, was thirty-six and begged off, citing a commitment to a polo tournament of all things. Doug Wilson, another main-stay of the blue line, was out with a back problem, as was Calgary's Paul Reinhart. The Oilers' Kevin Lowe had groin issues and he, too, was unavailable for selection.

So the defensive corps would be diminished. But the biggest change on Team Canada by far would be that, for the first time in the 1980s, the roster would not bear the stamp of the New York Islanders' dynasty.

Al Arbour's team won four consecutive Stanley Cups from 1980 to 1983, and, in the early part of the decade, his players had dominated the Canada Cup teams in much the same manner that the Oilers would dominate the '87 team. A check of the Teams Canada through the 1980s, in fact, reveals the shift in power from Long Island to the Alberta capital during those years.

The '81 Team Canada, which was drubbed by the Soviets 8–1 in the gold-medal game, featured five Islanders: Mike Bossy,

Bryan Trottier, Clark Gillies, Denis Potvin, and Butch Goring. The only Oiler on that team was Gretzky.

The '84 team also had five Islanders – Bossy, Trottier, Sutter, Bob Bourne, and tournament MVP John Tonelli – but they were offset, and then some, by a seven-player contingent from the Oilers: Gretzky, Messier, Coffey, Fuhr, Anderson, Lowe, and Randy Gregg.

The previous spring, the Oilers had snapped the Isles' Cup run and started one of their own. That development also created some interesting dynamics within the Team Canada locker room in the '84 tournament. Somewhere between their meeting in the '81 playoffs; the Islanders' sweeping the Oilers in the '83 Cup final; and the Oilers dethroning the Isles the next year, a fairly intense rivalry had developed between the two factions that made team building a difficult enterprise in the '84 event. In the early going, the five Islanders would dress in silence on one side of the room across from the equally icy Oilers. "There were some pretty strong characters in that room," says Doug Wilson, one of the few neutrals on the team. "You could feel the chill in the air."

Robinson helped start the thaw with some gentle diplomacy and a few good-natured barbs. Sather then brokered a sitdown between the two groups where the air was cleared after a few nervous moments. The Islanders, specifically Bourne, opened the meeting by stating, not too delicately, that they hated the Oilers. They hated them for singing, "Here we go Oilers, here we go" during their '81 playoff series. They hated their cockiness and their arrogance. But, mostly, they hated them for ending their streak of four consecutive Cups.

Gretzky then spoke, telling the Islanders how much he and his teammates respected them and how much they'd learned from them. He related the now-famous story from the '83 Cup finals, in which the Oilers walked past the victorious Islanders' dressing room, saw they were too tired and beat up to properly celebrate, and, for the first time, understood the price of victory.

The speech made the peace, and Canada would rebound from their humiliating '81 defeat with a gold-medal performance in '84, highlighted by an overtime win against the Russians in the semifinal. Fittingly, Bossy scored the game-winning goal on an assist from Coffey.

By the time the 1987 tournament rolled around, however, Sutter was the only holdover from the Islanders' Cup-winners who would make the team. Bossy's back had given out. Potvin was one year from retirement. Trottier would play for Team USA. Tonelli, the hero of '84, was starting the back nine of his career.

Their veteran presence would be missed, but their absences also created employment opportunities on Team Canada for an exciting new generation of players, some of whom were already proven NHL stars and others who were on the cusp of stardom. Clearly, the team would be led by the Oilers, but Keenan and his staff were also selecting from another layer of players who were taking their first steps into the spotlight. It might not have been the most impressive pool of Canadian players ever brought together for one training camp – in context, the '76 group was probably superior. But given the personalities involved and the time in their careers, it was certainly the most intriguing.

"Most of them were twenty-six, twenty-seven and were already experienced players," says Keenan. "Then we had the young guys who were trying to establish themselves. I know there's been some controversy since about players begging off but it didn't happen with them. They were excited about the opportunity."

That much was apparent when the camp opened on August 3 at The Forum in Montreal on a sweltering summer day. As mentioned, original invitees Lowe, Reinhart, and Wilson were nursing injuries and they would be replaced by Philadelphia's Brad McCrimmon, St. Louis's Rob Ramage, and Vancouver's Doug Lidster on the blue line. The mass defections as prophesied by the *Globe*, however, never materialized. Gretzky was there. All the Oilers were there. So were the game's greatest players. And what a group they were – young, confident, like Alexander the Great's army on the eve of battle. Together, they would embark on a memorable adventure. Together, they would make hockey history.

"I had them all at Rendez-Vous," says Perron, who had coached the NHL All-Stars at the two-game set. "I remember the power-play meetings in the video room at The Colisée [in Quebec City]. Wayne, Mario, Messier, Bourque, they'd be sitting there like school kids in a classroom, raising their hands and asking questions. What if we try this? What if we try that? I kept thinking, 'I want to get all their autographs.'"

"It was probably the best team ever," says assistant coach John Muckler, who had a front-row seat for the Oilers' dynasty. "It was certainly the greatest team I ever saw." Still, there were a few surprises in that original group. Just four goalies were invited to the camp – Fuhr, Hrudey, the Flyers' Ron Hextall, and Montreal's Patrick Roy – and many pundits wondered aloud why Hartford's Mike Liut and Calgary's Mike Vernon hadn't been extended a tryout. Goaltending, after all, had been an issue in '84, when Fuhr was injured, leaving the workload to Pete Peeters and Reggie Lemelin. The preponderance of grinders in camp was also noted. A gifted centreman like Chicago's Denis Savard hadn't been invited but Keenan's Flyers (Rick Tocchet? Derrick Smith?) were, as well as muckers like Claude Lemieux and Kevin Dineen. Who was going to score the goals in this lineup? Who was going to provide the offensive spark?

Then there was the issue at centre ice. Nine natural centres were invited to the camp and while it was clear not all would make the team, it was also clear some of them would have to play out of position. Gretzky, naturally, would centre the first line, but after him the picture was fuzzy. There was talk about moving Messier, arguably the second-best pivot in the game, to the wing, where he'd started his career. It figured Lemieux would centre a line but this would also be his first Canada Cup experience and no one knew what to expect from the young star. Behind that trio there was Hawerchuk, who was coming off his fourth straight hundred-point season in Winnipeg; Steve Yzerman, who'd made the '84 team as a nineteen-year-old; Gilmour who was coming off a breakout 105-point season with St. Louis; Sutter, who was a point-a-game player in those days, and, above all else, a Sutter; Flyers captain Dave Poulin, who'd played in Rendez-Vous '87; and New Jersey's Kirk Muller, who offered an enticing size-and-skill package. Somewhere in there, something had to give.

"Mike was in a panic because we had so many centremen," Serge Savard says. "I said, 'Don't worry about that. They can play the wing.' For players like that, it's not a big problem."

The final distinguishing feature of the training-camp roster concerned the age of so many of the players. As mentioned, the core of the team were all in their mid- to late-twenties, but they were greybeards compared to some of the other faces at the camp. Toronto's Wendel Clark was twenty and had scored 34 and 37 goals in his first two seasons with the Leafs. Boston's Cam Neely, twenty-two, had just enjoyed a breakout 36-goal campaign in 1986–87. Washington's Scott Stevens, twenty-three, had already played five full NHL seasons, including a 61-point, 283-penalty-minute year in 1986–87. Calgary's Al MacInnis, twenty-two, scored 20 goals that same season. Yzerman, twenty-two, had put in four full seasons in Detroit and was already the Wings' captain. Neely, Stevens, MacInnis, and Yzerman would go on to put in Hall-of-Fame careers, and only injuries would prevent Clark from reaching similar heights. But none, remarkably, would survive the final cuts.

"What a group they were," Keenan says. "But a lot of those players were boys compared to the guys who made the team."

No, for Keenan, most of the youngsters represented a great

unknown. And maybe that's fitting because Keenan certainly represented an unknown quantity to most of his players.

In three short years with the Flyers, the Whitby, Ontario, native had established himself as the brightest young coach in the NHL, but he was far from a proven commodity. The job, by all rights, should have belonged to Glen Sather, but the Oilers' overlord declined the position. Sather did encourage Muckler, his long-time lieutenant, to take one of the assistants' jobs, and Muckler would join Keenan's staff along with Tom Watt and Perron.

"It was kind of different for me being there without Glen," says Muckler. "In '84, it was Glen, Teddy Green [another Oilers' assistant], and me. It was an Oilers' act. [In '87], we had our differences but we got it together."

Sather, as we've seen, would accept one of the four GM positions doled out by Eagleson but never played a lead role in the team's affairs. That left the coaching position to Keenan, a logical choice given a) he was an Eagleson client and b) the Flyers' showing in the '85 and '87 Cup finals. It was also far from the safest choice Team Canada's management could have made and as is usually the case with Keenan, his personality and his methods were as much a part of the story as his coaching genius.

Keenan was just thirty-eight at the time of his appointment and his path to the NHL was as curious as the man himself. He'd earned a hockey scholarship to St. Lawrence College in upstate New York, where, as a defenceman/right winger, he played with long-time NHL coach Jacques Martin, was the lead singer in a frathouse band called Nik and the Nice Guys, and generally offered no indication that he was a Hall-of-Fame coach in the making. Keenan, in fact, would lose his scholarship and regain it before graduating with a Bachelor of Science from St. Lawrence. He then attended the University of Toronto, where he won a national championship playing for Watt, spent one year with the

Roanoke Valley Rebels, the farm team of the WHA's Vancouver Blazers, and retired at twenty-three, secure in the knowledge he wasn't big-league material.

Keenan would take a job at a high school in Forest Hill, a wealthy enclave in Toronto, and here it seemed he'd settle into a career as a teacher. But Keenan caught the coaching bug in a big way. At the local high school, he took over the girls' swimming team – roll that one around in your mind for a minute – and the boys' hockey team. He also coached the Junior-B Oshawa Legionnaires of the Ontario Hockey Association (OHA) where his first star was, ta da, Dale Hawerchuk. In those days, Keenan would rise at 5:30 a.m., drive in to Forest Hill to coach the girls' swim team, teach for a day, coach the boys' hockey team, then coach the Legionnaires, who also won back-to-back Metro Junior-B titles. At twenty-nine, those titles would land Keenan the coach's post with the Peterborough Petes, perhaps the most storied junior franchise in Canada. After leading the Petes to the Memorial Cup in 1979–80, Scotty Bowman, then the Sabres' coach and GM, hired Keenan to take over their Rochester farm team in the American Hockey League (AHL). In less than four years, Keenan had morphed from an anonymous high-school teacher and minor hockey coach to one of the rising stars of his profession. In Bowman, he also found his role model, his mentor, and the inspiration for his Iron Mike character.

Keenan worked under the great coach for only three years, but Bowman's influence would last a lifetime. From Bowman, Keenan learned how to manage the game. He learned about line matchups and allocating ice time. After most Americans' games, Bowman would call his young pupil and quiz him on different parts of the game. Those calls would generally last an hour or two.

But Keenan took other things from Bowman. There is an aspect to Keenan's personality that is warm, fun-loving, and caring, traits which aren't exactly consistent with great coaches. It's a similar story with Bowman, who, over time, developed a professional persona that was cold, aloof, inscrutable, and more than a little mean-spirited. Keenan saw this: he saw the way Bowman would freeze out certain players or give up on others; the way he'd stick players to the bench without a word of explanation. He also saw its effect on the team, how they never became too comfortable and how they never grew complacent. Keenan liked that. He liked that a lot. "Mike constructed a personality he thought he needed to be a successful NHL coach," says Dave Poulin, his former captain with the Flyers. "It included a large piece of Scotty Bowman and others who'd had an influence on him. But he loved that intrigue. He loved people not knowing him or what was coming next. Guys will tell you he was the best coach they ever had. But they'll do it begrudgingly and they'd never say it at the time."

"His reputation changed when he got to the NHL," says Larry Murphy, the Team Canada defenceman who had played under Keenan during his year in Peterborough. "Actually, it was like a different person. Maybe it was because he was coaching young kids and he had a different approach. But I didn't know him as Iron Mike. That came later."

After winning the Calder Cup with the Americans in the 1982–83 season, Keenan believed he was ready to move up to the NHL. Bowman, however, preferred the existing arrangement, and Keenan, who was never one to wait patiently for his opportunities, quit his job and returned to the University of Toronto for a year. That NHL season, the Flyers underachieved under head coach Bob McCammon and when new general manager Bobby Clarke took over, his first order of business was hiring a new coach. He interviewed Keenan along with long-time NHL assistant Ted Sator, Canadian national team coach Dave King, and Bill Laforge, who had had considerable success in the junior ranks. Clarke had his doubts about Keenan, doubts that were reinforced when Keenan sent him a letter outlining his philosophy.

"My approach in motivating the athlete is to maintain an imbalance of unpredictability in incorporating incentive, fear and attitudinal methods employed in a very dynamic environment," the letter read in part. "I would emphasize, however, within this framework of discipline and team organization . . . the players must be kept loose, their creativity unstifled and their intrinsic enthusiasm for the game maintained."

Clarke wasn't quite sure what that meant. "Imbalance of unpredictability"? "Attitudinal methods"? But he kept coming back to Keenan's record in Peterborough and Rochester, his emphasis on discipline, and concluded that's what his team needed. Clarke made the hire. He then stepped back and watched his young coach go to work. Darryl Sittler was supposed to succeed Clarke as the Flyers' captain but he was traded to Detroit for young Murray Craven as Keenan rebuilt on the fly. Youngsters like Tocchet, Derrick Smith, Peter Zezel, and Ron Sutter assumed expanded roles with the team. Poulin was named the captain. The lineup would eventually feature three rookies, seven second-year players, and, in many ways, represented the perfect canvas for Keenan. They were young and malleable. They would respond to his preferred speed-and-pressure game and, more importantly, his methods.

"Mike was a desperate man in those days," Clarke told Keenan biographer Jeff Gordon. "He partied with a sense of desperation. He coached with a sense of desperation. Everything in life was done with a sense of desperation."

Keenan does not disagree. "The media read me all wrong. They thought I was arrogant. I was just really scared. It's a great way to hide fear."

There are, of course, a million stories from Keenan's early years with the Flyers. When he was displeased with Zezel, he would have the Flyers' trainers move his equipment into a boiler room deep in the bowels of The Spectrum. Young Scott Mellanby – whose father, TV executive Ralph, was a close friend of Clarke – was a favourite whipping boy and Keenan would tell him the only reason he was on the team was because of his father's influence with the GM. In order to motivate Ron Sutter, Keenan would scratch his twin brother, Rich, from the lineup.

One story is particularly telling. In that first season in Philadelphia, Poulin approached Keenan and asked for an early practice on December 24 so the team could get a head start on the holidays. The Flyers brought in beer and pizza before the practice. They then went through a leisurely forty-five-minute session followed by a six-minute aerobic skate. But, as they were getting ready to head for the locker room, Keenan split the team into two groups, lined them up at either end of the ice, then bag-skated them for forty-five minutes. At the conclusion, he called in his exhausted players and said: "Expect the unexpected. Merry Christmas."

"My temper is a tool," Keenan told Gordon. "I lose my temper for the right reason, to make players better. My assistant coaches would tell me that I have to give in on some of the little ones to win the bigger ones. But I could never find one to give in on."

That year the Flyers would win sixteen of their last seventeen regular-season games to finish first overall. They then knocked off the Rangers, Islanders, and Nordiques in the playoffs before losing to the Oilers in the five-game final. Keenan cried on the plane on the flight back to Philly. The next season, goalie Pelle Lindbergh died tragically after he crashed his Porsche into a wall following a team party, but in 1986–87 Keenan was back with a team built around Hextall and extended the Oilers to seven games in the Cup final. That performance landed Keenan the Team Canada job the following summer and the coach, who was always looking for an edge, wasn't going to let this opportunity slip without getting something for his team. Seven Flyers were invited to the tryout camp. Poulin, who'd played at Rendez-Vous '87 the previous February, was immediately roomed with Gretzky. Tocchet, the young power forward, was roomed with Messier. Propp, Hextall, and blueliner Doug Crossman would all make the final cut, and players like Smith and McCrimmon were there to learn through osmosis. "It was staggering for me," said Poulin. "I walked into my room and Wayne wasn't there but I saw this bag with No. 99 on it. That was Mike Keenan at his best."

Poulin and the rest of the Flyers were familiar with Keenan's methods and knew what to expect when the workouts started. The rest of the team wasn't so sure. During the camp, players were perpetually grilling Poulin about his coach in Philadelphia. What's he like? How do you deal with him? Poulin could offer an educated guess, but he couldn't wrap up Keenan in a nice, neat package. Who could? The players – especially the Oilers, especially Messier – loved his practices. They were short in duration, forty-five minutes to an hour, but they were crisp, up-tempo, and everything was done with a purpose. There were four sessions a day: two groups, two practices. The drills stressed the transition game and quick counterattacks off turnovers. Those practices were as entertaining as the games that would follow.

"We'd put in new drills every other day and they just loved it because it was a challenge to them," says Muckler. "I'd seen some pretty good practices with the Oilers. But this was at another level. I remember one session we had a four-on-four drill where we changed on the fly. For over an hour, they went up and down and I can't remember a pass being missed. It was such a delight to watch it happen."

Gretzky, in particular, relocated his mojo during these sessions. Keenan tells a great story about watching Gretzky at the very first Team Canada practice. He'd worked through a line of interviewers, answering questions politely but woodenly. Then he stepped on the ice and his entire demeanour changed. His eyes lit up. His face relaxed. It was like he was freed from a terrible burden. Keenan doesn't miss much on the ice at the best of times and he certainly didn't miss this. "I understood him," says Keenan. "I understood the ice is the one domain where he's completely free."

Poulin, Gretzky's roommate, also remembers overhearing Gretzky talking to his father early in the camp. It seems he was worried about his play, which struck Poulin as a trifle odd because Gretzky, to his mind, had been brilliant in the training sessions. "He said, 'I just can't get into it,'" Poulin says. "And I kept thinking, 'Geez, I wish I couldn't get into it like that.'"

Keenan faced questions over how the various flavours on Team Canada would mix. His Flyers' teams favoured a straight-ahead, chip-and-chase style, but the coach understood he couldn't beat the Russians by giving up the puck. He didn't have a Gretzky, Lemieux, or Coffey on his Flyers' team but he knew how to deploy his most dangerous weapons on Team Canada to their best advantage. Tocchet, who had more than his share of battles with Keenan over the years, maintains that's what made him a great coach. "Mike could have gone in and said, 'This is the way we're going to play because this is the way we play in Philly,'" says Tocchet. "He still let the guys be themselves. It wasn't like he said to Messier, 'Mark, you're going to dump it in and hit everybody.' He let guys play their game."

Still, those flavours didn't always blend smoothly. Poulin recalls lining up with Anderson and Messier early in the camp. After a couple of days, he approached Messier and said: "I'm sorry. I have absolutely no clue what you're doing."

"Neither do we," Messier responded. "Isn't it great."

"[The Oilers] just spoke a different language on the ice," Poulin says.

Tocchet also remembers one of his earlier exchanges with Coffey. In Philadelphia, Tocchet's job was to keep the puck moving forward and forecheck with a single-minded purpose. Any deviation from those simple tasks would result in swift retribution from Keenan. It was with some surprise, then, that Tocchet learned from Coffey there was a different way to play the game. "[Coffey] said, 'When you get the puck on the wing, don't just chip it in. I'm coming late. I don't know what you guys in Philly do but I'm coming and I want the puck,'" says Tocchet. "I mean, I'd never heard of that before."

On the ice, then, there wasn't a lot of complaining about the coach's methods. The workouts were demanding and placed a premium on conditioning, but the players responded to Keenan's practices.

"It was a very difficult camp from the very first day," Hrudey says. "In fact, it was one of the most difficult camps I've ever attended. I can still remember it and that tells you how tough it was. I remember thinking, 'Holy cow, this is our first day and we've still got a month to go before we play our first game.' But when you work that hard as a group, and survive it, it brings you closer together."

They played just as hard off the ice. The Oilers, in particular, were an enthusiastic group of bon vivants and Keenan, who wasn't exactly a lights-out-by-ten sort, did his best to accommodate them. Practices were generally held around 4 p.m., which guaranteed two things: 1) The players would have recovered from any effects of the previous night's excesses and 2) The media could drag their sorry carcasses out of bed to cover the team. Keenan has always been adept at cultivating relationships with a few influential types within the press and in Montreal, he used to join a group of writers at a local watering hole, Grumpy's. The group in question was fond of Fifties music, which was right up Keenan's alley from his Nik and the Nice Guys days, and the evening's festivities would usually degenerate into a sing-a-long of dubious quality. Veteran writer Al Strachan remembers wailing to some doo-wop classic when he received a punch in the shoulder from Keenan for screwing up the words. "Always the coach," Strachan says.

The players, meanwhile, had their own rituals. Lunches were generally held at Chez Paree, an upscale strip club located on Stanley Street, of which Gretzky and Messier — and just about every player in the NHL come to think of it — were fond. The noontime gatherings became compulsory for the players and at least one of them remembers it as a valuable step in the team-building process. Gretzky had seen the rift between the Islanders and the Oilers on the '84 team. He was determined to bring this group together. Granted, the locale might have been a little unorthodox but it served the purpose.

Chez Paree, in fact, would become one of the meeting places for Team Canada and the media that covered the event. Gretzky had a favoured corner booth in which he hosted parties and would, on occasion, invite the press corps over to join him. Did we mention this was a different time? The booth became known to insiders as "Gretzky's Office," a play on the more common reference to the Great One setting up behind the opposition's net.

One member of the media troupe cites an anecdote to illustrate the difference between Team Canada's players and Team USA's. One night, several members of the fourth estate were enjoying the sights in Chez Paree when some American players walked in and sent over a round of drinks. Some time later, the Canadians walked in and sent over a dancer to entertain the scribes.

But Gretzky, by the standard of his teammates at least, was a relative choirboy. Messier got after it hard in those days but he always showed up ready to work. Anderson would tend to disappear shortly after practice and no one would see him until shortly before the next day's workout.

"The Oilers were a special group," said one of the players, who requested anonymity. "They partied hard. I mean, Anderson and Messier, wow. Anderson would play so hard, then you wouldn't see him until the next morning. He'd show up twenty minutes before practice, get dressed, work his butt off, then you wouldn't see him again until the next time we were together.

"Everything they did, they did all out."

That ethos was shared by most of the players. They were all of a similar age, at similar points in their careers, enjoying varying degrees of celebrity. There was also a different atmosphere around the game in those days, largely because the big money hadn't arrived. Sure, the players were dedicated pros and, when the puck dropped, they played like their hair was on fire. But away from the game things weren't quite as serious as they are now.

"We came together as a team pretty quickly," says Hawerchuk. "Everyone had a lot of respect for the other guys in that room."

As for the coach, well, that was becoming an issue. Keenan had already started, as he put it, to create "an imbalance of un-predictability in incorporating incentive, fear and attitudinal methods employed in a very dynamic environment." Yes, he did. And there was all kinds of unpredictability surrounding Team Canada.

For starters, Keenan didn't use the fabled Montreal Canadiens' dressing room at The Forum during training camp. That would be reserved for players who made the final roster. Until that time, the players could use the visiting team's dressing room and the symbolism of that move was not lost on anyone.

Then there was the matter of nutrition. Keenan had taken some pre-med courses at St. Lawrence and believed he knew something about the science of sport. He was one of the first coaches to utilize circuit and interval training methods. He was also a stickler for hydration and eating properly before games. The Flyers, for example, always ate chicken and broccoli before their games while the Oilers favoured the more traditional large steak-and-baked-potato entree followed by mounds of ice cream as their pre-game meal. This created your basic conflict when, before one pre-tournament contest, the Oilers entered the team's dining room and saw the trays of chicken and broccoli. Gretzky, according to Tocchet, took one look at the fare, walked into the kitchen, and proclaimed: "I need twenty freaking steaks out here (or words to that effect) and I need them right now." The Oilers got their steak and ice cream. The Flyers got a laugh out of it.

But it wasn't all mirth and merriment around the team. Gretzky and Messier, by Keenan's own admission, had gone out of their way to show their support for the Team Canada coach. Keenan now says both players had been instilled with a deep-rooted respect for the game's authority figures at a young age and you didn't have to look past their fathers – Walter Gretzky had been around the game all his life, Doug Messier had played and coached in the minors – to understand where that came from. But Keenan was a different story altogether and it wasn't long before his players were wondering just what the hell the coach was doing.

It started at the top.

"For all the respect I have for Mike, you don't treat Gretzky like a fourth-line player," Serge Savard says. "There were a couple of things that rubbed those guys the wrong way. Keenan would stand up in the middle of that room and say, 'I have no leaders.' Can you imagine saying that to Gretzky and Messier?"

Clarke, his boss in Philly, could. "It was a new experience for Mike," Clarke says. "It was his first experience with those kind of players and you could see him trying to prove he wouldn't be intimidated by that group. But with Mike, you never knew what he was thinking."

The players would come to understand this about their coach. Team Canada had flown out to the Maritimes from Montreal for a pre-tournament game in Halifax on August 20 before returning to Hamilton for an open practice at Copps Coliseum in front of twelve thousand fans the next day. Their flight from Halifax

landed in Hamilton at 3 a.m., and they took to the ice at noon
where, it was quickly revealed, they had nothing to give. Keenan
watched his exhausted players stumble around the ice for a few
minutes, then blew his whistle and summoned them to centre ice
for a lecture that wasn't well received by the troops.

"Keenan was going to show everyone who's in charge here
so he gathered everyone around and started giving us grief,"
Hrudey says. "We're looking at each other going, 'You showboat. You're only doing this because it's an open practice.'"

Hawerchuk, for his part, was reunited with Keenan for the
first time since his Junior-B days in Oshawa and he couldn't
help noticing a change in the coach. Hawerchuk, according to
Perron, had also shown up to camp a few pounds overweight,
which didn't endear him to Keenan. "He worked Dale's ass off
in practice," Perron says.

The players tolerated Keenan's act for the first month of
camp, until just five days before they met the Russians in the
final. But we'll get to that story in a bit. Team Canada still had
to be selected and if the men around him didn't have a clear
idea what Keenan was thinking, hockey fans all over the frozen
North were wondering the same thing by the time the final
cuts were made.

In looking at the Team Canada roster a couple of decades after
the fact, some of the personnel decisions made by coaches and
management seem almost comical. Kelly Hrudey over Patrick
Roy? Normand Rochefort over Scott Stevens? Doug Crossman
over Al MacInnis? Kevin Dineen over Steve Yzerman? You
could, in fact, build a team around the players cut by Keenan and
they would have been a threat to beat the team that represented
Canada in the tournament. But in August of 1987, the coaches
and management were confident they'd put together the best
team from the available talent. Given the results, you'd also have
a hard time disputing their choices.

"I know some of the decisions seem odd now," Keenan says. "But Scott Stevens wasn't what he'd become in '87. At that time, Normand Rochefort was a better fit for our team." Still, there were questions. Team Canada scrimmaged and practised for a week before playing its first pre-tournament game, against the Canadian Olympic team on August 9 in Sydney, Nova Scotia. They then met the Olympic team in St. John's before moving on to face the Americans in Ottawa and Montreal. After a lengthy meeting involving the four-man coaching staff and the four GMs, the first cuts were made on August 19, the day of their third straight meeting with Team USA. The casualties included Lidster, his Canucks' teammate Tony Tanti, Minnesota's Dino Ciccarelli, Muller, MacInnis, and, shockingly, Yzerman. The Wings' captain had made the team in '84. But this time around he didn't make it through the first cuts.

"I don't know if this means I'm getting worse or what," Yzerman said when he faced reporters. "This is a better all-around team. The last time, it wasn't really a team, it was just a bunch of talented players. This time, the guys seem younger and just as talented."

"He didn't deserve to make it and that's not a slight against Steve Yzerman," says Tom Watt, one of the Team Canada assistants. "That was the reality of that team. Every one of those teams in the Eighties there was a controversy because this guy or that guy didn't make it.

"We had Lemieux, Gretzky, and Messier as our centres and we had Hawerchuk and Gilmour playing the wings. We tried Steve at the wing in a couple of exhibition games and he didn't play well. We had to ask, was he better than Gretzky, Lemieux, or Messier. The answer was no."

Four days later, with the team now in Hamilton to face the Czechs, the second round of cuts came and, again, Keenan found himself in the middle of a hullabaloo. Neely and Clark were let go in that group, along with young Derrick Smith and blueliners Ramage and McCrimmon. Concerns were raised because Clark was one of the few natural left wingers trying out for the team. But the news of the day concerned the sixth player who was axed, Montreal Canadiens goalie Patrick Roy.

Roy was one year removed from his Conn Smythe performance in the '86 Cup finals, but he'd struggled through an indifferent campaign in the 1986–87 season. There was also some thought he'd chafe in the backup role to Fuhr, who'd been conceded the number-one job. At least, that's the way Keenan and others remember it.

Savard tells a different version of the story.

According to the Habs' former general manager, it was decided at a meeting the night before the cuts were announced that Roy would stay with the team. Savard then awoke to the news Roy had been released and realized he had a problem on his hands. "They played a trick on me with Patrick," Savard says. "I think he would have played a backup role. Then they changed their minds without talking to me. I had to live with Patrick on my team.

"Everyone knew he wasn't going to play in the tournament, but he still thought it was insulting and he blamed me. I thought about resigning after that. I thought that was really bad. But I wasn't going to quit."

When asked if he was ever able to repair his relationship with Roy, Savard answers, "I don't know. You'd have to ask him."

Keenan doesn't recall committing to Roy but he does remember Savard's reaction to the news his goalie had been cut.

"Serge didn't hide his displeasure or his support for Patrick," Keenan says. "He wasn't happy. We just weren't sure Patrick would accept a backup role. Grant was going to be the goalie and that was clear to everyone. The other guys weren't going to play unless there was an injury. Kelly Hrudey won the third-string job based on his performance in camp. I told him, Kelly, you've made the team but you're not going to play. And he was fine with that."

Well, maybe *fine* isn't the right word.

"I remember Al Arbour came to camp and I was mad," Hrudey says. "I talked to Al because I didn't want to be the third or fourth guy. I talked to Keenan about that. I said, 'I have no problem being the third guy but I want to know right away. I don't want to spend another week travelling around Canada, then be cut.'"

A number of the cuts did carry a bit of an odour. Keenan kept his goalie, Ron Hextall, over Roy. There were only two natural left wingers to make the team – Quebec's Goulet and the Flyers' Brian Propp. Tocchet, finally, was selected over several more accomplished players.

But while you could never put Keenan above that sort of politicizing, the final two cuts said a lot about the coach. The day before the tournament-opening game against the Czechs, the last two players released were Stevens, the hard-rock young defenceman from Washington, and Poulin, Keenan's captain and the heart-and-soul of his team. "This is the most difficult cut I've ever had to make as a coach," Keenan told reporters at a press conference.

But maybe not that difficult.

"Mike was always going to do what was best for the team," Poulin says. "He could remove the personal element as well as anyone I've ever been around."

Stevens, ever the competitor, was somewhere between distraught and infuriated over the news. Perron said he was almost in tears when the news was delivered. Savard remembers him being angry and that was the impression he left when he appeared before reporters, saying he wouldn't volunteer to play for Canada in the future.

"[Keenan] wanted me to stick around as the seventh defenceman but I said no. I want to play," Stevens spat. "I don't want to sit around and watch. I've got better things to do." Poulin, for his part, was almost relieved at the news. The previous season, his wife had delivered twin girls prematurely in October and the babies didn't come home until December. He also played the final three rounds of the playoffs that spring with three broken ribs. During Rendez-Vous '87, Poulin had centred a line with Hawerchuk and Dineen that was matched against the Larionov line in the two-game series. It was widely assumed he'd fill a similar role in the Canada Cup, but the younger players, particularly Gilmour, simply outplayed the gritty veteran. "It was deserved," Poulin says. "I would have loved to compete but it didn't happen. I'd been through so much. I didn't mind going home."

So Keenan had his team. "Pretty well everyone was involved in the process but in the final analysis it came down to the recommendations of the coaches," he says. Barring injury or an act of God, Fuhr would handle the goaltending. The defence would be anchored by Bourque and Coffey with an eclectic supporting cast behind them. Minnesota's Craig Hartsburg had been named the outstanding blueliner at the '87 world championship and he figured to play in the top four. Then there was the interesting tandem of Rochefort and Crossman. Finally, there were youngsters Murphy from Washington and James Patrick from the New York Rangers. Patrick, twenty-four, had played with Canada's national team for two years and the coaching staff believed his experience against the Russians would be invaluable.

"We had Bourque and Coffey," says Hartsburg. "The rest of us were decent players but we learned to lean on each other, whether we played five minutes a game or twenty minutes a game. I remember sitting on the bench with James Patrick one game and it felt like neither one of us got a shift for ten minutes."

Up front they knew they would be carried by their centre-man. Gretzky would be the engine that drove the team even though his two previous Canada Cup outings weren't exactly unqualified successes. In 1981, he led the team in scoring, but the team was crushed in the gold-medal game by the Russians. Gretzky would later call it the worst experience of his career. In 1984, he again led the team in scoring, but Tonelli was named the team's MVP. Behind Gretzky there were the dazzling young Lemieux and Messier – Gretzky, Lemieux, and Messier as your first three centres, not bad – but things got a little iffy after that. Only six natural wingers made the final roster – Goulet, Propp, Anderson, Tocchet, Dineen, and Claude Lemieux – and of those six, only Goulet resembled a goal scorer. It also meant Sutter, Gilmour, and Hawerchuk would be seeing the bulk of their ice time in an unfamiliar position.

Sutter didn't mind. He'd play goal if they asked him. "It was a special feeling just to be asked," he says. "The two things I had going for me [were] I was pretty adaptable and I had won."

Hawerchuk, meanwhile, wasn't asking any questions about where he'd play. Earlier in the camp, one of the assistants approached him and said, "You're making it tough on us. Quite honestly, we didn't have you pencilled in [to make the team]." But he made it and it was the high point of his Hall-of-Fame career. "For me it was an opportunity to measure myself against the best and I think it was that way for a lot of guys," Hawerchuk says. "You just didn't have that opportunity a lot."

Then there was Tocchet. If there was a long shot to make the team, it was the twenty-three-year-old Torontonian who'd played just three seasons with the Flyers and was coming off his first twenty-goal season in 1986–87. Tocchet realized a fruit fly had a better chance of surviving training camp than he did but he also understood there might be a spot on the roster for him. The phrase "energy player" hadn't yet fallen into the game's lexicon but that's what Tocchet envisioned for himself. And damned if he didn't make it.

"I was waiting for that sticker that said:'You're out of there,'"
Tocchet says. "But I was having a good camp and I came in in
great shape because I knew Keenan loved that. I looked at the
roster and said, 'If I'm going to make it, I'm going to have to
make it as an energy-type guy who might play two minutes or
might play eight minutes.'

"I've seen great teams who couldn't win because they didn't
have anyone to play that role. I knew that could be my slice of
the pie and I'm sure Mike had me on the team because I played
for him in Philly."

After four weeks of preparation and nine pre-tournament
games, they were ready. At least they seemed ready. But there
was still one more step in the process, one more trial that Team
Canada had to endure. Keenan now says he didn't orchestrate
the whole incident, but when pressed, he says simply: "I
wouldn't dismiss that as part of my coaching persona."

From the first Summit Series in 1972 to Salt Lake City in 2002,
the mythology of any winning Canadian entry in best-on-best
competition has usually included the story of one defining
moment that galvanized the team into the brotherhood of the
Leaf. In 1972, it was the defection of Vic Hadfield, Gilbert
Perreault, Richard Martin, and Jocelyn Guevremont prior to
the games in Moscow. In 1984, it was the peace between the
Islanders and the Oilers. In 2002, it was Gretzky's stirring – some
might say contrived – speech after the tie against the Czechs in
the round robin.

And in 1987, Team Canada came together as one in their hatred
for Keenan. Eagleson now says the trouble started at virtually the
first day of camp and by the time the round robin began,
the players were ready to stage a full-scale mutiny. Following
an exhausting two-week tour of exhibition games in eastern
Canada, the team flew to Calgary to make their final cuts and
prepare for the tournament opener against the Czechs on

August 28 at The Saddledome. With the tension building, a retreat was arranged in Banff before the game against Czechoslovakia and it seemed peace had been restored as the team left for Calgary. Wives and girlfriends, including Janet Jones, had been with the players. There had been a golf day in Canmore. There had been a gathering at Sather's spread. There had been bonding. Things, in fact, were relatively quiet and that was a problem for Keenan.

"I haven't heard one word of complaint from any player since I've been here," Keenan told reporters at the Alberta resort.

That's, at least, what he was saying for public consumption. Privately, the story was a little different.

"I remember Mike saying, 'It's too quiet. We have to provoke something,'" Savard says.

Keenan piled the players' significant others into a separate bus in Banff and had them follow the team into Calgary. Team Canada then played the Czechs to an uninspired 4–4 tie in the tournament opener, which didn't do a lot to lighten Keenan's mood. "All night we didn't see much defence, and I mean defence includes everyone on the ice," Keenan groused.

"Adolf was not very happy," said one member of Team Canada, using the players' preferred nickname for the coach.

After the game, and with the wives and girlfriends waiting, Keenan told Bill Tuele, the team's director of public relations, he saw no reason why the players should go out. They were then bussed back to the hotel for a postgame meal. And that's when the trouble started.

According to the people who were there, Messier stood up and said, "There'll be none of that."

Eagleson was then contacted and a hasty meeting was called the next morning with Gretzky, Messier, Bourque, and the team's management. Keenan now says that meeting lasted a couple of minutes and ended with Gretzky and Messier apologizing profusely after Keenan explained why he'd been so tough on the players. "I said, 'Wayne, whether you understand it or not you're going to be playing the best team Team Canada has ever faced and this is the level you have to prepare,'" is Keenan's version of the events. "Wayne said, 'Sorry we had to do this. It won't happen again.' And that was about it."

But that's not quite the way it went down according to others.

Clarke and Perron remember the players were mightily pissed off and wanted Keenan removed or straightened out. The meeting was held early the following morning and while Clarke is vague on details, he remembers the overriding sentiment in the room. "They were really, really mad," Clarke says.

"There was too much stress on the team and Clarke could see that," Perron says. "He said, 'I don't want a riot in the dressing room.'"

And the riot was averted for the time being. "Part of the regimen was to develop team discipline and together-ness," Keenan later said when the story broke. "I think [the meeting] opened up communication and turned into a very positive thing."

Maybe. But Eagleson says the incident in Calgary was actually "a minor skirmish and resolved easily" and the real con-frontation occurred five nights later after the Canadians had defeated Team USA in Hamilton. Following that contest, the team flew to Montreal to prepare for a meeting with Sweden. According to the Eagle, two of Canada's top players knocked on his door in the early hours of the morning and requested Keenan be removed permanently. Eagleson listened, said he would discuss the matter with Keenan, and prevail on him to ease up. Firing the coach, however, wasn't an option. Eagleson has never identified the players and he wouldn't for this book. But it's generally accepted Gretzky and Bourque were the spokesmen for the players.

The next day at a team luncheon, Eagleson brought together Keenan and the players and told them to work things out. Keenan agreed to compromise. Sort of. And the players agreed to let the matter die there.

"I don't think that it's a big secret Mike is a tough man," says Gretzky. "Away from the rink I happen to think he's a good guy. But he wanted every player to be as intense and prepared as he was and it was tough in August. The level of intensity and determination wasn't where it should have been and Mike could see that.

"We weren't very good to start the tournament. We sat down and talked it over and Mike lightened up. After that we came together pretty quickly."

Hawerchuk gives Messier, who was the alpha male in the dressing room, credit for helping to negotiate the peace. But whoever was responsible, Hawerchuk and others also agree it was a turning point for the team.

"Mess went up to [Keenan] and said we don't need the mind games," Hawerchuk says. "These guys are going to be ready and they're going to play. We don't need the bullshit. That's all it took. After that, we looked after things."

The next night, they beat Sweden 5–3 as Gretzky scored a goal and picked up three assists and Messier led the way with his physical play. Two nights later, they tied the Russians to capture their pool.

"The matter was over," says Eagleson. "I had no further complaints."

"The bottom line was everyone had the same goal," says Larry Murphy. "Everyone wanted to win. Everyone wanted to get to the same place. That's why everything worked out."

But that wasn't exactly the end of it, because the media also got wind of the attempted mutiny. Scott Morrison of the *Toronto Sun* did most of the work in breaking the story and was in the process of writing it in Montreal when he got a call from Eagleson. The Eagle begged Morrison to spike the story, "for the good of the country." When Morrison asked if the story was inaccurate, Eagleson responded, "Hell no. I just don't want it to come out now." By the time the team hit Hamilton a day later, the story was out. This created a few nervous moments for Morrison when Keenan was asked about the veracity of his reporting. Keenan paused for a few seconds, then answered: "I know this reporter and he's usually very accurate. I have no reason to believe that isn't the case this time." Morrison breathed a sigh of relief. He also thought he saw Keenan smiling at him.

CHAPTER 2

Red Army

J ames Patrick played two full seasons for the Canadian national team from 1983 to 1985, which meant he saw as much of Viktor Tikhonov's team as any North American player of that era. He played against them at the '84 Olympics in Sarajevo. He played against them in tours and international tournaments. He played against them all over the world. And he no more understood the Soviet players or their system than he understood Swahili.

"I can remember seeing them in track suits running in the hotel parking lot or doing their exercises outside the arena," Patrick says. "You'd be staying in the same hotels but there were always security people around and you never had any inter-action with them. They were still isolated. There was still no exchange. They trained eleven months of the year and the only thing I knew about them was their conditioning was way above ours. I don't think the mystique wore off until they started playing in the NHL."

Patrick remembers seeing four or five of the Soviet players walking around the Olympic village in Sarajevo after winning the gold medal in '84. They'd obviously been drinking in celebration of their victory and that moment stands out because it was one of the few times Patrick saw them showing a human face outside the rigid team structure. Dave King, Patrick's coach on the Olympic team, remembers the same thing. "We played them thirty times a year and they were still a mystery," says King, who coached Mettalurg in the Russian elite league in the 2005–6 season. "They'd play the game, get on the bus, and within ten minutes they were gone, back to their world. You never saw them apart. They were always together. You'd think sometimes in a city you'd see three or four of them together out for dinner but it never happened. Their lives were like their hockey, very well ordered."

To Patrick, King, the players on Team Canada, and virtually every other hockey fan in North America, the Soviets were still the automatons from the Evil Empire; a soulless collection of robots who'd been programmed to excel by the black genius Tikhonov. A lot had changed since 1972 and change was coming to the USSR. But outside the Motherland, the perception of the Soviets hadn't altered appreciably since the first Summit Series.

"There was hate there," says Tocchet. "There's no question. In 1972, they brought a TV into my classroom and we watched the game. I mean I was eight years old. That was vivid in my mind when I put [the Team Canada] jersey on. When I was growing up, it was always the Russians, the Russians, the Russians."

And there was something comforting in that for Team Canada.

"It wasn't about hockey," says Keenan. "It was about capitalism versus communism."

As a young man, Keenan had travelled to Poland with the University of Toronto and when the plane set down in Warsaw, he was shocked to see armed guards with machine guns in the airport. This, he thought, was a clear indication of what life was like behind the Iron Curtain. "That still very much existed and it was at the forefront of the competition," says Keenan. "We had to win this for our way of life."

As for the Russians' way of life, a revolution was underway. Mikhail Gorbachev had risen to power in the mid-Eighties and a new feeling permeated the USSR. Even the players in Tikhonov's tightly controlled world could sense it. But Tikhonov still had the power to create his own order. In 1987, he could make a man's career and an easier life with the snap of his fingers. He could crush them just as easily. There might have been new ideas creeping into the Soviet Union, but Tikhonov was a product of the old system and he liked things the way they were.

His players knew that. They also knew he wasn't going to surrender his power without a fight. Sergei Nemchinov was twenty-three in 1987 and sitting on the periphery of the national team. Maybe the great stars could at least think about playing in the NHL but that was a pipe dream for a player like him. "This was impossible," Nemchinov says. "Why even think about something that's impossible."

"It was like everything was trying to grow, but the hockey was still the same," says Larionov. "If you said anything you'd be punished. That's just the way it was. Tikhonov was a product of that system. He was sixty years old and he wasn't going to change. It was impossible. Whatever happened in politics at that time, it was still the same in hockey. The game was still being run by the hardliners. Nothing had changed."

As much as Keenan tried to convince his players they were about to face a super-team in the Canada Cup, the reality was the Soviets weren't at the height of their powers in the fall of 1987 and Tikhonov was hearing about it at home. The Soviet national team, shockingly, had failed to win the world championship in Vienna that spring when ties against Canada and Sweden gave the Swedes gold. They'd won the worlds in Moscow in '86, but they had also lost to the Czechs in Prague the previous year, a defeat that had huge political implications in the Soviet Union.

True, they were still capable of memorable performances – just prior to the world championships in '87, they'd split the two-game Rendez-Vous series with a team of NHL All-Stars coached by Perron, winning the second contest 5–3 in Quebec City on two goals by the brilliant young sniper Valeri Kamensky. But they were far from the team that had gone 38–0–4 through four world championships in the 1980s and placed their famed five-man unit – the KLM line with Krutov, Larionov, and Makarov and the defensive pairing of Fetisov and Kasatonov – on the tournament All-Star team in 1983 and again in 1986.

Some blamed Tikhonov, which was astonishing. Anatoli Firsov, one of the great Russian stars of the 1960s, wrote a scathing review of the coach's program in *Red Star*, the military newspaper. Among other things, Firsov claimed Tikhonov was trying to play a North American–style game, there were no new stars coming up in the system, and Russian hockey, in general, was on the decline. It was a stunning critique because, as Larionov says, "Tikhonov was like God." But it also missed the mark.

The more deep-rooted problem lay with the players' disenchantment with Tikhonov and the Soviet system. In the early 1980s, they were a machine: technically flawless, relentless in their preparation and execution. They played with a grim sense of purpose but they also played beautiful hockey. For most of the players, it was the one joy they received from playing for Tikhonov.

"He did not spare himself," Larionov wrote in his 1990 autobiography. "Give him that. He worked nights on end without sleep, watching video tapes of the matches, twisting them this way and that, analyzing them. You cannot take that away from him. I will not take away all the coaching talent of Tikhonov. The back side of his coin was his fanaticism."

But sometime in the mid-1980s, something changed with the Soviet team and cracks started to appear in the great wall. Mistakes were made. The effort was not as consistent. There were times the players almost seemed disinterested. There were a couple of reasons for this. The national team and Red Army – both coached by Tikhonov, essentially the same team – had gone unchallenged on the world stage and within the Russian league for too long. Their sharp edge had been dulled. A malaise had set in.

"For five years winning the national championship has brought no joy or interest to me," Larionov wrote. "Sometimes you are ashamed when you see that a team does not want to compete against or is unable to compete or both."

King could see the same thing from his vantage point. In the early part of the decade, the Canadian national team and their collection of marginal talents couldn't touch the Russians. By the late 1980s, they were starting to register results on a consistent basis. "You could tell there was something going on," says King. "They were so good in the early part of the Eighties. Then they got hot and cold. Some nights they were into it. Some nights they weren't."

The larger problem facing Tikhonov had to do with forces beyond his control. He was a Stalinist, a man who'd started working at age twelve, who'd been drafted into an Air Force team run by Stalin's son Vasily, who'd started his career at Dynamo, the team of the KGB, then, after coaching in Latvia, took over the fabled Red Army team. Everything he had – the power, the prestige, the respect, the gold medals – he owed to the Soviet system. But as brilliant a coach as he was, he was also of a different time and didn't seem to understand his world was changing.

"All that I know of myself is that nothing was ever given me without effort, not when I first stepped out on the ice or now when I am carrying the coach's burden," Tikhonov said. "Stubborn labour, self-sacrifice, fanatical devotion to a favoured activity, tireless perfection of athletic professionalism – these are, in my understanding, the key to success for every hockey player and every athlete. And these principles I always and everywhere defend."

As mentioned, a good-time Charlie he wasn't.

Any good Marxist-Leninist, however, has to be aware of the currents of history and in 1985, Gorbachev arrived and a curtain was pulled back on the Soviet Union. He was a new man for a new era. He introduced a series of reforms at the Party Congress in 1986 – together they were called perestroika (restructuring) – and they were designed to move Russia toward a market-based economy and a more democratic system of government. He also talked about glasnost (openness) and the importance of discussing publicly the USSR's current and historical problems. These were new, dangerous ideas that would eventually bring down Soviet totalitarianism in Eastern Europe. In 1985, they represented something very exciting to people like Larionov. "I had a somewhat enthusiastic perception of the new leader of the country," Larionov wrote. "I read, listened, talked, discussed, and argued, and I was happy that a time had come when people could calmly, easily speak out because it could apply to hockey players too. Until perestroika I felt hopeless. It was a blind alley."

It's hard now to conceive of how brutal and dehumanizing Tikhonov's system was and even more difficult to understand how the players could tolerate it. Admittedly, they had a better deal than the average Russian, whose life was tougher than a night in jail. They got to play hockey for a living. They were adored by the masses. A car and an apartment went along with that adoration. Kasatonov, the Tikhonov suck-up, lived in Tikhonov's former flat, a spacious three-room unit in the upscale section of Moscow. Fetisov drove a big blue Mercedes. Every Christmas, Alexander Mogilny reports, they received a box of goodies that included coffee and rye bread. They also travelled, which presented opportunities to acquire Western consumer goods and hard currency. Admittedly, it wasn't life in Boca Raton, but those sorts of perks were only available to the party brass and the politically connected. There wasn't a lot of sympathy for the plight of the national team and Red Army players within Russia's borders.

"It was the chance of a lifetime for a Russian hockey player," says defenceman Igor Kravchuk. "We had this expression, 'After you get the Red Army jersey, you can play anywhere.' Everybody dreamed about this. It was like playing for the Montreal Canadiens. They dictated the style of the game. They dictated the direction of the game. It was the biggest thing in my country."

But there was a fearsome price for obtaining that jersey. In return for the Russian version of the good life, blind obedience was demanded. Even the greatest stars were simply parts of the machine that could easily be replaced, and Tikhonov took great pains to reinforce that point.

"That was the system," says King. "If you wanted to be an elite player, get the holidays at the Black Sea, an apartment in Moscow, maybe a car, you had to pledge allegiance. You just kept your mouth shut and you played."

The training centre, Archangel, was a three-storey facility located near parkland on the banks of the Moscow River about half an hour from the capital, and the hockey team trained there nine months of the year. Preliminary camp would start on June 25. The official camp would run from mid-July to mid-May, which left about a six-week summer holiday for the players. Then they'd return and start all over.

Conditions at the complex, by Russian standards, were comfortable, but they wouldn't quite make the Michelin Guide. The first floor featured a cafeteria, sauna, medical rooms, and a recreation room with a malfunctioning TV and a ratty old pool table. The second floor housed the national soccer team. The third floor was the dormitory for the hockey team. There were eighteen rooms per floor, two players to a room. Each room was big enough for two single beds, a night table, and a lamp. There were two toilets per floor and one telephone.

A typical day began at 7:15 a.m., with a wake-up call followed by calisthenics and jogging at 7:30. Breakfast was at 9 a.m., before the team split into two groups. The first group would work out in the weight room at 10:00, then hit the ice at 11:00. The second group, the lucky dogs, received another hour for breakfast before weights at 11:00 and an on-ice session at 12:30. Players were then given a break before a full practice was held from 5 p.m. to 7 p.m. Then it was supper, massage, and a choice of lining up for the phone, watching TV, playing cards or pool, or reading. Lights out at eleven. The next day they got to do it all over again.

But it wasn't all hard work and sacrifice. The players were allowed to go home every Sunday until August 1, then one evening every ten days or so according to Tikhonov's whims. Of course they had to be back for calisthenics at 7:30 the following morning because the coach was paranoid about his players getting loose on a bender. That fear was also justified in a number of cases.

Larionov notes the room-and-board was free. The players' salaries were about 350 rubles per month, the equivalent of sixty dollars at the time. In the early 1990s, and we swear we're not making this up, a Russian travel company offered tours and a chance to train at the famous complex.

"We have known no other way," Larionov wrote. "The country cares for and feeds its athletes and for this the athletes are expected to perform. This was the same in every sport, not just hockey."

In his autobiography, Larionov describes the manner in which the state ensured its athletes were fully prepared for competition. Three to four weeks before the world championship, the national team players were prescribed injections over a week-long period at Archangel. Larionov never uses the word *steroids*. But he does write, "We didn't know what was in them but we had our suspicions."

"They told us it was vitamins and you'd get a boost," Larionov now says. "Something, in my opinion, was wrong."

He also described a testing procedure where he walked into a washroom and a lab assistant handed him a urine sample from behind a toilet. Larionov maintains, despite threats from Tikhonov, that he and his linemates refused to take the injections before the 1982 world championships in Helsinki and were never asked again.

"But others went along – and were still doing so at the Moscow championships in '86 – afraid of losing their positions," Larionov wrote. "And Tikhonov left no doubt about that."

Larionov, one of the most remarkable men in the history of the game, beat his head against that system for eight years before he finally won his freedom. He first came to Tikhonov's attention in the late 1970s when he was starring for Khimik, the team in his hometown of Voskresensk. At the time, Tikhonov was looking for a centre to play on the national team's top line with the gifted wingers Krutov and Makarov. He'd tried Viktor Zhluktov, a big, strong pivot in the Messier mould and a notorious Tikhonov toadie, but Zhluktov lacked the skill to complement Krutov and Makarov. Larionov, on the other hand, was a brilliant passer who was blessed with an uncanny sense for the game.

Early in the 1980–81 season, Red Army played Khimik in Voskresensk, and Larionov, who had no desire to leave his hometown or to play for Tikhonov, was summoned to a meeting with the national team coach behind the team bus. There, Tikhonov invited the young centre to Red Army and the national team. Well, maybe *invited* isn't quite the word. "If you leave for another team, it's all the same," Tikhonov explained. "We will draft you into the army. In general, Igor, think it over. Weigh it all carefully. We are talking, you know, about your future."

That night Larionov recorded five assists against Tikhonov's team in a 5–5 tie. He would join Red Army a few weeks later. He would be placed between Makarov and Krutov in the fall of 1981. And together, they formed arguably the greatest line in hockey history. "That somehow lightened my spirits," Larionov said of the day the KLM line was formed. With the defence pairing of Fetisov and Kasatonov, the threesome played on the winning Russian side at the '81 Canada Cup, then simply took over international hockey for the next five years. Like the five Oilers on Team Canada, they were a fascinating study. Larionov and Fetisov were of a type, intelligent, worldly, fiercely independent. They would ultimately win some semblance of freedom for all Russian players and they drew strength from each other in the battle with Tikhonov.

Fetisov was the unquestioned leader of the team and one of the five greatest defencemen ever to play the game. He was a squatter version of Ray Bourque and had the same attributes: a physical edge, toughness, smarts, creativity but was more explosive. At twenty, he was named the outstanding defenceman at the '78 world championships and shortly thereafter named captain of Red Army and the national team. Gretzky called him the best defenceman he ever played against. He was named Russian player of the year three times and Soviet Honoured Master of Sports three times.

He wasn't as confrontational as Larionov was toward Tikhonov but he was in the middle of the fight. "We needed each other," Larionov says. Fetisov also played through personal tragedy. In the summer of 1985, he was involved in a car accident that claimed the life of his younger brother Anatoly. The great defenceman said it took him some time to recover from the death of his brother. There is some belief he was never the same player after the accident. "I spent too much strength on coming back without giving myself time to rest, to think, to stop," he said at the time. "I wanted to prove to myself that I could still play and I wanted to bring some joy to my parents by doing what they asked. And that's probably when the fall in my game happened." Nevertheless, Fetisov was still named to the '87 Canada Cup all-tournament team.

As for the others, Krutov was from the big city, Moscow, but wasn't a terribly complex individual. "He's a very simple guy," says Igor Kuperman, the Russian journalist who covered the team. "He knew one thing. Hockey. He didn't like the spotlight." He was a professional goal scorer from an early age who was loyal to the system but equally loyal to his linemates when the fight for freedom erupted in the late Eighties.

Makarov was the wild card, a stubborn, brilliant individualist who hailed from Chelyabinsk, an industrial city located near the Urals and, like Larionov, he fought long odds to make it to the apex of Russian hockey. Makarov grew up idolizing the great Valery Kharlamov and he was the one player in the history of the Russian game who came closest to emulating Kharlamov's dazzling combination of speed and skill. At Chelyabinsk, Makarov developed away from the mainstream of the Russian system and, despite winning a gold medal at the '77 World Junior Championship, doubts persisted about his game. His one champion, however, was Tikhonov and in 1978, the national team coach made Makarov a surprise selection for the world championship in Prague. There the Russians won gold for the first time in three years and the next year, Makarov was promoted to Red Army, where he joined Krutov. The pair were joined with Larionov in 1981, the same year Kharlamov died in a car crash.

Makarov became the best right wing in Europe and a three-time player of the year in Russia. But he remained fiercely independent and gave Tikhonov as much trouble on the ice as any of his players. He wasn't any easier when he got to the NHL. While playing in Calgary, then Flames coach Terry Crisp tried to explain some fine point of the game on a greaseboard to

Makarov, who simply turned away from him, saying, "Tikhonov, good coach, bad guy. You, good guy, bad coach."

Kasatonov, finally, was the perfect partner for Fetisov but he was also the outsider of the group after he sold himself to Tikhonov. A native of Leningrad and a partier, Kasatonov credited Tikhonov for making him a player and remained loyal to the chief, to the disgust of Larionov in particular.

"The relationship started going bad in the last couple of years when we started thinking about playing in the NHL," he says. "We were going in different directions. On the ice it was professional and we got the job done. Off the ice we didn't talk." Kasatonov doesn't dispute that version of events.

"It was later our relationship started to go bad," he says. "It was a different time and they had a different understanding of what was happening. It was the situation. They made a decision and I wasn't part of that decision. I went my own way."

But somehow, these parts meshed together beautifully on the ice like the accents in a good bottle of wine. King says Larionov was the key because he had so many responsibilities on the line. He had to do most of the dirty work in the defensive zone. He had to make the pass to spring Krutov or Makarov. He had to read off his two wingers, which wasn't the easiest chore. If they were up, he had to be back. If they wandered, which they were wont to do, he had to cover for them.

"Larionov was the architect," says King. "And the proof is in the pudding. Who lasted the longest of all those players?"

"That was the best structure of a line I've ever seen," says Jean Perron. "You had the great playmaker in the middle and you had these two incredible talents on the wing. But they complemented each other. Krutov was good in the corners and had the shot. Makarov was more dangerous off the rush. Then they had the two quarterbacks behind them to start everything. It's not like you could key on one of them or say, 'We'll try to take this away from them.' They were all dangerous."

And that was the best part of the unit. It's possible to neutral-ize great players and great lines by making them the focus of a team's game plan. But how could you stop this group? All five players handled the puck like a centre. Krutov was a pure sniper. Makarov was the greatest individual talent. Larionov is one of the most intelligent players in the game's history. Fetisov and Kasatonov could both play in the rough going without sacri-ficing any of their skill.

"There was so much talent on that line and we were very competitive," Larionov says. "We kept challenging each other. We had this magnificent chemistry and it didn't matter what the coach said to us before the game. We just went out and played by improvising and reading off each other. There's no doubt that's the kind of hockey they're trying to play now, but it's a hockey that has to come from the players."

At the time, Fetisov said the same thing, more or less.

"The greatest happiness of us five was to find unexpected solutions in any situation, however standard," the defenceman was quoted as saying. "To me, improvisation for a hockey player is the same as for a jazz musician. But, for the whole to impro-vise, it is possible only when every player is strong, well-versed in his tactical scope and rich in technical repertoire; when all together they understand one another with half a word and half a glance and even without one or the other; when to every one, it seems tedious to move only according to the plan of the hockey textbook." In other words, they played their own style and they were good at it.

Led by the Green Unit, so named for the green jerseys they wore during practice, the Soviets won the world championships in 1981–83 and 1986, the Canada Cup in 1981, and, most signifi-cantly, in the Motherland, Olympic gold in 1984. But the friction between Tikhonov and the players was growing with each passing year and the tension was starting to hit critical mass by the time the '87 Canada Cup rolled around. King now says, as impressive as the Soviets' record was, it could have been even better if Tikhonov would have learned to relax his grip on the team.

"He was never satisfied, always pushing," King says. "He never understood the law of diminishing returns. It was just push, push, push. Tikhonov understood the tactical part of the game, the conditioning part of the game, the systems part of the game. He didn't understand the psychological part of the game."

No, that was something he would not, or could not, grasp. He knew only the old way, the way it had been done in the USSR for fifty years. Change might be coming to his country, but it wasn't coming to Tikhonov.

Larionov, as he'd been for years, was the lead actor in that drama. An engaging, outgoing sort, he quickly mastered English when he began touring North America and was the one Russian player who would socialize with outsiders.

You can guess how that went over with Tikhonov.

Larionov even committed the ultimate heresy when he talked with reporters in North America about one day playing in the NHL. Tikhonov listened to all this for a while, then he acted.

In December 1985, Larionov was preparing for a Red Army tour of six NHL cities when he was told there was trouble with his passport and he wouldn't be going. "Trouble with your passport," of course, could mean a million things behind the Iron Curtain and Larionov was left to stew for a couple of days before he was told it was all a mix-up. He would be going. Then he was told he wasn't. Then he sat in Moscow for a couple of weeks wondering what the hell was going on.

In North America, reporters were told Larionov had health problems including, of all things, chronic tonsillitis. Red Army returned and immediately set out for Italy and the European championship. Again, Larionov stayed behind. The national team had three exhibition games scheduled in Sweden. This time Alexander Tretiak, the former national team goaltending great who was now a lieutenant-colonel, told him he was going.

And at 4:30 a.m., the morning of his scheduled departure, Red Army assistant coach Boris Mikhailov – old Needle Nose from the '72 series – told him he wasn't going.

Finally, in February, Larionov was summoned to a series of meetings with high-ranking officials and his offences were read to him. In a scene right out of a Solzhenitsyn novel, it was revealed that Larionov and his parents had received a visiting Canadian girl in their Moscow apartment. At the next meeting, he was told his mother had been speculating in video equipment on the black market. And, at the third meeting, they finally got to the crux of the matter when Larionov was grilled about his fondness for the West. If you like life over there, he was told, it means you could be passing on information. What about all your friends in North America? And what about all those interviews?

In the end, Larionov was let go with a warning and a clearer understanding of how the Soviet system worked. After a punitive training session in Leningrad, he was restored to the national team in time for the world championship, which, not coincidentally, was played in Moscow. Tikhonov's team won the gold medal and the Green Unit was again named to the tournament All-Star team. Larionov was married in August 1986 and told all was forgiven. But until he left for the Vancouver Canucks three years later, he was always looking over his shoulder.

"I endured it for eight years, fighting the system whenever and however I could," Larionov wrote. "It was as though I were in chains."

In an interview for this book, Larionov was asked how he could play for Tikhonov without going crazy. "The Russians are resilient people," he said. "And I didn't have a lot of choice. I had to play and believe common sense would prevail. My other choice was to go to Siberia with the army."

Larionov says the first time he was asked about the possibility of playing in the NHL was during a North American tour for the

'82 Super Series. At the time, that prospect seemed as realistic as manned space flights to Jupiter. Five years later, the idea didn't seem so far-fetched.

"Journalists would ask me about playing in North America and I'd say, 'Maybe in the future, sooner or later it might happen,'" Larionov says. "It was just my opinion but you couldn't say it out loud in those days. The KGB people were all around. Every story was translated by the embassy people."

That began to change under Gorbachev. The real revolution in Russia started with ideas, and when the country's new leader introduced the concepts of openness and reform, he opened doors that couldn't be closed. For the first time, Larionov says, he and his countrymen could speak their minds. They could ask questions. They could express themselves in a way Russians hadn't been able to for three generations. "We saw that," Larionov says. "We knew what that meant."

What they saw was the Iron Curtain starting to come down as Russia opened herself to the rest of the world. There were trade missions and cultural exchanges. Soccer players were allowed to play in France and Italy in the prime of their careers. There was a feeling that new things were possible. True, the hockey system was different than the soccer system but even for all his influence, Tikhonov wasn't strong enough to hold back history. But that wouldn't keep him from trying.

Fetisov became the first Russian player to be drafted by the NHL. Back in 1978, when he was just graduating to the national team, the Montreal Canadiens took a flyer on him in the twelfth round. Five years later, he was still in indentured servitude to Tikhonov when the Devils stepped up and took him in the eighth round of the 1983 draft. That same year, the Devils selected Kasatonov and the Flames took Makarov. Two years later, the Vancouver Canucks drafted Larionov. And in 1986, the Canucks nabbed Krutov.

All of this had absolutely no effect on Tikhonov or the Russian federation, who seemed to delight in toying with the NHL teams that came calling about their players. Flames GM Cliff Fletcher, whose first experience in this regard came in the 1970s when he was in Atlanta and tried to get forward Anatoli Firsov out of Russia, would make annual inquiries about Makarov's availability and was repeatedly stonewalled. Not this year. Maybe next year. Or the year after. It's hard to say.

Canucks GM Pat Quinn, whose owner Frank Griffiths was aggressive in his pursuit of Larionov and Krutov, ran into the same roadblock. The Canucks were told Larionov wanted to play in the NHL as early as the spring of 1985. They brought Anatoli Tarasov, one of the seminal figures in Soviet hockey, and the great goalie Vladislav Tretiak to their training camp in 1986. Tarasov returned in 1987 and even had hip surgery in British Columbia. Quinn would have half a dozen meetings with Soviet officials and there were times he allowed himself to become optimistic. But at the next meeting, it was like they'd never talked.

The NHL, then, wasn't an option but, through the 1970s and 1980s, veteran Russian players were allowed to play out their careers in Europe and Japan with the understanding they'd return to the Motherland and contribute to the Soviet system. Alexander Yakushev, one of the stars of the '72 Summit Series, went to Austria when he was thirty-three and played three seasons there. Vladimir Shadrin, Yuri Liapkin, and, later, Helmut Balderis spent time in Japan. Makarov's older brother, Nikolai, went to Finland and played with Jokerit Helsinki after thirteen years at Traktor Chelyabinsk. All would leave and get a taste of a better life. But all would return.

By the summer of 1987, however, the players were looking beyond Europe and Japan. The veterans of the national team, who had all toured North America a number of times, were aware that the evil capitalists in the United States and Canada weren't sucking the life's blood out of the working class. NHL players, in fact, had a pretty good deal, better, even, than spending eleven months of the year at Archangel. The Russians were also aware that, as they entered their late twenties, the clock was beginning to tick on their playing careers. In Russia, they could count on being replaced by the time they hit their early thirties, which left a very small window for Larionov and his pals.

"We didn't have a lot of years left," says Larionov, who, astoundingly, would play for seventeen more seasons after the '87 Canada Cup before retiring in 2003–4. "We thought our turn was coming."

Kasatonov was aware of the same thing. Even though he was dedicated to Tikhonov and the national team, he saw that world changing. During the '81 and '84 Canada Cups, the team operated under the old rules. They stuck together. They didn't talk to outsiders, especially in the hockey world. But as the 1980s rolled on, things began to change. Virtually every year of that decade, the national team or Red Army toured in North America, and Tikhonov couldn't keep them in their isolation chamber forever.

"There was more freedom," says Kasatonov. "It was more like democracy. We'd played so many games in North America and we began to see the differences in their way of life and our way of life. We see these people, and they're friendly to us. Coaches and GMs start speaking to us. The other players started speaking to us. We see they're just like us. They want to play hockey."

And, as Larionov says, their turn was coming.

In August of 1987, as the Russian team was training in Stockholm for Eagleson's tournament, Jim Proudfoot of the *Toronto Star* wrote a column under the headline: "Five Soviet stars headed for the NHL." While the column was vague on details, Proudfoot suggested that Larionov, Makarov, Krutov, Fetisov, and Kasatonov would all play in the NHL sooner rather than later, and Tikhonov even paid lip service to the concept, admitting it had been discussed at the federation level. Fetisov, the spokesman for the group, said he was aware of his value in the NHL and there had been offers through the years. But, like others who were allowed to play outside of Russia, he would play in North America only if he was allowed to return to his homeland.

"Hockey players grow up with a strong love for the Motherland. It is part of us. There is a bond that some of us would never break. To go away with no chance of returning – that is impossible to imagine," Proudfoot quoted Fetisov in the article.

That, at least, was his position for public consumption. Fetisov was willing to play along to a point and he hoped his many years of service to the national team would allow him to play in the NHL. But he was also growing more militant and more outspoken within the system. During the Canada Cup, the Soviet captain would appear before the press with a Devils' pin displayed conspicuously on his lapel. He'd also worked out a deal with a Swedish manufacturer to wear their helmets during the Canada Cup, an outrageous act of defiance. Fetisov was a singular figure on the team and if the Russian players were going to win any freedoms, they were going to be won through their captain. Larionov was a willing fighter but he wasn't Fetisov. Krutov was a follower. Makarov was far too calculating to take the first step. Kasatonov was a federation man.

As for the rest of the team, they were either too young, too old, or lacked the wherewithal to stand up to Tikhonov. Beyond the Green Unit, in fact, most of the '87 Canada Cup team was young and just finding their way onto the national team. Lomakin, Sergei Nemchinov, and defenceman Alexei Gusarov were twenty-three. Valeri Kamensky, Kravchuk, Belosheikin, and Alexander Semak were twenty-one. Players like Vyacheslav Bykov, Andrei Khomutov, and Anatoli Semenov were a little older but they were also replaceable in Tikhonov's scheme of things. And the more intriguing names in the Russian system –

Alexander Mogilny, Pavel Bure, Sergei Fedorov – were still a couple of years away from establishing themselves in the international game.

"At that moment it was absolutely impossible to leave," says Kravchuk. "Guys regretted they couldn't play in the NHL but we couldn't do anything. Later on the opportunity arose.

"It was a different time. [Tikhonov] got the power because of his success and he was a powerful man."

And he wasn't going to relinquish that power easily.

"On the ice it was easy for us to take care of any situation," Larionov says. "Off the ice we were fighting the big Soviet machine and you needed support in your team. Slava gave me and so many others that support."

As we've seen, while there might have been a lot of high-minded talk about international goodwill and the spirit of sportsmanship surrounding the '87 tournament, most of Team Canada still regarded the Russian team with a healthy dose of suspicion and contempt. The underlying current was still us-versus-them and the Canadians believed they were defending everything that was good and proper in the world. "They were still a Communist country," says Hawerchuk. "It was the last big tournament before the Iron Curtain fell, but there was still a lot of that feeling. We're playing for our way of life. We don't like what they represented. I hate to say it but it almost felt like war. Everyone did what they had to do to win."

There was, however, one voice within Team Canada who didn't believe the Russians ate their young and it was a fairly significant one. Wayne Gretzky was the one Canadian player who, over the years, had familiarized himself with the Russian players and the inner workings of Tikhonov's team, which to most of the Canadian players represented a great unknown. "We didn't have a great scouting report on them," says Hawerchuk. "We knew about the big line and Fetisov and Kasatonov and that was about it." But Gretzky seemed to understand the personalities and the history of the Soviet team as well as some of the Soviet players. Midway through the tournament, he was asked about his impressions of the Russians.

"Of the Soviets' top five players I think only Larionov is playing at the level we saw a few years ago," he said, launching into a lengthy dissertation. "How many good, young players have they had to break in lately? Maybe one, Valeri Kamensky.

"I think the lack of competition in their league really hurt their program. Almost all the good players are on the Red Army team, which always wins. They're always ahead, never behind, and they get no practice at how to handle it. They were supposed to do some things to make the league better but I asked the players and they said they didn't know anything about it.

"We always say before we play them that if you stay close or get ahead they aren't the same team. And it's still true."

It was an insightful assessment of the Russians in 1987. It also revealed Gretzky's fascination with the Russian game.

Gretzky's connection to Russia reached back to his grandfather Tony, who emigrated with his family from what is now Belarus to North America shortly before the First World War. When they reached the States, the family split up, half of them staying, half of them moving on to Argentina. Gretzky's grandfather then moved to Chicago but enlisted in the Canadian army and served overseas during the war. After the armistice he returned to Canada, where he married a Polish immigrant named Mary and, in the 1930s, bought a farm just outside of Brantford with money he borrowed from the War Veterans Act. Gretzky's parents, Walter and Phyllis, lived in Brantford but the farm was a second home to the young Great One. He watched the '72 Series with his grandfather.

"I was thrilled by the win and at how great Phil Esposito was," says Gretzky. "But I always remember how excited my grandfather was to see the Russian players. He didn't like the Communists and he knew how difficult the life was for the average Russian. But my grandfather saw those players as people and that's what he passed on to me."

Tony Gretzky always told his grandson he wanted to return to Russia and see his country one more time, but he never got the chance. One year after watching the Summit Series with his grandson, he died. Wayne Gretzky, for his part, always dreamed of travelling to Russia and playing in a reprise of the '72 Summit Series in Moscow. "Maybe it was because of my grandfather," he says.

Gretzky's first exposure to the highest levels of the Russian system came during the '78 World Junior Championship when, as a sixteen-year-old, he authored a breakout performance on a very good Canadian team in Montreal. Gretzky, who would always regard that tournament as a seminal point in his develop-ment, counted eight goals and seventeen points in six tournament games. But after going undefeated in the round-robin portion of the tournament, the Canadians fell to a Russian team that fea-tured Fetisov, Larionov, Krutov, and Kasatonov and finished third. During the competition, Gretzky had pictures taken of himself with Larionov and Fetisov that he kept throughout his career.

Gretzky faced off against that same group in the '81 Canada Cup and also began to form a friendship with Vladislav Tretiak. The next summer, Gretzky, his family, then girlfriend Vicky Moss, her mother, and long-time hockey man Charlie Henry and his wife flew to Moscow to film a TV special through a Winnipeg-based production company. The idea was Wayne and Walter would show their training techniques to young Russian players and the Gretzkys would be taught the Russian system through Tretiak. The entourage spent a week in Russia, filming, seeing the sights, and being shepherded around by Tretiak and Anatoli Firsov. They toured Red Square. They saw the Moscow circus. The changing of the guard in front of Lenin's Tomb left a deep impression on Wayne, who arose from a sleepless night and watched the ceremony half a dozen times. The Gretzky boys also dined at Tretiak's apartment and Wayne's younger brother Brent, in particular, formed a bond with the great goalie.

In the ensuing years, Gretzky would form relationships with other Russian players. Following the '84 semifinal between the two teams, he and Larionov went out for dinner and beers in Calgary. He had a deep and abiding respect for Fetisov's ability. He also went out of his way to be friendly with the Soviet players and they called him Vanya, the Russian version of his name.

Old Vanya wasn't above trading for Russian caviar, either.

"Maybe it was because of his grandfather but Wayne was always talking to us," says Kasatonov. "There was something about him. He wasn't just a good player, he was a good guy. He was interested in seeing who we were as people."

It should come as no surprise, then, that Gretzky would return the hospitality he was shown in Moscow by Tretiak. Five years later, after Canada met Russia in an afternoon pre-tournament game, Gretzky invited his Russians pals to a barbecue at his parents' house in Brantford. The original idea was to invite Larionov only but things were never that simple with Tikhonov.

"This was all done through channels, but it started off when I invited Igor," Gretzky says. "Then Igor wanted to invite his linemates. Then Fetisov had to come. Then Tikhonov got wind of it and he had to come. Then, because Tikhonov came, the KGB guys had to come. We were pretty crowded."

Gretzky eventually had to explain the dinner was planned for his parents' house, not a hotel, and the numbers would have to be kept to a manageable level. Normally, Tikhonov wouldn't have let the players out of his sight – "KGB rules," Larionov says – but the Russians had clobbered the Canadians 9–4 in the game and Gretzky's father, Walter, spoke to Tikhonov.

"Tikhonov was always in a good mood when we won," Larionov says. "Wayne invited us and we said, 'We don't know.'

Then he talked to Walter and Walter got the message to Tikhonov and it was all right."

That evening, a bus pulled up to the Gretzky household and out popped Larionov, Fetisov, Makarov, and Krutov along with Tikhonov and two unsmiling gentlemen of undetermined purpose. "They said one was a translator and the other was a friend," says Dave Poulin, who also attended the event.

The group then sat down in the Gretzkys' backyard, where Walter and Phyllis had laid out a spread complete with beer and soft drinks. Tikhonov immediately banned beer consumption and, for a long uncomfortable spell, the guests just sat there and didn't say much.

"It was getting kind of comical," says Poulin.

Poulin and the Wayner's brother Keith, however, would save the day. After dinner, the players repaired to the basement and the Gretzky trophy room. There they admired the many mementoes from the Great One's past while Keith Gretzky quietly passed around some beers, which improved the atmosphere considerably.

Upstairs, Tikhonov, the translator, and the friend continued to stare at the Gretzkys while, downstairs, the Gretzky boys, Poulin, and their Russian friends engaged in the time-honoured Canadian tradition of pounding back the ales.

"It was amazing," says Gretzky. "My parents lived in a nice middle-class home but the Russians thought it was a mansion. It was nice just to relax and get to know them as people. That's when I found out how badly they wanted to play in the NHL."

The Russians also found out something about Gretzky.

"I've always remembered that day," says Larionov.

A week later, the tournament would start. And a lot of people would remember the days that followed.

Eagleson's Round Robin

Twenty years after the fact, the perception is every-thing in the 1987 Canada Cup followed a tight script that built toward a thundering crescendo and maybe that's how it should be. Canada and the Soviet Union did meet in the final with the two teams at the peak of their powers. They did produce three transcendent games that will be remembered as long as hockey is played. The series was decided by, if not the most famous goal in the game's history, certainly the most artful. Nothing can diminish the grandeur of those three nights in September.

Yet the runup to the final was your basic dog's breakfast that produced sparse attendance, a schedule which seemed to be written on a cocktail napkin, and inconsequential hockey. The Canada Cup field consisted of the six pre-eminent hockey nations in the world – Canada, the USSR, Czechoslovakia, Finland, Sweden, and the USA – playing a full interlocking schedule over nine days with the top four teams advancing to the semifinal round. The winners then met in a best-of-three final. Had

Czechoslovakia held on to its 2–0 second-period lead over Canada in the semifinal game, in fact, this tournament would be remembered as the greatest calamity in Canada's international hockey history. As it was, the Canadians would come back to beat the Czechs and fight their way into the final.

"It was a roller-coaster ride for our team," says Craig Hartsburg. "There was nothing that came easy for us right from the first game against the Czechs to the last minute of the last game against the Russians. There wasn't a time in that whole tournament where we thought we had it under control."

And that applied to everyone connected with Team Canada, especially Alan Eagleson. Before the tournament started, hockey's overlord was suggesting this could be the last Canada Cup he would stage and his dark mood was the direct result of paltry gates and massive public indifference. Then again, those problems didn't grow out of a vacuum. They first became apparent during the 1984 event in which the great semifinal showdown between Canada and Russia had been played before twelve thousand fans in Calgary and the two-game final between Canada and Sweden didn't fare much better. By 1987, Eagleson's problems had intensified. Russian teams seemed to be touring North America on an annual basis and the novelty of a Russia–Canada showdown had long since worn off. There was resentment over the exorbitant ticket prices – as high as thirty dollars per ducat! Three games were moved – one to Regina and two to Sydney, Nova Scotia, of all places – when ticket sales tanked in Ottawa and Calgary. "I didn't think the '84 Canada Cup was a great success and I was worried [about '87]," says Gretzky. "I thought maybe it had run its course."

He wouldn't get any argument from the Swedes. As a result of the improvised schedule, two of Sweden's games were moved and the Scandinavians played their round-robin games in Calgary, Hamilton, Regina, Montreal, and Sydney over nine days. They would fly some ten thousand kilometres and play in four different time zones in that span and after meeting Finland in Sydney on the night of September 6, they had to get up at five the next morning to catch a 7 a.m. flight from Halifax to Toronto before meeting the Russians the next day in the semifinal and falling 4–2 to the Red Machine. Canada, for its part, played three games in Hamilton and one in Montreal after they opened their tournament in Calgary. This development did not escape the Swedes' notice.

"We are only a team to fill up the tournament," said Curt Bergland, the head of the Swedish hockey federation. "We are like supporting actors."

But the schedule wasn't the only thing the Swedes were complaining about. "In Calgary, we were served chicken for three straight days," said head coach Tommy Sandlin. "I've had to send players out to buy their own food. When we're in Russia, it's a different food culture but they do what they can for us. Here we're being treated like animals." Which at least gave the phrase, "chicken Swedes" a new meaning.

Alan Eagleson wasn't exactly sympathetic. He'd tried to balance the wants and needs of the six teams while giving special consideration to the host side, but the embarrassing situation in Ottawa and slow sales in Calgary forced his hand. He flew to Sydney, met with the mayor, and decided the city presented a better alternative than Ottawa. "I didn't want the teams playing to empty arenas," he says. "I had to preserve the tournament."

As for his assertion that 1987 would be his last Canada Cup, Eagleson said he was frustrated by the slow ticket sales. But just before the round-robin portion of the tournament, he was also talking openly about a twentieth-anniversary reprise of the '72 Summit Series between Canada and the Soviets.

He had at least one enthusiastic supporter for that concept.

"Is this the last Canada Cup?" Eagleson asked rhetorically on the eve of Canada's opening game. "If you asked me that a week ago, I would have said yes. But now that it's all coming together, there will probably be another one in 1992. Gretzky would like to do a rehash of the '72 Canada–Russia series, so we're looking at that."

"I'm excited and I think everybody in the room is excited," Gretzky said of the proposed eight-game series.

But whatever the new format looked like, it was apparent something had to be done because the Canada Cup no longer held the hockey world's imagination. The day Canada played their first game against the Czechs in Calgary, *Philadelphia Daily News* hockey writer Jay Greenberg wrote: "Under cover of apathy, the best hockey players in the world have gathered this week to determine which country plays the sport the best."

And that was an accurate depiction of the atmosphere surrounding the tournament. The Canada–Czechoslovakia game, played in Calgary's new Saddledome, drew 8,458 fans. That same night U.S.A.–Finland drew 8,508 fans in Hartford. And those were two of the larger crowds of the round robin. Just over 3,000 fans watched Sweden play the Soviets in Calgary. Canada–Finland produced a crowd of 9,624 in Hamilton. A crowd, if that's the right term, of 3,262 attended the Russia–Finland game in Halifax. Czechoslovakia–Finland drew some 3,000 fans in Sydney. Even in Montreal, just 12,360 fans showed up at The Forum to watch Canada versus Sweden.

Clearly, the novelty of the event had worn off in Canada and the story wasn't any happier for Eagleson in the States, where American coach Bob Johnson, who put together a strong team, decried both the fan support and the media support in his home country. Among other things, Johnson noted just five U.S. daily papers were covering the tournament and, "One of the writers told me we had to keep winning or they're sending him home."

But the biggest reason for fan apathy was simple enough. Canada–Russia was the only matchup the hockey public wanted to see and the round-robin games were little more than an exercise designed to arrive at that point. Everyone connected with this tournament was aware of this reality – "I understand Eagleson's problem," said Sweden's Bergland.

They also knew they were the warmup act and Canada–Russia was Sinatra. After a time, hockey fans got the show they wanted to see.

Team Canada assistant coach Jean Perron notes there is a certain pattern most Canadian entries follow in best-on-best competition. They start slowly. There is usually a crisis. But, "When the chips are down, the guys respond," Perron says. "And the bigger the challenge, the better the guys play." You might say Mike Keenan's team followed this pattern in the early part of the round robin.

They led off with the uninspired 4–4 tie against the Czechs, beat the undermanned Finns 4–1, then edged the Americans 3–2 before seventeen thousand fans in Hamilton. The Americans iced their best-ever team to that point in their hockey history – John Vanbiesbrouck and Tom Barrasso in goal; a defence with Chris Chelios, Rod Langway, Kevin Hatcher, and Gary Suter; Pat LaFontaine, Brett Hull, and Bobby Carpenter up front. But after opening with a win over Sweden and the one-goal loss to the Canadians, they were blitzed 5–1 by the Soviets, then dropped a 3–1 contest to the Czechs and fell out of a playoff spot. The Americans outshot the Czechs 37–25 but couldn't solve Dominik Hasek, then a twenty-two-year-old tenth-round draft pick of the Chicago Blackhawks who was playing with Pardubice in the Czech Elite league. (Hasek wore the number two in the tournament.)

Canada, meanwhile, finished with a win over the Swedes and a 3–3 tie with the Russians when Gretzky scored with two minutes and twenty-seven seconds left in the game. That tie gave them first place in the round robin, but the more significant development occurred in the area of team building where, once they decided they weren't going to lynch Keenan, players and coaches went about sorting out roles and playing time. For some it was easy. Gretzky was going to centre the top line and, with Lemieux, key the offence. Messier and Anderson, who was playing through a sprained knee, would form the nominal second unit. Bourque and Coffey would eat up most of the minutes on the blue line.

For other players, things weren't quite as straightforward. Hawerchuk, Gilmour, and Sutter were all natural centres and at least two of them were playing out of position. Tocchet, Claude Lemieux, and Kevin Dineen were similar players – grinding two-way wingers who weren't going to scare anyone offensively. Propp would end up seeing duty on the first line with Gretzky in some games and would be used sparingly in others. Keenan, of course, loved this. He loved moving players around, trying to find the best matchups while keeping everyone fresh and on edge. He was a master manipulator and this team, which featured so many interchangeable pieces, was perfectly suited to him. "We had a meeting and I asked how many minutes of ice time are available," Keenan says. "Larry Murphy sticks up his hand and says, 'sixty.' I said: 'Well, Murph, actually there's seven hundred and twenty. There's six men a side who play for sixty minutes. Now one of those is a goalie who'll probably play for sixty. That leaves three hundred for the whole team. Now, do you guys mind if Wayne plays twenty-five? And Mark plays twenty-five. And Ray plays twenty.' I went down the list and Tocchet finally sticks up his hand and says, 'Mike, there's four minutes left. Do you mind if I get that?'

"They started to understand what this was going to look like, that not everyone was going to get the star minutes. They understood that pretty well."

Some understood better than others. Brent Sutter was on board. He knew he was going to play right wing. He knew he was going to be cast in a checking role. On Long Island, he was a twenty-minutes-a-game centreman but he had no problem with his Team Canada role. He didn't even have a problem with Keenan. "I had a lot of respect for Mike Keenan," Sutter says. "He was my coach for two Canada Cups and he traded for me when I was in Chicago. I know what kind of coach he is. My job as a player was to go out there and do what was asked of me."

Then again Canada had a number of those guys. Tocchet started training camp as a long shot to make the team but opened the tournament playing on a line with Gretzky and Propp and scored Canada's first goal on a pass from Gretzky. You might say that left an impression on the twenty-three-year-old winger.

"Did you see that pass," Tocchet said. "It was unbelievable. Sometimes this whole thing is unbelievable when you stop and think about it. But you know something? After a couple of days of camp, I felt I belonged.

"In 1984, Canada won with guys who people said they couldn't win with. Guys like me, grinders like John Tonelli and Brent Sutter. Guys who like to win. I think guys like Claude Lemieux and I owe them a debt of gratitude for proving that, even on this level, that kind of hockey can still win."

And would win again.

Hawerchuk, for his part, was moving freely in and out of Keenan's doghouse throughout the round robin. The Winnipeg Jets centre scored in each of Canada's first two games and reasoned he'd earned a regular shift. But he was used sporadically over the next three games until the semifinal contest when he started the comeback against Hasek and the Czechs with Canada's first goal.

"With Mike you never knew," Hawerchuk says. "He'd play you every second shift and you'd think, 'Wow, he really has confidence in me.' Then you wouldn't see the ice for five minutes. Finally he'd come down the bench and go, 'Are you ready to start playing?' You'd be thinking, 'I thought that was the idea.'"

Apparently, Hawerchuk was ready against the Czechs. Hasek, who'd played four games in the '84 Canada Cup as a nineteen-year-old, had a 2–0 lead midway through the second when Hawerchuk fired a slapshot that ticked off defenceman Bedrich Scerban and flew past the Czech goalie. That goal ignited the Canadians. Forty-two seconds later, Mario Lemieux scored on a partial breakaway when he zipped a wrister over Hasek's shoulder from the right faceoff circle. Students of Foreshadowing 101 please take note. Less than two minutes later Lemieux scored again. Goulet and Propp would finish off Hasek in the third period.

"I think we smelled blood after [Hawerchuk's goal]," said Messier after the game.

But that wasn't the last time the hockey world would hear from Hasek.

"The Czechs were already saying he was the best goalie in the world," says Hrudey. "You saw him and he was this skinny guy with this weird equipment. But he could stop the puck. That was pretty obvious."

Years later, Hawerchuk would play with Hasek in Buffalo and remind him of his goal. "I used to give it to him all the time," Hawerchuk says. "I'd go, 'Dom, I blew that by you. You couldn't see it.' He'd go, 'No, no, it deflected off the defenceman.' I never let him forget that."

Hasek was asked what he remembers about Hawerchuk's goal almost twenty years after the fact. "It was a deflection, a slight deflection but it was definitely deflected," he answered quickly.

Anything else?

"Canada underestimated us. We were up 2–0 and Rosie Ruzicka had a breakaway. If he scores there, I think we win."

For Canadians, the other lasting memory from the semifinal win concerned Lemieux's two goals in a one-minute-and-forty-three-second span. The two markers gave him seven goals to lead the tournament, but, more importantly, it signalled the first time in his career that he produced when the pressure was at its highest. Lemieux, just twenty-one at the time, had endured endless criticism for his failure to lead the Penguins anywhere, for his spotty work ethic, for his perceived lack of commitment. But this was a new Lemieux the game was witnessing.

"I'm here to win the Canada Cup and give everything I've got," Lemieux said in mid-tournament. "I admit it's a lot of fun being in this dressing room with all these great players."

The Russians' story arc, meanwhile, tracked the Canadians' closely. A week after the barbecue at their pal Vanya's place in Brampton, Tikhonov's team opened the tournament with a shocking 5–3 loss to a Swedish side that was without NHLers Hakan Loob, Thomas Steen, Tomas Sandstrom, and Pelle Eklund. "It was great," said Sweden's Mats Naslund. "We all admire the Russians. I guess we don't like them." The Swedes played the perfect game against the Soviets, opening a 4–3 lead on Belosheikin after two periods, then trapping them to death in the third. The Red Machine were great front-runners, but, as Gretzky noted, they weren't the same team when they were challenged.

That wasn't a problem in their next game. Behind diminutive goalie Sergei Mylnikov, the Russians beat the Czechs and Hasek 4–0 in Regina, then followed that up with a sloppy 7–4 win over the Finns. In their fourth outing, however, they flexed their old muscle, pounding the Americans 5–1 in a wild affair. Late in the first period, with the Russians leading 1–0, American defenceman Gary Suter broke his stick over the fine facial features of Andrei Lomakin and earned a major for his troubles. Makarov scored on the ensuing power play and the Americans were finished. "That was always one of the tactics they used against us," Larionov says. "They never understood it didn't work. We'd bend but we didn't break."

The win over the States set up a first-place showdown between Canada and Russia in Montreal in which the Canadians came back from a 3–1 second-period deficit to tie the game and take the round robin. The matchup between the two rivals also featured a bizarre scene when Tikhonov reached over the boards to grab the jersey of linesman Kevin Collins midway through the third period, ostensibly to discuss the nature of the officiating. American referee Mike Noeth, who'd also worked the Russians' earlier loss to Sweden, had the power plays 5–0 for the Canadians, including a bench minor to Tikhonov, in the exciting affair.

"It's a pride thing to finish first in the round robin," Messier said afterward.

"They can't play any better than that," said Canadian coach John Muckler. "And I'm not sure we can, either."

But both teams could.

The Russians joined the Canadians in the final with a sharp 4–2 semifinal win over the travel-weary Swedes, in which they allowed just twelve shots on goal over the final two periods. Krutov scored a goal and added two assists as did Makarov. Larionov also scored and Fetisov contributed two helpers.

"It seems we were always arriving someplace at 5 a.m., or leaving at 5 a.m.," said Swedish defenceman Tomas Jonsson.

"If you want my opinion, we should keep our mouths shut," said Mats Naslund. "All we ever do is complain."

Scott Morrison, who covered all three Canada Cups in the 1980s, was constantly amazed at Eagleson's ability to upstage the best players in the world during his tournament. He was always available to the media and always providing lively copy. Sometimes it was a controversy he'd dredge up involving one of the European teams. Sometimes it was an insight into the inner workings of Team Canada. To the favoured, he'd serve up a scoop or two. It was all designed, of course, to keep the Canada Cup in the news, and Eagleson had an incredible ability to give the media what they wanted.

The stories that emerged from the live action in the '87 event were rich enough to stand on their own. But that didn't stop Eagleson from insinuating himself into everything that occurred from training camp in early August to the final in mid-September. There was the intrigue over the twentieth-anniversary restaging of the Summit Series. There was his fussing over the future of the Canada Cup. There was no such thing as a slow news day when Eagleson was around. "He always gave you something to write about and the media loved every minute of it because he was gold," says Morrison.

And, in the end, Eagleson loved every minute of this tournament because it worked out the way he'd envisioned. After the slow start, Canada and Russia would meet in the best-of-three final. That would ensure massive media coverage and sellout crowds for Game 1 in Montreal, Game 2 in Hamilton, and, if necessary, the deciding contest back at Copps Coliseum. A Canada–Russia final also ensured huge television numbers. The '87 Canada Cup would be a success on and off the ice, which meant Eagleson would meet his financial obligations to Hockey Canada, under whose auspices the tournament was run, and the NHL Players' Association, whose pension fund would benefit greatly from the event.

The tournament, in fact, would generate millions in revenue, though how much exactly was a mystery because Hockey Canada's financials were less than detailed. There were questions, of course, about the accounting, about Eagleson's handling of the tournament's business, about Eagleson's questionable practices. But that's all they were, questions, and that's all they'd been since the Eagle got his talons into international hockey.

It was only after Russ Conway, the courageous and indefatigable sports editor of the Lawrence *Eagle-Tribune*, dug deeply into the paperwork that a truer picture would be revealed. Conway would report that seventy-two cents out of every dollar in '87 Canada Cup revenue went toward expenses and there was little information to explain where that expense money went. He would also uncover irregularities over the board advertising that benefited Eagleson greatly.

In a famous memo sent to the PA in 1989, Eagleson wrote: "Neither I nor any member of my family nor any company with which I have been associated has ever received money directly or indirectly from any international hockey event."

Eight years later, Eagleson would begin serving an eighteen-month jail sentence after pleading guilty to three counts of fraud and theft in an Ontario courtroom and to three more counts in a Boston courtroom.

"I don't know if [Eagleson's involvement in Canada Cups] was a lightning rod [for investigators] but that's where he seemed to benefit the most," said player-agent Rich Winter, one of the men responsible for bringing Eagleson down. "That was the exchange for lying down for the owners. He got international hockey."

And the cost was great for all concerned.

Hockey Canada, under whose aegis Eagleson conducted the Canada Cups, was founded in 1969 following a recommendation by a federal sports task force headed by Charles Rea, a Toronto businessman. At the time, the country's hockey establishment was reeling from a series of lopsided losses at the hands of the Russians and other European countries at the world championships, and Rea's task force, among other things, recommended the formation of a non-profit organization to raise money and operate a national hockey team program. Hockey Canada was officially formed on February 24, 1969, at a meeting chaired by John Munro, the federal minister of health in Pierre Trudeau's cabinet. Those present included newspaper columnist and politician Douglas Fisher, Leafs co-owner Stafford Smythe, Canadiens co-owner David Molson, Father David Bauer, Earl Dawson, and Gordon Juckes from the Canadian Amateur Hockey Association (CAHA), and Eagleson, then the head of the NHL Players' Association and the game's most powerful player-agent.

Eagleson was originally named chairman of the new group's

public relations committee and seemed to play a minor role in the early going before his profile increased as Hockey Canada pressed for the participation of NHL and minor pro players at the world championship. Early in 1970, they thought they'd convinced the IIHF and its president, the conniving Bunny Ahearne, to allow the pros into the 1970 world championship, set for Winnipeg. But after some backroom manoeuvring, not only was the use of professional players rescinded, the tournament was taken away from Winnipeg and moved to Sweden. That led to Canada pulling out of all international competition and set in motion the events that would lead to the '72 Summit Series.

Now, of course, the perception is that Eagleson was the driving force behind the '72 Series, and he has done little over the years to discourage that perception. But the more accepted version of events had Joe Kryczka, a Calgary lawyer and the CAHA president, and Juckes, the CAHA's executive director, laying the groundwork for the history-making series after several high-level meetings at the '72 world championships in Prague.

According to observers, Eagleson wasn't invited to those meetings, but he did mysteriously appear in Prague just as negotiations were drawing to a close. Eagleson was eventually named to an eight-man board that would run the series and, through the influence of the Players' Association and the strength of his own personality, he emerged as the drama's central character. He was front and centre with the media. His infamous entourage – a loose collection of doctors, dentists, lawyers, photographers, and other Eagleson bootlicks, distinguished by their Team Canada blazers and who, at their peak, numbered nearly thirty – made its first public appearance. By the time the series moved to Russia, Eagleson was as visible as the game's greatest stars and he cemented his place in the Canadian sporting conscience in Game 8 when he was shepherded across the ice by Team Canada players at the Luzhniki Ice Palace after a confrontation with Soviet soldiers.

Through the '72 Series, Eagleson also came to learn about the wealth of opportunities international hockey might afford an enterprising young man. It seems unbelievable now, but when the TV rights for the Summit Series originally went up for auction, it received only one bid, for $500,000 from McLaren Advertising. Eagleson took one look at that offer, partnered up with Leafs co-owner Harold Ballard, and ended up purchasing the rights for $750,000 under the company name Ballard-Orr Enterprises Ltd. Bobby Orr was Eagleson's most famous client. Orr, as you might have guessed, didn't know his agent had committed $375,000 of his money to the project.

"In '72, he could see what international hockey could be and that's when he made that turn," says Conway. "He also saw what it could do for Al."

The Eagle hit a home run in the series. A TV audience of 16 million would tune in for Games 7 and 8 in Moscow and Ballard-Orr realized a profit of $1.2 million. Expenses for the tournament, meanwhile, rang out at a hefty $1 million – as mentioned, there were a lot of those guys in blue blazers – leaving $700,000 to be split between Hockey Canada and the PA's pension fund. Again, no one really knew where all the expenses went, but the $350,000 for Hockey Canada represented a huge windfall to a non-profit organization that was trying to operate itself on private money. The organization saw the dollars generated by the '72 Series. They reasoned there was more where that came from. And they essentially sold themselves to Eagleson. In 1975, the federal government named Eagleson the chief negotiator for Hockey Canada. Suddenly a whole new world was laid at the Eagle's feet.

Eagleson's first endeavour at his new posting was an unqualified success, both aesthetically and financially. In 1976, he realized a long-held dream when he hosted the first Canada Cup, an international best-on-best tournament loosely based on soccer's World Cup. A stacked Canadian team defeated the Czechs in a memorable final on Darryl Sittler's game-winning goal. The event turned a $3-million profit. Hockey Canada, which had been guaranteed $600,000 up front, ended up with $1 million. And that money bought Eagleson considerable influence and favour within Hockey Canada. He made the most of his new prestige. Canada would return to the world championships with professionals in 1977. In 1981, a second Canada Cup was undertaken. Eagleson was given almost complete autonomy in the organization and execution of these events and Hockey Canada wasn't completely uncomfortable with the arrangement. In 1981, 1984, 1987, and 1991, they received a handsome payout while expending minimum effort. True, Eagleson wasn't the easiest person to deal with and questions were starting to be asked about his business dealings – what were all these secretarial and administrative charges? What about the board advertising? What about all those guys in the blazers? – but they weren't asked too loudly.

"There wasn't a great deal of suspicion at Hockey Canada level," says Ron Robison, who started at Hockey Canada in 1985 and was its president when Eagleson was forced to resign in 1993. Robison is now the president of the Western Hockey League (WHL). "He always met his obligation to Hockey Canada. Everyone was satisfied the event was well-managed and it was successful.

"Hockey Canada always felt they were getting their money's worth. He was essentially treated as an independent contractor. It was his project. He had his people."

Oh, he had his people all right. Eagleson maintained he never drew a salary from Hockey Canada and, technically, that's true. Eagleson hired out his secretaries and staff to work on the Canada Cups, then billed Hockey Canada inflated sums for their employ. He charged Hockey Canada for office expenses when working out of Maitland House, the building from which he also ran the Players' Association and his Sports Management Limited agency. Bill Watters, his right-hand man at Sports

Management Limited, held seven different positions with international Canadian teams from 1976 to 1979, including GM of Team Canada at the 1977 and 1978 world championships. His Hockey Canada salary exceeded $100,000 between 1977 and 1979 and that money was also deducted from his Sports Management salary.

It was a similar story with Rick Curran, another employee of Sports Management, who would become one of the most influential agents in hockey. Curran's jobs with Hockey Canada ranged from chauffeuring IIHF officials at the '76 Canada Cup to coordinating Canada's entry at the '77 World Junior Championship in Montreal. His Hockey Canada salary was also deducted from his Sports Management salary. For the '87 Canada Cup, Sam Simpson, Eagleson's director of operations for the Players' Association, signed a $72,000 agreement to serve as comptroller and liaison to Team Canada. Eagleson didn't see anything wrong with this. "The guy works for me and if I can put him to work and make a million dollars, it's my million dollars not his," he crowed to *Sports Illustrated* in 1984. "If I pay my guy $30,000, and rent him for $50,000, that makes me smart."

And Eagleson had figured out all the angles. Conway's investigation into Hockey Canada's financials was exhaustive but he also concluded it was hard to know the precise amounts the Canada Cups generated. The statements were one-line entries that revealed nothing in the way of detail. The 1987 and 1988 financial statement says simply that Eagleson's International Committee expenses for those years totalled $1.9 million. That figure included $795,298 for salaries and benefits, $323,078 for office expenses, $154,368 for accommodations and meals, and $108,836 for insurance and other costs. That was it. No explanation. Just one line with a big number. When he was asked about the business of the Canada Cup, Eagleson employed a variety of methods to discourage the inquisitive. If a player asked him about where the money went, he'd tell them that was Canada Cup business and not a player's concern. If a Hockey Canada official questioned him, he would counter-attack aggressively and profanely and that would quiet any dissent. Eagleson was fond of saying, If I raise the money, I'll tell you how to spend it. And there weren't a lot of people at Hockey Canada who disagreed with him, especially when he turned over a fat cheque at the conclusion of each Canada Cup.

· Then there was the matter of the rinkboard advertisements. Conway, who would uncover further improprieties in the '91 Canada Cup, learned that for the '87 Canada Cup, Air Canada agreed to purchase $84,000 in rinkboard ads. Rather than pay in cash, however, Air Canada honoured twenty-eight flight passes from March 30, 1987, and December 31, 1989, worth an average of $3,000 apiece. Some years later, Hockey Canada determined that approximately $60,000 worth of those tickets were used from the Canada Cup. Between 1989 and 1993, Eagleson flew to London three times, twice to Frankfurt, twice to Chicago, and once each to Zurich, Vancouver, Tampa, Paris, and Nice. Between 1989 and 1991, Eagleson's wife used $37,000 in Air Canada travel passes in return for Canada Cup advertising, including one trip to Bombay. His son Trevor used the passes. His son's wife used the passes. Howard Ungerman, an employee of his law firm, used them.

Add it all up and the system Eagleson built resembled a high-level crime organization in which he, as the boss, took a taste of every transaction in the neighbourhood. There were four parking spaces at Maitland House, the site of Eagleson's law offices and the home of the NHLPA. The PA was billed $500 a month for three of those spots and the fourth was supposedly thrown in for free. For the '91 Canada Cup, Eagleson rented six parking spots to Hockey Canada for $600. That means he'd rented out the four parking spots ten times. Those blue blazers didn't come cheap, either. For the '91 Cup, a $100,000 bill for suits and ties was forwarded to Labatt. Eagleson also included

$28,000 worth of invoices for his own suits that Labatt refused to pay.

Now, it seems impossible that one man could wield that much power and influence while helping himself to whatever he deemed fit. But such was the force of Eagleson's personality, his cunning and his bravado, that he could take control of a hockey world that was not without its own levels of corruption.

"I kept thinking, Al, why are you doing this," Conway answers when asked what was going through his mind as the truth about Eagleson revealed itself. "You've got a thriving business. If you want more money, why don't you just go to the PA? You don't have to steal. There wasn't a nickel went by that he didn't take a piece of."

He even had the perfect cover story. Eagleson would tell the players, I'm doing all this for you, for the association, for your pensions. And that was just another part of the elaborate shell game he'd constructed. The Players' Association's share from the Canada Cup was supposed to pay for the players' pension fund. That might have been Eagleson's most ingenious trick of all. The owners were supposed to match the players' contributions dollar-for-dollar, but their share, as Carl Brewer and a group of former players would learn, was paid for out of an existing surplus within the pension fund. If that wasn't enough, Eagleson would use the pension issue to deliver the players to the owners in five separate negotiations over a new collective-bargaining agreement. Thus, while every other professional sport in North America was making huge advancements in free agency and salaries, NHL players, who were still shackled to a near-feudal system, were placated with modest gains in their pensions.

In 1979, when the NHL needed the players' assent to ram through the merger with four WHA teams, the players backed off free agency in exchange for a small increase in their pension. The players held all the leverage in that negotiation. They'd also seen a significant rise in their salaries because of the WHA. But, despite the threat of militancy, they caved when the owners made their oft-repeated claim that free agency would ruin the game and drive several franchises out of business, costing the union scores of jobs in the process. Eagleson also did his part for the owners. At a crucial juncture in the talks, he took aside then PA president Phil Esposito and made an impassioned plea to "to do the right thing for all the players." Esposito recommended the PA accept the deal. He would come to regret that decision.

"I was like [Eagleson's] puppet," Esposito told *Sports Illustrated* five years later. "I admit that."

It was the same story in 1986, when it was clear the NHL was lagging behind the gains made by players in Major League Baseball, the NFL, and the NBA. Again, there was talk of pressing for change within the system. Again, the threat of a strike was issued. But in the end the players were bought off with a lump-sum bonus of $250,000 to be paid out at age fifty-five to those who'd played four hundred career games. The owners also paid for their share of that increase out of the pension fund's surplus.

The authors of *Net Worth*, the fine 1991 book that also exposed Eagleson, called this, "the biggest sucker play in the history of professional sports" and few would disagree.

"There is a fine line between loyalty and naivete and we crossed that line," says former player Ray Ferraro, who was involved with the Players' Association during his career. "[Eagleson] took advantage of us because we weren't paying attention."

But it still took a brilliant engineer to construct the machine Eagleson controlled. As the chief negotiator for Hockey Canada, he had access to the tournament's financial levers and he manipulated those levers to his own advantage. He used the Canada Cups to strengthen his position with the players through the marvellous job he was doing in building their pensions. By making the pensions the focal point of collective-bargaining negotiations, instead of free agency, he also secured a cozy working relationship with the owners. It all ran through Eagleson and it made him the most powerful man in hockey. And that suited management just fine.

"Al delivers us the players and we give him international hockey," an NHL general manager told *Sports Illustrated* in that same 1984 article. "It's that simple."

But, it was starting to get a little more complicated for Eagleson by the time of the '87 Canada Cup.

It says something about his unassailable position within the game that he was able to hold off outside forces for another six years, but questions were being asked about the Eagle and the power he held. One of the earliest and most persistent of Eagleson's critics was Bruins defenceman Mike Milbury, who attended Colgate before playing twelve seasons on the Bruins' blue line. As far back as 1979, Milbury and his Bruins' team-mates commissioned Price Waterhouse to survey all 460 NHL players on whether they wanted a full-time executive director for their union. One hundred and fifty-four players responded, and 101 said they wanted a full-time director. Milbury distributed the results at a PA meeting in February 1980. Eagleson immediately said if the players wanted to replace him, he'd step down. A four-man selection committee was then struck, which, incredibly, included Eagleson. It met once later that year and never again. In 1983 and 1984, Eagleson also survived two votes from the player reps, who tended to be Eagleson allies. The vote was conducted publicly by a show of hands. Milbury always believed it would have been a different story with a secret ballot.

Player agent Rich Winter, who'd just graduated from law school and was in the process of establishing his practice in Edmonton, took up the cause in the mid-1980s and Winter, along with L.A.–based agent Ron Salcer, would eventually play an instrumental role in bringing down Eagleson. At the time, Winter represented a handful of players, most notably Czechs

Frank Musil and David Volek, and, like every other agent in the game, he'd heard stories about Eagleson's methods. Unlike a lot of those agents, however, Winter resolved to do something about it.

"I think it was the rapid increase in salaries in other sports that finally got the players' attention," he says. "If Al would have done his job half-assed and salaries would have gone to $500,000 and $600,000, I think it might have died there."

As it was, the sheer absurdity of the situation still strikes Winter. Owing to active and more militant unions, the players' lot in other professional sports had undergone dramatic changes in the 1970s and 1980s. In hockey, where things never seemed to change, the union was run by one man who couldn't or wouldn't deliver the rights and freedoms, to say nothing of the salaries, won by players in other professional leagues. That man also seemed uncomfortably close to the owners. And you could never be certain from day to day or week to week who he was representing or where his allegiances lay.

"It was a pattern of ongoing complaints voiced by the players," says Winter. "I looked at it and said, 'This doesn't make any sense.' This guy doesn't act like a union leader. He doesn't seem to stand up for the players. I didn't know the influence this guy had. I thought people would put me on a white horse for helping them. I was from a town of five thousand [Drumheller, Alta.], and I was naive.

"Once I got into the battle, it was me against Al and I couldn't get out."

It was big things with Eagleson. And it was little things. Jim Fox was the L.A. Kings' player rep from 1985 to 1989 and one of the first to align himself with Winter and Salcer. In talking to players and union officials from other sports, he was told that public disclosure of salaries had been a huge benefit because it gave all concerned access to the same information. Eagleson always belittled that suggestion, but that wasn't what bothered

Fox. What bothered him was his union chief forming that opinion without examining the available data.

"Shouldn't he be on our side?" Fox asks rhetorically. "Shouldn't he be looking into these things? You started to look at the way the PA was run and those questions came up over and over."

Fox had also joined the fight early when the anti-Eagleson faction was few in number. Was he nervous about taking on the most powerful man in hockey? "Was I nervous?" he replied. "Yeah. At the time there were still concerns about who controlled your job. But when we finally started talking to others and realized a lot of people felt the same way, it made things easier."

About the time Winter and his allies began taking a longer look at Eagleson, *Sports Illustrated* ran a lengthy piece in July 1984 that was one of the first public investigations into the PA chief. The magazine spent eighteen months examining Eagleson and drew attention to many of his methods. "Because he holds the ultimate bargaining chip – 100 per cent of the world's best professional hockey players – scarcely anything of import can happen in the sport without the approval, if not the direct participation, of Eagleson," John Papanek wrote, neatly summing up Eagleson's place in the game. "However there's evidence that Eagleson has at times abused his multiple powers as head of the NHLPA, chief negotiator for Hockey Canada . . . and personal representative of many of the NHL's stars specifically for his personal gain and the gain of his friends."

Papanek also wrote: "Eagleson rules hockey from atop a sort of international pyramid, because he's likely to be negotiating today against the side he'll be representing at a different bargaining table tomorrow," and Eagleson saw no problem with that.

"I consider [Blackhawks owner] Bill Wirtz a friend except at the negotiating table, when I consider him the enemy," he responded. "Everything I do is out front. If the players don't like it, all they have to do is fire me."

Eagleson was interviewed more than a year before the piece

ran and he refused subsequent requests from *Sports Illustrated* as they uncovered irregularities in his business practices. The story, in fact, was a commendable effort that presaged the work of Conway and others. But it didn't exactly shake the game to its foundation.

Papanek wondered about a man who represented all NHL players as head of the Players' Association but also represented fifty players individually as their agent. He wondered about Eagleson's chummy relationship with NHL president John Ziegler and many of the owners and pointed out that, unlike unions in other sports, the PA never fought for free agency. He wondered about some of the problems with insurance and why Eagleson didn't fight for players like Glen Sharpley and Murray Wilson who'd suffered career-ending injuries. Papanek wondered about many things but he lacked the hard data to make any of the charges stick.

"There were a lot of allegations in those days, but there wasn't a lot of hard proof until Russ Conway came along," says longtime hockey man Brian Burke.

And Burke was intimately familiar with this reality. In the summer of 1985, Burke was among the leaders of a dissident group of agents, which included future PA chief Bob Goodenow, who drafted a letter to Eagleson seeking reforms to the Players' Association. The language in the first draft of that letter was direct and to the point. "Mr. Eagleson's position is that the union is his own personal fiefdom and that the role people like us play is superfluous to the bargaining procedure . . . I am going to recommend that each player/agent present (and any others who wished to attend but could not) instruct each and every player he represents to abstain from the NHLPA until such time as Mr. Eagleson either adopts a program in line with ours or resigns." A softer version of that letter was eventually sent to Eagleson but it still demanded audited NHLPA financial statements and proposed an agents' association that would serve an advisory role to the PA.

Eagleson was magnanimous when he was presented with the demands. "Their representation was reasonable, sensitive, and positive," he said. "I might as well have written their proposal. These were the basic things I've been talking to the owners about over the years."

But a face-to-face meeting between Eagleson and the dissidents produced predictable results. Burke, Pierre Lacroix, and Gus Badali sat down with the Eagle to drive home the agents' agenda but they weren't quite as tough in person as they'd been on paper. Lacroix, according to Burke, agreed with everything Eagleson said. Badali showed up in a ski ensemble because he wanted to head to the Laurentians. "Eagleson said, 'Yes, yes, I agree totally,' to everything we said," Burke now says. "Then he put it in the paper shredder."

Burke maintains that, at the time, Eagleson's involvement in international hockey wasn't the most pressing issue for the agents. More important was wresting away control from Eagleson of the Players' Association, the institution from which his powers flowed.

"[The dissatisfaction] was widespread but it was always met with this outraged arrogance from Eagleson," says Burke. "It was like, 'How dare you question me.' There was great unanimity and militancy among the agents. But it wasn't shared by the players. There were enough who thought Eagleson had done a good job for them."

And many of those players continued to believe in Eagleson until Conway and others came along. "There was a paper trail," Conway says. "There were always questions and innuendo around Al but nothing could be proven.

"He beat the Milbury challenge. He beat *Sports Illustrated*. The PA never got to him. They tried to audit him and it went nowhere. All the stories wouldn't put him in jail. The paper trail put him in jail."

The Great One, Wayne Gretzky,
Team Canada Captain

Doug MacLellan / Hockey Hall of Fame

Mike Keenan,
coach of Team Canada

Doug MacLellan/Hockey Hall of Fame

Legendary Soviet coach Viktor Tikhonov

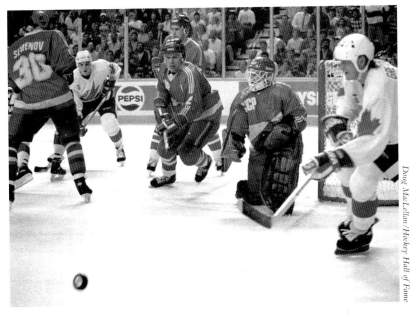

Viacheslav Fetisov chases the puck and Gretzky

Smooth–skating Ray Bourque

Mike Gartner and Brian Propp are all smiles

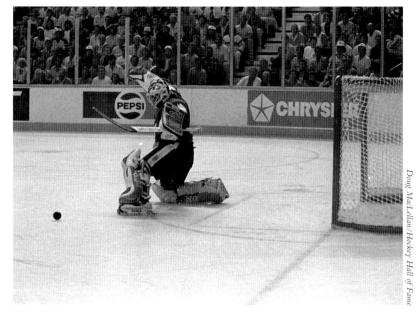

Canadian goaltender Grant Fuhr turns aside another shot

The Magnificent One, Mario Lemieux, breaks in on the Soviets

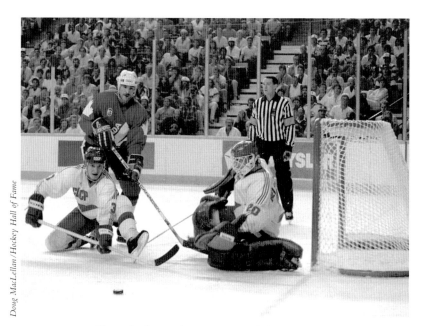

Glenn Anderson buzzing around the Soviet net

Mark Messier causing problems in front of the Soviet goal

CHAPTER 4

A Slow Start

The first game of the 1987 Canada Cup featured a Canadian goal on their first shot of the game, four consecutive goals from the Russians, which caused much consternation at The Forum in Montreal, a four-goal rally by the Canadians, which came out of the blue and gave them a one-goal lead with just under three minutes left, a tying goal from the Russians thirty-two seconds later, and a brilliant overtime winner from Alexander Semak after Grant Fuhr made two highlight-reel saves.

And it was the worst game of the three-game set. It's true what they say about all things being relative.

Thirty-nine days after Team Canada had assembled for their first day of camp, the much-anticipated final began. There had been several notable developments on both sides before the puck was dropped. Canada was without the services of wingers Kevin Dineen, out with an ankle sprain incurred against the Americans, and Claude Lemieux, who was out with another ankle injury. Rick Tocchet meanwhile was badly hobbled with a sprained left knee, suffered in the earlier 3–3 tie with the Russians but was ready for spot duty. James Patrick, the seventh defenceman, was also available for the odd shift on the wing.

"We've got ten and a half forwards," Keenan observed dryly before the contest. "Sure with only ten forwards, the more Mario, Gretz, and Messier play the better we should be," said Muckler, the Team Canada assistant. "But if we have to play three games with the Soviets, there are going to be times when we need that fourth line. There's not too many lulls in a game with the Soviets. They have two speeds: fast and faster."

The Soviets, for their part, had lost forward Sergei Svetlov, who scored two goals against the Canadians in the round robin, when the explosive winger broke his arm in the semifinal against the Swedes. But, while the injured players represented interesting sidebars prior to Game 1, by far the biggest piece of news to emerge was the appointment of Canadian referee Don Koharski at the request of the Russians.

"This is unusual with a Canadian team playing," noted broadcaster Dan Kelly in the lead item to his pre-game remarks.

"I was as surprised as anyone," says Koharski, who became the second referee in NHL history to work fifteen hundred regular-season games in 2005–6.

He had plenty of company. In just his third full year of refereeing, the fifty-two-year-old Maritimer had worked several of the round-robin games and assumed his tournament was over when Russia met Canada in the final because international protocol called for neutral officials to be assigned to games. The problem was the Russians didn't trust any of the Europeans and, as we've seen, they weren't overly enamoured with the work of American referee Mike Noeth.

Prior to Game 1, Eagleson and NHL supervisor of officials John McCauley met with representatives from Canada and the U.S.S.R. Koharski, for his part, went to play golf near his Burlington, Ontario, home and was surprised when the pro at his course told him to phone home for an important message.

"Honestly, I thought I might be the standby official," Koharski says. "Then I got a hold of John and he said, 'This is unbelievable. They want you to do all three games.' He had his own ideas and he wanted [American referee Paul Stewart] to do one of the games. I said fine. I was thrilled just to be considered."

"That broke the ice as far as the international game went," Koharski continues. "Now, they just select the best officials. Before it was very political and anything could happen."

Eagleson now says he convinced the Russians that Koharski was the best available referee, but it wasn't exactly a tough sell. Koharski had worked a number of the Soviets' games when they toured North America and Tikhonov's team always seemed to do well under Koharski's watch.

"Maybe they thought I was a good luck charm, but I can tell you, they didn't need my help," Koharski says.

The appointment also made for some lively copy the day before the game and Koharski was the subject of considerable attention from the assembled press corps. That was noted by Mark Messier, who said something unkind to the portly arbiter early in the game. The Moose's disposition toward Koharski didn't improve in the third period, when he ruled a Messier goal had been kicked in.

"I heard about that," Koharski says. "The good old Canadian press ripped me a new one."

The good old Canadian press had plenty of targets that night, particularly through the first thirty-nine minutes and eighteen seconds of the game when it looked like the Russians would make short work of Keenan's crew.

Canada actually started the game well enough, scoring on the third shift of the contest on a play started by Rochefort. The Nordiques' defenceman, who'd never be confused with Bobby Orr during his career, broke up a Soviet attack in his own end, charged through the middle of the ice, then fed Lemieux at the

Russian blue line, who relayed to Mike Gartner. Gartner, who had a step on Russian defenceman Anatoli Fedotov, beat Sergei Mylnikov with a slapper from a sharp angle.

"The Russians' problems start in goal," said colour man Ron Reusch. "There's just no way you're going to replace Vladislav Tretiak . . . That guy [Mylnikov] is trying to fill skates that are ten sizes too big for him."

It wouldn't be the last time goaltending was discussed in this series.

A minute and a half after Gartner's goal, Sergei Gusarov hauled down Glenn Anderson in the neutral zone, sending out, if not the greatest power play in the history of the game, certainly the greatest collection of mullets in the history of the game.

Twenty years after the fact, the pedigree of that unit still boggles the mind. The points were manned by Bourque and Coffey, with Messier playing right wing, Lemieux playing the left side, or his off-wing, and Gretzky orchestrating the play from the half-wall and behind the Russian net. The cost alone, to assemble that group in their prime on one team in the pre-salary cap NHL, is astounding. Their first time up the ice in Game 1, Coffey started the rush with a pass to Bourque, who hit Lemieux, who fed Messier, who found Gretzky, who then set up Lemieux with a clean-scoring chance that Mylnikov turned aside. The whole sequence took about ten seconds and all five players on the ice touched the puck. Messier also threw in a huge hit against Krutov along the boards.

Five seconds later, they were back at it again. This time the play went from Bourque to Coffey to Lemieux to Gretzky to Messier, and back to Gretzky, who just missed on a backhand. The puck was always moving. It was also finding the most dangerous man on the ice. It seemed as though the five men had been playing with each other all their lives. "Honestly, we didn't practise the power play a lot," Keenan says. "It was just those great individual talents at work."

The Russians, however, had some talent of their own and midway through the opening frame they announced their presence. Canada's problems started when Coffey, as was his wont, was caught up-ice on a rush, forcing Brent Sutter to defend against the Soviets' second line of Bykov, Kamensky, and Khomutov. Sutter eventually hauled down Kamensky in front of the net during the ensuing scramble and the Russians' power play took to the ice for the first time.

It wasn't too shabby either.

It took just twenty-seven seconds for the Russians to capitalize when Kasatonov's point shot deflected off Gilmour and past Fuhr, and while the goal was flukey, it completely changed the complexion of the game. Larionov's line came out and immediately produced two good scoring chances. A couple of minutes later, Hartsburg was sent off for tackling Semak and again the Russian power play produced a goal when Krutov collected a Fetisov rebound and pulled the puck around Fuhr. That made the Russians two-for-two on the power play and with just over two minutes left in the first period, Makarov scored a short-handed goal against the vaunted Canadian power play. Krutov started the play when he picked off an ill-advised Messier cross-ice pass at the Russian blue line and sent his linemate in alone. Makarov, who was as nimble as Nureyev, made Fuhr look bad with a forehand-to-backhand deke and, suddenly, there was great dissatisfaction in The Forum.

The crowd's spirits didn't improve early in the second when Fuhr fanned on a Kamensky slapshot from just inside the blue line. Canada was now down 4–1 – "a shocker," said Reusch – the Russians had scored four goals on fourteen shots, and the booing among the faithful was now audible.

And that was precisely the time Fuhr boarded up the net and gave his team a chance to fight their way back into the game.

"As a goalie you have to have a short memory," says Fuhr, who now passes on that advice as the Phoenix Coyotes' goalies' coach. "You can't worry about the ones that have gone by you. You have to worry about the next one. I figured out at a young age you're going to give some goals up. That's just the nature of the position. To get flustered by it only makes it harder."

Now, of course, Fuhr is remembered as the greatest money goalie of his generation, a keeper whose performance rose in direct proportion to the pressure of the moment, and while it's difficult to determine when the Fuhrian legend began, it was secured during the '87 Canada Cup with his performance against the Russians. His overall numbers for the tournament, by contemporary standards at least, are ordinary: 3.34 goals-against average with a .893 save percentage. They were even more pedestrian in the final – 16 goals on 116 shots in just over ten periods of work. But what those statistics don't reveal, and what was at the core of Fuhr's genius, was his uncanny ability to make the pivotal save when his team needed it most. In the three-game final, he let in sixteen goals but not one of those goals gave the Russians the lead in the third period. True, he would surrender the overtime winner in Game 1 on a perfect shot by Semak, but in reviewing the championship round, it's clear Canada won because a) they had Fuhr in goal and b) they had Keenan behind the bench.

"He always had the reputation he could make the save at the right time but that cemented it," says Hrudey. "In a 5–5 game, some other goalies would succumb to the pressure after letting in five. Not Grant."

"He was the perfect goalie for that team," says Hawerchuk. "He'd give up a couple of questionable ones, then he'd shut it right down. He'd just say, 'OK boys, they aren't going to get another one. Just go ahead and play your game.'

"You can't overestimate how much that helped us. We could just keep on attacking, knowing he was back there and he'd make the save. We had the kind of team who had to play to top speed and had to get after it."

That was also the way the Oilers played and Fuhr's unique game was born from Glen Sather's great teams. To that point in his career, he'd shared the regular-season workload with Andy Moog, but he was the Oilers' meal ticket in the playoffs, largely because he could handle the heat and didn't seem to take it personally that his teammates weren't exactly obsessed with defence. It was the same story with Team Canada, whose personality was essentially an extension of the Oilers', and Fuhr's unflappable demeanour, coupled with his ability to deliver in the clutch, were ideally suited for the pressure cooker of the Canada Cup.

"We knew he'd provide the kind of goaltending we needed to win," says Messier. "We'd seen it so many times."

"The game was never over in his mind and he got that mentality from the Oilers," says Tocchet. "You might get three behind him but you're not getting the fourth, and all of a sudden the Oilers would start to get their legs. It was the same in that series. There were a couple of times they could have blown us out but he kept us in and we started getting our legs going."

Fuhr was just twenty-five that September and he was an original, both on and off the ice. Of mixed race by birth, he was adopted as an infant and raised by Robert and Betty Fuhr in the middle-class enclave of Spruce Grove, Alberta. He was twenty-three when he met his birth father for the first time in a bar after the Oilers had won their second straight Stanley Cup. Fuhr was celebrating when a man he'd never met told him he was a hell of a goalie. Fuhr looked at the man's face and knew it was his father. The goalie asked him if he'd ever given up a son for adoption. The man said yes, he'd been sixteen when his boy was born and the mother was thirteen.

"It all worked out for all of us," Fuhr told *Sports Illustrated*.

Young Grant wasn't much at schooling, but he was a remarkable athlete who was drafted by the Pittsburgh Pirates as a left-handed catcher as a sixteen-year-old. That year he opted to concentrate on hockey and moved to Victoria, where the Oilers made him the eighth pick of the 1981 draft. Sather went into that draft vowing he wouldn't take a goalie but was swayed by his two chief scouts, Barry Fraser and Lorne Davis, who sold the Oilers' coach and GM on the young goalie.

Fuhr would start the next season in Edmonton, where he would become the final piece in the Oilers' dynasty. If he had a care in the world in those days, it never showed. He was guileless, hopelessly naive, a rare innocent. Andy Moog made more than him, even though Fuhr played the bulk of the games in the playoffs and maybe that was for the best because he was clueless with money. Earlier in his career, he paid Sather, his coach and GM, $100 a month to do his accounting. He once had to settle a debt for almost $500 in unreturned video tapes. He was asked about his seemingly extravagant lifestyle. When my clothes get dirty, he answered, I just throw them in the closet and go out and get new ones. That also explained the unreturned tapes, he noted, because sometimes they ended up under the pile of clothes.

According to Oilers' legend, Fuhr once rented a car, then attempted to sell it. Sather heard about this and interceded on Fuhr's behalf, which wasn't the only time Sather saved both his goalie and the organization some embarrassment.

"I'm sure if it wasn't for Glen, things would have been a lot worse," says a member of the Oilers' organization. "Money wasn't a priority with Grant."

"I was having the fun of playing," Fuhr said at the time. "And I couldn't spend the money they were paying me. I had money. I spent money. No big deal."

Sather caused an uproar in those days when he said Fuhr's problems arose from being "a kid who is dumb." Fuhr responded by sarcastically referring to Sather as, "our glorious leader," but he also admitted his priorities were skewed in those days.

"At the time, I didn't care what was said," he told *Sports Illustrated*. "My first couple of years I lived life to the fullest. I had fun. I wouldn't give those days up for anything. They were some of the best I had. And you know why? I learned. You live and learn. If I had it to do all over again, I'd do it the same way. I've closed a few bars in my day. I'll probably close a few more, too."

Fuhr, by all accounts, wasn't dumb. He just couldn't be bothered with details that seemed insignificant to him. Money wasn't important to him. Contracts weren't important to him. Playing goal for the Oilers, on the other hand, was important to him. And so was golf.

During the 1985 Stanley Cup final, Fuhr warmed up for one of the games by playing thirty-six holes of golf. He was asked how he could possibly play thirty-six holes on the day of a Cup-final game. "Because there wasn't time for fifty-four," he responded. By the time the '87 Canada Cup rolled around, he was limiting himself to eighteen holes the day of a game but he also played virtually every day of the tournament. Hawerchuk, who loved golf and was a three-handicap at the time, became Fuhr's default partner. Initially, he loved playing most every day with the goalie, but the Jets' centre couldn't begin to match Fuhr's insatiable appetite for the game.

"He wanted to play every day and somebody had to play with him," says Hawerchuk. "I never thought I could get tired of golf but I couldn't keep up to him."

It was on the ice at the Canada Cup where Fuhr authored the more memorable story, combining that carefree mien with his preternatural athleticism. Goaltending in the late 1980s, Hrudey says, was a far different position than it is today. It changed in the 1990s, when the Patrick Roy–style – with its emphasis on positioning and a strong butterfly technique – came into vogue. Fuhr had those elements in his game. But mostly he relied on his instincts and reflexes, which is why he was so pleasing to watch. It was also more effective against the Russians, who changed the point of attack more quickly than NHL teams and could open up a slower goalie like a can of tuna.

"Like all of us back then, he made saves as opposed to block-ing the shots," says Hrudey. "It's a more exciting [style]. I grew up watching Doug Favell and Mike Palmateer. That's how they played. There's nothing better than that full-on glove save."

Fuhr would make that save several times against the Russians, usually finishing in a full split. But when asked what he remem-bers most about Fuhr in that tournament, Hartsburg comes back to his personality and its role in keeping the team loose. "He was the most confident guy on the ice," says Hartsburg. "When you see that and [hear] that behind you, it kind of rubs off on you. You've got a guy who's all nervous and yelling and it's hard to stay calm. But there were times Grant was laughing back there. If a goal went in on him it wasn't a big deal. It was never you got to do this, you got to do that. It was just, 'Don't worry, boys. I'll get the next one.'"

That was the story of Game 1 – and Games 2 and 3, come to think of it – but it would take Fuhr's teammates some time to draw inspiration from their goalie.

Shortly after Kamensky's goal, the Canadians drew an extended five-on-three and their vaunted power play produced nothing as the booing grew louder in The Forum. In search of a spark, Keenan unleashed the wounded Tocchet on the un-suspecting Russians and the Flyers' winger promptly took a stupid penalty when he crosschecked Russian defenceman Igor Stelnov into Mylnikov. With Tocchet in the box, Hartsburg then crosschecked Krutov in the back behind the play and the Russian sniper had to be helped off the ice.

Koharski missed the call. Krutov, however, would miss just one shift.

"To me the best guy on that line was Krutov because he was the toughest guy," Hartsburg concedes. "He was a miserable bugger to play against."

Fuhr would make saves off Bykov on the Russian power play shortly before Khomutov hit the post, producing more grumbling in Montreal. Bourque took another brain-dead penalty, negating a five-on-three for the Canadians. Still more grumbling. Late in the period, Fuhr had to make one of those full-on glove saves on a backhander by Lomakin.

With just over two minutes left in the frame, Koharski gave Canada a gift when he sent off Anatoli Fedotov for high-sticking after an exchange with Goulet. The Canadian power play again failed to produce anything resembling a scoring chance for the first minute before Gretzky dropped a pass between his legs to Bourque, whose harmless-looking wrister from the boards deflected off Kasatonov and past Mylnikov with forty-two seconds left in the middle frame.

It didn't look like much at the time, but it was actually the start of the '87 Canada Cup final.

For a series that was destined to be a classic, the first two periods of the Canada–Russia showdown were relatively un-inspiring and lifeless. That was also the way Tikhonov's team liked it. The crowd in Montreal was out of the game. Team Canada was flat and playing with little emotion. There was no speed or urgency to their game. But that all changed over the final twenty minutes of regulation play when the long-time rivalry finally caught a spark and the series erupted into what we remember.

Right off the third-period faceoff, Fuhr was forced to make an acrobatic glove stop off Larionov. "That might have been a game-saver right there," Kelly said as Makarov tapped Fuhr on the pads. Seconds later, Krutov just missed on a two-on-one with Makarov. Back came the Canadians. Gilmour, playing on a makeshift line with Gartner and Lemieux, got in on the forecheck and pressured Gusarov into an errant pass up the boards. Hartsburg relayed the turnover to Gartner and the Capitals' winger shovelled a centring pass that found Gilmour through two Russian players. Gilmour, who was never much of a shooter, got off a half-slapper from his back foot that bounced through Mylnikov and into the net. Russia, 4, Canada, 3, and the game was on.

Today, of course, it hardly registers as a surprise that Gilmour would play a starring role in the Canadian comeback because, during the course of his remarkable twenty-year NHL career, the diminutive centre became one of the premier clutch perform-ers of his generation. He played a leading role on the Flames' '89 Stanley Cup team. He almost single-handedly carried Toronto to the Conference finals in 1993 and 1994, a two-year period when he might have been the best player in the NHL. He was that rarest of players who was more productive in the post-season than the regular season, averaging 1.03 points per game in 182 career playoff games and .955 points in 1,474 regular-season games.

But most of those heroics came later in his career. In 1987, Gilmour wasn't regarded as a money player and, outside of St. Louis, he was barely regarded at all. On Team Canada, in fact, he was the original just-happy-to-be-here guy, thrilled to be rubbing shoulders with Gretzky, Messier, and Bourque, thrilled to be playing the game at its highest level. Four seasons earlier, he'd graduated from the Cornwall Royals and, against all odds, made the Blues as a twenty-year-old rookie on his checking ability and his outsized heart. But no one saw one of the game's great young stars in those early years in St. Louis. No one saw the kid who'd play a key role for Keenan in the '87 Canada Cup. What they saw was the quintessential long shot, a scrawny, pugnacious rink-rat who was more likely to be killed than make it to the NHL.

"He was an unknown, that's for sure," says Mike Liut, the Blues' goalie during Gilmour's early days in St. Louis. "He wasn't a player who was on anyone's radar screen. They listed him at 175 but if he weighed 150 in those days I wouldn't have been surprised. But what was immediately noticeable was he was a tenacious player. He ran at big guys. He played in the high-traffic areas. He was literally fearless."

"He was this little guy but he'd charge into the pile and throw himself at people, then bounce off them like someone hit an eject button," says Bernie Federko, the scoring star of those Blues teams. "We still laugh about him. He came to play on and off the ice."

Gilmour joined the Blues in the 1983–84 season, and if few expected him to make the NHL team that, or any other, year, at least he'd had some experience with being underestimated. Hawerchuk, whose connection with Gilmour went back to peewee hockey when he was starring for Oshawa and Gilmour was playing in Kingston, says his old rival always had that certain indefinable something that appears in great players. It just took the rest of the hockey world some time to realize what Hawerchuk and most everyone else who came into contact with Gilmour already knew.

"Anyone who knew him knew he was going to be a player," says Hawerchuk. "Anyone who didn't know him just saw this kid who was never going to be big enough."

In Cornwall, Gilmour played a third-line role behind Hawerchuk and future NHLer Scott Arniel on the second of back-to-back Memorial Cup championship teams in 1981 and he also went undrafted in his first year of eligibility. The next year, while Hawerchuk was winning the Calder in Winnipeg, Gilmour put together a 114-point campaign, which at least prompted the Blues to invest a seventh-round draft pick in him. The following year, he rang up 177 points with the Royals but that was his third year of junior, he was still vertically challenged, and the beer leagues were full of big junior scorers who couldn't make the jump to the next level.

But there was also something different about Gilmour and that became evident his first training camp with the Blues. He'd been a draft of then GM Émile Francis but the Cat had moved on to Hartford and been replaced by Ron Caron, who hired Jacques Demers as his coach in Gilmour's rookie season. Caron had told his coach that the new kid might be a player, but Demers had no clue who Gilmour was or what his game was about.

He'd discover soon enough.

"He was at an NHL camp, so he must have done something good somewhere along the line," says Demers. "But the first time I saw him he looked so small and so frail, I didn't think there was any way he'd last. Then we started scrimmaging and you could see he was special. I would say a week into that training camp he made the team."

In a reprise of his junior career, Gilmour would spend his rookie season stacked up behind Federko and Blake Dunlop in a checking role, but he still managed to accumulate 25 goals and 53 points. The Blues, a largely veteran group, also fell in love with their new centre and his irrepressible passion for the game. Brian Sutter hung the nickname "Killer" on him and he was also referred to as "Charlie Manson" by his teammates in those years. He spent two more seasons checking, killing penalties, and working his ass off before his breakthrough performance in the 1986 playoffs when he counted 21 points in nineteen games as the Blues upset Minnesota and Toronto in the first two rounds before falling to Calgary in seven games in the Campbell Conference final. The next season, Federko got hurt and Gilmour stepped up with a 42-goal, 105-point season.

It was an astonishing campaign for someone who'd been typecast as a checker in his first three seasons and it earned Gilmour an invitation to the Team Canada camp that summer. But he was also one of nine natural centremen vying for a spot and three of the positions were already conceded to Gretzky, Messier, and Lemieux. Gilmour took one look at the competition, reasoned he didn't have a hope in hell of making the team, then proceeded to do what he always did, which was play as if his mortal soul was on the line.

It had worked before. It would work again.

"My god, the talent on that team and I was just a kid," Gilmour says. "Then they cut Stevie Y and Kirk Muller and all the guys I was hanging around with. I made it to the final cuts and it came down to me and Dave Poulin and I thought, 'There's no way.'"

But Gilmour had some champions within the Team Canada dressing room. Gretzky, for one, lobbied Keenan on his behalf and as much as it pained the coach to cut Poulin, his captain with the Flyers, Gilmour had been the better player in the runup to the tournament. He was given a fourth-line role with the team and expected to spend most of the tournament watching from the bench. Against Finland in the round robin, he then took an ill-timed penalty, got an earful from Tom Watt, and was made a healthy scratch the next game against the Americans. That was also the game Claude Lemieux went down with an ankle injury and Gilmour was reinstated for the next contest, where he started to work his way up the team's depth chart.

"I'd gone full circle," he says. "I started out my career as a checker, had one season as a scorer, and I was a checker again. But I would have done anything they asked me on that team."

By the time the final rolled around, Gilmour was one of nine healthy forwards Keenan could call on and his versatility made him an invaluable piece of the Team Canada puzzle. He played a lot on the wing with Lemieux in a feature role, centred his own line in a checking configuration, and, with Sutter, was the team's top penalty killer. He was also reliable defensively, could handle the minutes and the pressure, and, other than Lemieux, he was the only Team Canada forward to register more than one goal in the final.

"He wanted to play in that series," says Federko. "You could sense the excitement when he talked about it. There was a great deal of pressure and he just loved to play in those kind of games."

"Early in the tournament neither one of us played very much and I can distinctly remember sitting on the bench and talking to him," says Hawerchuk. "We figured our chance would come because guys weren't going to stay healthy with the amount of hockey we were playing. Maybe there were guys at the start of the tournament who didn't know what kind of teammate he would be but, by the final, there wasn't any question about what Dougie brought to the table."

There wasn't any question what Gilmour's goal did for Game 1 either as The Forum, which had been uncomfortably quiet, came to life along with Team Canada. On his next shift, the unlikely tagteam of Gilmour and Gartner both ran at Fetisov, Hanson brother–style, and smashed him into the boards. There were chances at both ends. With the play running toward the Canadians, Messier took a penalty when he elbowed Gusarov in the head, crosschecked him in the back, then high-sticked the Russian defenceman across the shoulder, narrowly missing his nose. Messier should have been tossed. Instead, Koharski called a minor for high-sticking, which Gretzky had the temerity to come off the bench to argue over.

"He got away with the first one, but I think the penalty got called on the rest of them," Reusch noted.

No matter. Fuhr stopped Fetisov from the high slot on the Russians' only chance of the power play and, after coming out of the box, Messier was in the thick of it again. This time, he was skating through the neutral zone when Gretzky threw an awkward pass in his general direction. Stelnov, the Russian defenceman, thought he had the Moose lined up. Or maybe he was just in the wrong place at the wrong time. Either way, the two men's courses collided, Messier's elbow flashed, and Stelnov went down like he'd been shot. The play happened so quickly, TV cameras missed the full extent of the blow but subsequent replays revealed Messier's elbow landed squarely on Stelnov's chin. The result was also self-evident.

After spending some time on his hands and knees, the

unfortunate blueliner was helped to the Russian bench. The TV cameras later found him making his way to his team's dressing room, bent over and using the wall for support, like a man who'd consumed far too much alcohol. It wasn't quite as spectacular as Messier's elbow on Vladimir Kovin in the '84 Canada Cup, but it was close.

"I've known Mark and his family for a bunch of years and Mark comes by it honestly," says Hrudey, who grew up in Edmonton with the Messiers. "Doug [his father and a hockey lifer] is a hard man. He ran the junior teams the same way as Keenan. If you're losing, we'll fight. Mark used to get so wound up for those games against the Russians he scared me."

Twenty years later, Messier was asked if he ever felt he crossed the line on the ice or if he ever did anything he regretted. Who me? he answered.

"Back then that was the way the game was played," Messier says. "As hockey became more widely viewed, and the idea of what was politically correct changed, you had to change. Things happened then that probably wouldn't be acceptable now. We never took a backward step. It was tough hockey. And the Russians weren't any slouches in that department."

Tikhonov wasn't happy that Messier's hit went unpenalized. He was extremely unhappy when, moments later, Kasatonov jumped off the bench on a line change, played the puck a beat early, and the Russians were penalized for too many men on the ice. Tikhonov gestured theatrically at Koharski, waving six fingers in the air and pointing toward his eyes, but the referee was unmoved. Out came Gretzky, Lemieux, Messier, Coffey, and Bourque. And for the next two minutes Canada did everything but score the tying goal.

Thirty seconds into the power play, Koharski was in the middle of another hey-rube when Messier directed Gretzky's centring pass behind Mylnikov with his skate. Now, the goal would have counted because Messier didn't make a distinct kicking motion. Then, it was an easy call for Koharski despite the animated protests of Messier and Gretzky.

The next day, Gretzky was asked what he'd said to Koharski. "I asked him how his summer was," he said.

"He appealed to my patriotism," Koharski said.

Canada continued to buzz the Russian net after the non-goal, coming close on wild scrambles a couple of times. At the end of the power play, Coffey missed Gretzky alone by the left post, firing a waist-high slapper instead that Mylnikov caught easily as Gretzky broke his stick over the crossbar.

Mylnikov, to that point in the game, had outplayed Fuhr but the Russians' fatal flaw was exposed with just over five minutes left in the third period. Messier started the play when he gained the Soviet zone, then fed Anderson coming through the high slot. Anderson, who'd suffered a knee injury in the round robin, let go with an indifferent wrister through Gusarov, which beat Mylnikov badly and tied the game.

It would be Anderson's only goal of the final series but it ignited another dazzling exchange between the two teams. Mylnikov came back with a big stop off Goulet. Fuhr made a remarkable sliding save off Krutov. And eighty-two seconds after Anderson's goal, Gretzky gave Canada the lead on one of those plays only he was capable of producing. Bourque had dumped the puck into the Russian zone, then regained possession at the point when Tocchet's aggressive forecheck created a turnover. Bourque was on the right-wing wall when he turned and fired the puck toward the Russian net. Gretzky, meanwhile, had been hiding along the left-wing boards as the play developed and when Bourque let fly, No. 99 headed for the net. Halfway there, he could see Bourque's shot would miss on the short side and Gretzky readjusted his course to the point where the puck caromed off the boards. He was there when it arrived and even though he partially whiffed on the shot, Mylnikov was still miles out of position when the puck crossed the goal line.

"You expect something is going to happen when you play against Wayne," Larionov says. "Something magical. Something unusual. That's why we all played the game." Gretzky's goal, his only one of the final, came with just under three minutes left and The Forum crowd was still on its feet when Khomutov tied the game thirty-two seconds later. Bykov did some nice work against Gretzky, ironically, behind the Canadian net, but his centring pass into a crowd took a crazy bounce off Gretzky's skate and off Khomutov, who was wrestling with Bourque in front of Fuhr. Fuhr had stopped twenty-three straight Russian shots before that goal. It took a double deflection to beat him.

The ensuing overtime was just the second in the history of the Russian national team and it would end on a far happier note than the first one in the '84 Canada Cup semifinal against Canada. Bossy's goal on a deflection off Coffey's shot gave the Canadians a 3–2 win, but you can also make the case that that goal marked a huge turning point in the fortunes of the two great hockey nations. Prior to Bossy's goal, the Russians had an aura of invincibility about them. They'd crushed Canada 8–1 in the '81 Canada Cup final. They'd won the world championship with laughable ease in 1981, 1982, and 1983. They'd won the gold in Sarajevo in 1984, and they'd also pounded the Canadians 6–3 in the round robin meeting at the '84 Canada Cup. But, in the way Mike Tyson was never the same fighter after he lost to Buster Douglas, the Russians were never the same team after Bossy's goal. They had their moments, but they would go on to lose the 1985 and 1987 world championships and they'd never regain that mystique they'd worked so hard to create. Still, it came back for one night. Canada looked the aggressor in the early part of overtime and mounted a couple of dangerous-looking rushes without producing a clean scoring chance. Then, about three minutes into extra time, the ice began to tilt in the

Russians' favour. Fuhr stood his ground to stop Makarov before Coffey made a sliding block on Larionov. Fuhr just got a piece of Larionov's slapper. Three shifts later, the Soviets ended the affair on a goal by their fourth line.

Fetisov started the rush innocently enough, moving slowly through the neutral zone before finding Lomakin, who tipped it to Semenov. Semak, who was near the end of his shift, had been trailing the play but put on a little burst to get to some open ice at the top of the faceoff circle. The puck was on his stick for a split second before he snapped a wrister over Fuhr's shoulder, off the back crossbar and into the Canadian net.

As the Soviets poured off the bench, a few boos could be heard in The Forum but mostly there was silence. Then, after a few seconds, sustained applause broke out as the fans in Montreal saluted both teams. Semak would later become part of the second wave of Russians to play in the NHL, joining the New Jersey Devils in 1991–92 from Dynamo. He would enjoy a huge season the following year, scoring 37 goals and adding 42 assists, but that was his only successful season in a four-team, six-year NHL career. He finished his career bouncing around the NHL, the minors, the Russian league, and Germany.

"Boy, what a shot," Reusch said. "There was nothing Fuhr could do at all. You hate to see a team lose. The Soviets have won this one but the series is far from over."

Tikhonov pumped his fist and something approaching a smile came across his face as his team left the ice. The Soviets had taken Canada's best shot in the third period and gave a little but, when pressed, they responded with a display of courage and character that was supposed to be the Canadians' birthright.

"I've always admired Canada's ability to come back and have hoped that quality would rub off on our players," said Russian assistant coach Igor Dmitriev, who would become the team's spokesman in the final. "Maybe tonight it did."

Kasatonov shared that sentiment. Throughout his career, he'd heard about the Canadians' heart and relentlessness. Never mind that in best-on-best, the two teams were virtually equal. Team Canada supposedly had this mythical ability to rise to the occasion when the stakes were highest.

"Maybe we still believed that," Kasatonov says. "But we had this great feeling after Game 1. We played so hard and now we just had to win one more game."

The Canadians, for their part, bemoaned their slow start but conceded nothing to Tikhonov's team. That defiance wasn't shared by the Canadian press, who fretted that Keenan's men had expended too much energy in their comeback and now had to face the Soviets in less than forty-eight hours with depleted ranks. Still, the Canadian players didn't seem overly concerned about the challenge facing them.

"Some guys, some teams it would affect," said Gretzky. "But there are too many winners in this room for that to happen."

Gretzky hadn't enjoyed his best game but he did produce a goal and an assist and his third-period marker put Canada in a position to win the game. But after the contest, Gretzky met up with his father and an unsmiling Walter Gretzky greeted his son with a pointed bit of criticism. Gretzky *père* told Gretzky *fils* he'd stayed on the ice too long on the shift that produced Khomutov's goal. "You cost your country the game," Walter Gretzky said, and the message was Wayne had played selfishly during the most critical part of the game.

"That was quite a shocker," Gretzky says. "It wasn't the best thing to hear after a loss, but I remembered that for a while."

Keenan, meanwhile, was asked for this book what he recalled about the team's mood after Game 1.

"They were unhappy with the results in Montreal but I never sensed there was anxiety," he says. "It was a confident group, especially in their offence, and they expected a lot from each other. They were very, very ready for the next game. They just felt they'd get it done."

CHAPTER 5

The Truth of Things

In the aftermath of the first battle, it was hard to tell who'd won Game 1, the Soviets or Canada.

Keenan, in the off-day stories, noted the Canadians had carried the play in the third period with a shortened bench and scoffed at the notion of the Russians' superior conditioning. "In the third period, were we fatigued or were they?" the coach asked rhetorically. "We pretty much went with nine forwards and four defencemen yet we made them back off. Now is that a relationship of fatigue and fitness or a relationship of motivation and psychology?"

Okay, no one was quite certain what Keenan was talking about, but Messier crowed about how the Canadians' pressure game had flustered the normally unflappable Russians. The Canadians, after all, had overcome a 4–1 deficit and had played only twenty minutes of the game. Just think of what they could do with a complete sixty-minute effort. "I haven't seen the Russians unravel like that in all the games I've played them," said Messier. "I've never seen them break down like that under pressure and there's no question it did a lot for our confidence."

Winning might have done a little more. But as the Canadians talked up their moral victories, there were concerns within their locker room. They were down to nine forwards for Game 2 with Tocchet joining Dineen and Claude Lemieux in the infirmary. That meant, in an elimination game against one of the best teams in the history of the sport, they would dress one player under the limit. Keenan again utilized James Patrick as a seventh defence-man and occasional right winger for Game 2, but with those shortened numbers, fatigue was bound to play a role in the series.

That, at least, was the popular theory.

"I get a little tired of hearing about the Russians' superior conditioning," Keenan spat. The other worry for the Canadians was the play of their stars in Game 1. Gretzky picked up a goal and an assist and Lemieux had a couple of helpers, but neither player was a dominating figure. Canada's player of the game, in fact, was Gartner. Russian stars Makarov and Krutov, mean-while, both had a goal and an assist and Krutov was named the Soviets' player of the game.

Fuhr, finally, had turned in a subpar effort by his standards, fanning on Kamensky's long slapper and surrendering six goals on forty-three shots. Heading into the final series, it was a given that Canada's one great advantage lay in its goaltending. That wasn't the case for most of Game 1.

"We need nothing more than a Grant Fuhr game," said Gretzky. "He's got to stand on his head."

But Fuhr had the rare ability to simplify complex problems.

"We have to win two out of two," he said. "Simple to figure out."

Before the puck was dropped for Game 2, a juicy storyline again erupted over the referee assigned to the contest. The consternation over Don Koharski's appointment to work the first game of the final was nothing compared to the selection of American

referee Paul Stewart, whose prior NHL experience had consisted
of part of one game when he'd come down from the stands in
Boston to fill in for an injured Dave Newell. "[An] interesting
situation will be the referee for tonight's game, Paul Stewart,"
said Reusch as Stewart skated around a jam-packed Copps
Coliseum before the game. "He's got a lot of pressure on him."

"My greatest game was my first game," Stewart now says from
his Boston-area home. "I can remember every moment, every
detail of that game."

Stewart, who'd been serving a minor-league apprenticeship,
was actually scheduled to begin working NHL games that
season and had worked an earlier tournament game but was no
more qualified to officiate a Canada Cup final than he was to
clone sheep. He'd watched Game 1 in a bar in Boston, then
flew to Toronto the next day for the start of the officials' training camp. That night, John McCauley, the NHL supervisor of
officials, called a meeting with Stewart, Newell, and Andy Van
Hellemond. Stewart assumed he was going to be a standby
official, but McCauley, a revered figure among officials of that
era, motioned him outside and said: "Well, big guy, you're
going to get your chance. I know you're up to it," then broke
the news to the other officials.

"John said, 'John D'Amico is going to work the lines. Don
Koharski is the backup, and Paul Stewart is going to be the
referee,'" Stewart recounts. "You could have heard a fucking
pin drop."

Stewart, at that point, was just four years removed from a
nomadic career as a minor-league tough guy who also had short
stints with the WHA's Cincinnati Stingers and the NHL's Quebec
Nordiques. Stewart's grandfather Bill had been an NHL referee.
His father, also named Bill, worked at the collegiate level.
Stewart himself received an ivy league education at Penn and
graduated with a degree in Asian history. But after college,

he moved on to the North American Hockey League, where he developed a fearsome reputation as a fighter.

"Paul Stewart was as tough as any player I've ever seen," says Rick Dudley, his former teammate in Cincinnati. "He actually liked to fight. He'd fight anyone, anywhere, at any time and you had to admire him for that."

The Stingers would call up Stewart midway through the 1977–78 season after some of their better players were pounded in a brawl with the infamous Birmingham Bulls. In Stewart's second game with Cincinnati, the Stingers met the Bulls in a rematch and Stewart fought noted goons Frank Beaton, Gilles "Bad News" Bilodeau, and Serge Beaudoin. In his third game, he fought Jack Carlson, the reigning WHA heavyweight champ, twice. After the WHA merger, Stingers coach Jacques Demers took Stewart to Quebec with him, where his most notable achievement was fighting Terry O'Reilly, Stan Jonathan, and Al Secord in the same game against the Bruins. Between the WHA and the NHL, Stewart would play eighty-six career games, score five goals, add six assists, and pick up 362 penalty minutes.

While he was still playing, Stewart began working high-school games in the Boston area and, in 1983, enrolled in Bruce Hood's referee school. He would work in the NHL for sixteen years, but his debut remains the most memorable moment of his career. "I remember all those nights sitting and listening to my dad and my grandfather tell stories," he says. "I've never been more ready for anything in my life."

Stewart still has a picture of him dropping the puck for the opening faceoff in Game 2 and when he says he remembers every detail of that game, he doesn't exaggerate. He remembers having lunch with D'Amico before the game and the support the veteran linesman gave him. He remembers wearing his grandfather's watch that day. During the pregame warmup, he remembers running into Team Canada's Gartner, a former teammate with the Stingers, who took one look at Stewart and started laughing.

"Nobody would believe this," Gartner said.

"What, that I'm here or you're here," Stewart responded.

As for the game, he can rattle off plays and penalty calls like they happened yesterday. At the end of the first period, he skated off the ice at the Zamboni entrance and was greeted by a gentleman in a blue blazer who was screaming at him: "Give us a chance, Paul. You're fucking killing us."

"Who was that?" Stewart asked D'Amico.

"Eagleson," the linesman responded.

Stewart waved off a Russian goal in the first period when Nemchinov planted Fuhr in the Canadian goal. Later, Stewart is clearly heard on the broadcast of the game telling a player: "Watch that fucking lip or I'll run you out of here." After four hours Lemieux finally ended the affair with a dramatic goal in the second overtime at which point every player on the ice and the rookie referee, who'd acquitted himself well, was exhausted.

"It was up and down, up and down, up and down," says Stewart. "I was dying. I'm getting dehydrated and thinking, 'Someone please score.' You look at Mario's goal and I'm right behind the net. I don't know who was happier. Mario, Wayne, or me."

After the game, Stewart was in the officials' room taking off his skates when McCauley walked in. He tapped Stewart on the foot, rubbed his head, and said, "Superb," then walked out. Later McCauley told Stewart: "There were a lot of people who wanted you to fail."

As Stewart tells this story, he has to stop a couple of times to compose himself. He's also shouting instructions to his young son to get ready for bed. His boy's name is McCauley.

"I was just proud because I validated the confidence John showed in me," Stewart says. Stewart wasn't the only official who felt that way about McCauley. Koharski, who worked Games 1 and 3 of the series, also credits McCauley for his NHL career. During the 2005–6 season, Koharski became the second referee after Kerry Fraser to work fifteen hundred NHL games. His partner for many games during that season was McCauley's son Wes.

"Wes asked his mother, Irene, why his dad and I were so close," Koharski says. "She thought about it for a minute, then said, 'You know what, Koho was a little chubby like your dad.'

"God bless John McCauley, is all I can say. He was my mentor, a father-figure, and I owe my career to him. I can't tell you how cool it is for me to work with Wes."

John McCauley would succumb to cancer in the summer of 1988, just one year after his two disciples worked the greatest hockey series ever played.

For Game 2 of the Canada Cup final, Keenan started a line of Messier, Anderson, and Hawerchuk behind the quizzical defence pairing of Crossman and Rochefort. Tikhonov countered with the Green Unit. About fifteen seconds into the very first shift, Fetisov grabbed the puck in his own end, took a return pass from Krutov, and found Makarov with a spectacular back pass as he was spinning to the ice. Makarov relayed to Larionov, and Fuhr ended the sequence with a sliding save off Makarov at the goal-mouth. With Larionov and Makarov caught deep, Hawerchuk took the rebound, skated through the neutral zone, then found Messier streaking down the wing. The Oilers' centre beat Kasatonov to the outside, circled the net, and fed Rochefort, who, to the surprise of everyone in the building, had jumped into the slot. Rochefort's one-timer beat Russian goalie Evgeny Belosheikin easily and Team Canada poured off the bench. The game was forty-three seconds old. The fans at Copps had already witnessed two spectacular plays. There would be a few more before the night was over.

There have been more dramatic games in hockey's history. Game 8 of the 1972 Summit Series certainly qualifies. So does U.S.A.–Russia at the 1980 Winter Olympics. But for pure hockey – the speed and flow of the game, the skill on display, the setting and what was at stake, to say nothing of the individual stars – Game 2 is indisputably the greatest game ever played. The 1975 New Year's Eve classic between Red Army and the Montreal Canadiens is sometimes mentioned in the same breath, but doesn't come close. That game ended in a 3–3 tie. Red Army produced thirteen shots on Canadiens goalie Ken Dryden. They were two club teams. The game was essentially an exhibition contest.

Game 2 was set against the backdrop of the Canada Cup in a best-on-best format. The stars, and there were a boatload on each team, were at the peak of their game, except for Lemieux, who was in the process of announcing his genius to the world. The two teams produced 111 shots on goal between them and almost as many scoring chances. Lemieux scored three times. Gretzky recorded five assists. And for all that, the most memorable play in the game is made by twenty-one-year-old Russian forward Valeri Kamensky, who went one-on-four in the last minute of regulation time and scored the tying goal.

The game they played defied description – literally. Scott Morrison remembers the problem of writing the story of Game 2 on deadline. Normally, as the game winds down, a scribe will glance up only momentarily from his laptop to watch the action while he's trying to compose his game story. But Morrison and the rest of his colleagues couldn't take their eyes off what was transpiring at Copps.

"It was absolutely mesmerizing," he says. "There'd be a stoppage in play and you'd try to get something down but the minute the puck dropped, you had to watch. It wasn't the best way to write on deadline."

"You knew you had to be your best every shift because one

shift could change the complexion of the game," says Hartsburg. "Both teams could score so quickly and that was the story. As much as you were exhausted physically, you were exhausted mentally because you had to concentrate so intently every minute of every game."

"It got to the point where the intensity was so high, guys were barely watching the game," says Hawerchuk. "You had to catch your breath and get ready for the next shift because if you were half-a-step out of position, it could mean a goal. You couldn't go more than thirty seconds a shift playing like that. It was the first time that ever happened to me."

Following Rochefort's goal, Keenan put out a line with Gretzky, Sutter, and Goulet against the Russians' second line of Bykov, Khomutov, and Kamensky and late in the second shift of the game, Bykov dug out a loose puck behind Fuhr about the same time as Coffey and Kamensky were moving to the Canadian net. Kamensky, with no help from Coffey, bumped into Fuhr, who took a swing at the Russian forward, spun, and went down. He was still on all fours looking into his net when Khomutov tied the game. Fuhr said a couple of words to Stewart, who was standing by the net but that was the end of the controversy.

The game was now eighty-seven seconds old, the score was 1–1, and, if anything, the action only accelerated from that point.

Seconds after Khomutov's goal, Lemieux almost scored again when Belosheikin made a brilliant glove save after Lemieux had faked Anatoli Fedotov to his knees and moved in front of the Russian goalie. On that same play Gilmour was penalized for high-sticking Belosheikin. Out came Larionov's line, who'd produced two power-play goals in the first period of Game 1, and they immediately held the puck in the Canadian zone for a full minute without scoring. As Gilmour was about to step on the ice, Gretzky intercepted a pass near the Canadian blue line, carried it through the neutral zone, and found the irrepressible

Rochefort, who again had jumped into the play. Rochefort, who never accumulated more than twenty-four points in a season during his NHL career, drove wide against Stelnov, then found the trailing Gilmour with a nifty back pass and Gilmour's so-so snap shot beat Belosheikin from the high slot. Of the six goals scored against the Russian goalie in Game 2, Gilmour's goal was about the only one on which he could be faulted.

"I think Rochefort thinks he's Bobby Orr out there," Reusch said.

As if they needed it, the go-ahead goal gave the Canadians a further spark and for the next five minutes, they were all over the Russians. Messier just missed on a power play before Belosheikin dove to smother a loose puck during a furious goal-mouth scramble. Hawerchuk hit the post. Team Canada, if you can believe it, outshot the Russians 13–2 through the first seven minutes of the period, and while he wasn't earning any style points, Belosheikin kept his team in the game with some desperate goaltending.

Shortly after the Canadian flurry, Lemieux came out to play right wing on a line with Gretzky and Propp, the first time during the final the two superstars had played together five-on-five. They almost produced a goal when Belosheikin had to reach back into the crease to grab Coffey's slapshot as it was trickling toward the goal line, but seconds later, Messier, who wasn't always conscientious about the deployment of his stick in this series, took a minor when he slapped Gusarov across the face with his twig.

Now it was the Russians' turn to carry the play. Kasatonov ripped a wrister off the post from the high slot and Fuhr made an acrobatic save on another Kasatonov drive. Fuhr followed with three straight saves before Bykov appeared to tie the game on a backhand during more wild action in front of the Canadian net. This time, however, Stewart nullified the goal, penalizing Crossman and Nemchinov, who ended up on top of Fuhr as

Bykov was scoring. In truth, Kamensky's interference on the first Russian goal was more blatant but Nemchinov, who was deep in the crease, didn't make any effort to avoid Fuhr. That didn't quite explain why both players were penalized but a higher justice might have been served by the call.

The first twelve minutes of the first period had produced three goals, a disallowed goal, at least fifteen scoring chances, a couple of five-alarm saves, and two clear changes in momentum. After Bykov's non-goal, Reusch asked of Kelly: "Have you ever seen such a pace to a hockey game, Dan?"

"Not really," Kelly replied. "This is something else. And I'm not sure Grant Fuhr or Belosheikin have seen such a pace."

"I don't think people understand the level of hockey that was played those final two games in Hamilton," says Gretzky. "The speed and intensity of the games was like nothing I'd ever seen. We were also one shot away from elimination for both those games and that only added to it."

After Messier returned to the ice, Gretzky, who was winding up a long shift, picked up a loose puck behind the Canadian net and carried through the neutral zone as both teams changed on the fly. Gartner, however, jumped off the Canadian bench ahead of the play, and Gretzky found the speedy Washington winger going down his off-wing. The resulting play was a fairly straightforward two-on-two rush, but Coffey, who jumped on the ice shortly behind Gartner, charged into the open ice as the trailer. Gretzky, who was partially covered, saw this before anyone in the rink and motioned toward Coffey with his stick. Gartner missed the cue, but his pass toward Gretzky got through Stelnov, and the Great One was able to flip a pass toward Coffey, who was flying down main street all by himself. The Oilers' defenceman took the pass in stride, made a sweet move to his forehand, and beat Belosheikin, giving Canada a well-deserved 3–1 lead.

Coffey's play in this series went underreported but watching the tapes of the final gives a fresh appreciation of the Oilers' defenceman and his singular game. He was, of course, a brilliant skater, maybe the best to ever play the game. Bobby Orr, who wasn't bad himself, said: "I couldn't skate like Paul Coffey and I'm not just being humble. We're not going to see anybody skate like him again. It was like he was floating. The acceleration, the speed. One day, my dad said to me, 'Did you see that Coffey skate? He's a better skater than you are.'

"I asked him, 'Am I even close?'"

Coffey, who worshipped Orr, scoffed at the comparison, but against Tikhonov's team, who weren't exactly plodders, his skating is still clearly superior to every other player on the ice. He's always in motion during the three-game final, gliding into and out of the picture frame with preternatural grace, breaking up the play at one end, leading the rush at another, then racing back into position to do it all over again. Hockey fans of a certain age saw it hundreds of times during Coffey's career but this was the Russian national team he was playing against, not the Winnipeg Jets in Game 42 of the NHL's regular season.

This series, in fact, was tailor-made for Coffey. The game was predicated on speed and skill. There weren't a lot of physical confrontations. In the NHL, Coffey was regarded as something of a defensive liability, and even Sather had his moments when he doubted his great blueliner. At one Oilers' practice, Sather pleaded with Coffey to play tougher in front of Fuhr, to engage his man in front of the net the way every other defenceman played in the NHL. "No," Coffey said. "I like standing over by the post. I can see what's going on better."

And even after he'd established himself as one of the NHL's best two or three defencemen, his game met with some resistance on Team Canada. GM Savard, who was the anti-Coffey during his playing days, said he had trouble watching Coffey during the series. "I can tell you Paul Coffey almost gave me a heart attack," says Savard. "He was always up on the play and it always looked like he was going to get caught. It didn't matter if it was the first period or there was thirty seconds left."

But Keenan and his teammates understood what Coffey brought to the table. Canada's defence in the final essentially consisted of Bourque, Coffey, and whoever Keenan had a mind to stick out there. Rochefort, for example, tended to play a lot early in the game, but seldom saw the ice in the third period. Crossman's and Murphy's ice time tended to increase in the latter part of the game, and Murphy would become a huge factor for Team Canada as the series unfolded. But Bourque and Coffey were the foundation Keenan built his blue line around and they were both magnificent in the series.

"The thing about Paul was he never panicked," says Hartsburg. "Maybe that's because he was so confident in his skating and his ability but you never saw him lose his cool. He was so different than the rest of us. We had to be more aware defensively. But Paul could get to places so quickly, he could take chances offensively and defensively that we couldn't take. He was something to watch."

Following Coffey's goal, the period's frenetic pace slowed half a beat and stayed that way until the intermission and early part of the middle frame. Canada killed off a penalty to open the second period with Fuhr making a big stop on a nifty one-handed deke from Kamensky. A Canadian power play produced a flurry around Belosheikin with Gretzky and Lemieux just failing to connect a couple of times. Canada, however, was playing a more careful, calculated game than they'd played in the opening twenty minutes and it started to catch up to them.

Crossman was sent off for tackling Krutov, and shortly thereafter, Fetisov whistled a drive from the point that ricocheted off Rochefort past a screened Fuhr.

The game was on again.

A couple of minutes after Fetisov's goal, Nemchinov was sent off for holding Anderson. From the faceoff deep in the Russian end, Makarov jumped on a loose puck, sped through the neutral zone and across the Canadian blue line, then spun away from Coffey and back over the blue line, before picking his way through Gretzky, Lemieux, and Messier, none of whom seemed all that interested in checking him. By the time Makarov had turned back to the Canadian blue line, Krutov had caught up to the play. He took a pass from his linemate and from the right faceoff circle beat Fuhr with a snap shot from his off-wing just inside the post, à la Messier.

The score was now tied and goals seemed to be lurking on every rush. On the same penalty-kill Bykov just failed to give the Russians their first lead of the game when he mishandled the puck on a two-on-one. The next time up the ice, Bykov failed to get the puck deep on a rush and Fetisov was trapped as Bourque slapped a pass up to Gretzky, who was alone with Lemieux on a two-on-one against veteran defenceman Vassily Pervukhin. The pair hadn't played a lot together in five-on-five situations since the first period but now they had half the length of the ice to work their magic. Gretzky cut over to his favoured left side to improve his angle, Lemieux cocked his stick the minute he crossed the blue line, and the pass was delivered right into his wheelhouse. He beat Belosheikin easily with a wicked one-timer.

"I don't know what Belosheikin thought but he's got the two greatest forwards in the game today coming at him," Reusch said. "What are you going to do? There's not much you can do. Watch it go by."

It was Lemieux's first goal of the final and Gretzky's third assist of Game 2 but, more importantly, the goal consummated the union between two superstars and they would play together for the rest of the series. Through nine pretournament games, five tournament games, and Game 1 of the final, Keenan had looked down his bench at the two greatest forwards to ever play the game and hadn't put them on the ice together. "It would be counter-productive," he'd reply cryptically whenever the question was raised, and it was raised frequently. But midway through the final, with Canada already down a game and in a dogfight just to survive, he unleashed the pair on the Russians and changed the course of the '87 Canada Cup.

Why?

"I thought about it in training camp and during the whole tournament, but I wanted a trump card," Keenan says. "I knew it would take something special to beat that team and, in the end, that's what we needed."

Perron, who worked with Keenan the whole series, says the entire Team Canada bench took notice when Gretzky and Lemieux were paired together. "I was surprised he didn't play them together at first but I think in the back of his mind, he knew that move was always there if he needed it," says Perron. "And when he did it, there was no warning. It was a genius move. When it happened, everyone on the bench looked at each other like, 'What's he doing?' It was a shocker. It turned out to be the best move he made in that series."

With twenty years of hindsight, however, you wonder what took Keenan so long. Gretzky was the best player in the game and the best passer the NHL has ever seen. In Lemieux, he had a bigger, stronger, more skilled version of Jari Kurri, his right winger and triggerman in Edmonton, and that's saying something. Lemieux had the instincts of a sniper but he was also the only other forward in the history of the game who could think and play at Gretzky's otherworldly level.

Now it seems so obvious. But it wasn't at the time because the Lemieux of '87 wasn't quite the transcendent figure he would become later in his career. It seems preposterous now but there was actually some question whether Lemieux would even make the team in the early part of training camp. Lemieux, who was just twenty-one, had played three seasons in Pittsburgh and there was no denying his talent. But, owing to a series of well-documented incidents, he was also regarded as moody, a trifle selfish, lazy, and self-centred. The Canada Cup would be his coming-out party and Lemieux has never denied the role it played in his development. But as much as it changed him as a player, it also changed the way he was perceived by the hockey world and it all happened over the three nights in September 1987.

"I scouted Mario when he was in junior [at Laval] and he was just so-so," says Perron. "You'd see flashes you wouldn't believe and then there'd be nothing for a long time.

"Mario was kind of a happy-go-lucky kid but he learned how to win from Wayne in that tournament. There was no question Mario got better every game in the tournament because of Wayne. When Keenan put them together, Mario understood he had to deliver because now he was playing with the best."

Lemieux, of course, was blessed by the hockey gods at an early age and most everyone in Quebec was keenly aware of his prodigious talents by the time he hit puberty. When he was twelve, then Montreal Canadiens coach Scotty Bowman went to scout him playing peewee in Granby. At fifteen, he had his first meeting with his agent Bob Perno and told Perno he was going to break the Quebec junior league scoring record and become the NHL's first overall draft pick. "How big a contract do you think you can get me?" he asked Perno.

Perno worked with Gretzky's agent, Gus Badali, and, that same summer, Lemieux was invited out to Badali's golf tournament in Toronto. There, the fifteen-year-old Lemieux went out for dinner and beers with Gretzky and, according to one Lemieux biographer, a significant event in young Mario's life took place later that night. Very significant, if you catch our drift.

If the story is true, it wasn't the last time Lemieux scored on a setup by Gretzky. In 1981–82, his first season playing in Laval, Lemieux ripped off 30 goals and 66 assists and, just as quickly, started developing a reputation as a floater. He promptly quit school. He was advised against the move by Perno, Badali, and even Gretzky, but Lemieux said he would be able to train more often with free time. Ice time was then made available for him at the Laval arena, which he never used. His junior teammates seldom saw him work out or jog. He started smoking at a young age.

The next year he counted 84 goals and 100 assists with Laval but questions persisted about his commitment to the game. Over Christmas, he played for Dave King at the World Junior Championship in Leningrad but didn't like the way he was used. He told his family he'd never play at the world juniors again. In the playoffs that year, Lemieux's team was knocked out in the first round by an expansion Longueuil team coached by Jacques Lemaire.

Looking back, it seems Lemieux was going through an awkward maturation process common to all teenagers. In Lemieux's case, that process was complicated by the fame and notoriety that found him when he was barely out of short pants. He once remarked that if someone told him to speed up, he'd slow down just to prove a point. But by the time his draft year rolled around, he started to apply himself and the hockey world was stunned at what he produced.

Stung by criticism, Lemieux actually began working out the summer before his final campaign in Laval and when the season started, he went off like a Roman candle. He'd eventually make good on his prediction to Perno, setting Quebec league scoring records with, wait for it, 133 goals and 149 assists for 282 points. Late in the season, Gretzky and the Oilers were in town for an Oilers–Habs playoff series and No. 99 and Coffey took in a game where Lemieux counted five goals and six assists against Longueuil to break the Q's scoring record.

Still, it wasn't all sweetness and light in Lemieux's world. Brian Kilrea replaced King as coach of Canada's entry at the world juniors that year but Lemieux, true to his word, refused to suit up for his country. He was then suspended by the Quebec league but took the case to court and won an injunction. That year, Laval won the Quebec league title but they also tanked in the Memorial Cup tournament, losing all three games. Lemieux entered that summer as the NHL's top-rated prospect, and the Penguins had worked hard to secure the first pick in the draft. In 1983–84, they'd traded Randy Carlyle, their best defenceman, to Winnipeg for a first-round draft pick. They also sent their best goalie, Roberto Romano, to the minors and called up the immortal Vincent Tremblay. The Pens lost their last six games that year to finish 16–58–6. They also averaged 6,700 fans per game that season, were more than $6 million in debt, and had posted losing campaigns in thirteen of their seventeen seasons. Yet, there were still voices in the Penguins' organization who wanted to take Guelph's Kirk Muller with the first pick because Muller represented a safer bet. He might not have Lemieux's upside but Muller would play and he wasn't going to be the giant pain in the ass Lemieux was proving to be.

The problem, naturally, was his contract. Lemieux wanted an unheard of $1 million over three years in his first deal and the Pens were offering $700,000. Lemieux told the Penguins he wouldn't appear at the draft, which was held in Montreal, unless he got his dough. After Gretzky counselled him to at least show up at the draft, Lemieux attended but didn't, as per custom, go down to the Penguins' table when he was selected. He was booed in his hometown, His mother, Pierrette, who was in attendance, cried. An unrepentant Lemieux told reporters: "I didn't go to the table because negotiations aren't going well. I'm not going to put on the sweater if they don't want me badly enough." Following draft day, Lemieux was savaged in the press, but he would eventually settle on an incentive-laden deal with the Penguins.

His first NHL training camp was hardly auspicious. As part of the Pens' physical, players were required to bench press 180 pounds ten times. Lemieux couldn't complete a single rep. He also couldn't finish the three-mile run that was required. But, about the time the Penguins were wondering if they'd made a mistake, Lemieux scored a memorable goal in his first shift of his first NHL game against the Boston Bruins. He finished his rookie year with 43 goals and 57 assists for 100 points, edging out Montreal's Chris Chelios for the Calder Trophy.

With some reluctance, and at Eagleson's urging, Lemieux even attended the world championships in Prague that spring. But Lemieux quickly soured on the experience when he suffered a groin injury and the Canadians were pounded 9–1 by the Russians in the round robin. He told Eagleson he wanted to go home. He told Perno to make arrangements to get him out of Prague. While he was stewing, he also watched his teammates drop a game to the U.S. and, for whatever reason, that loss engaged him to the Team Canada cause. He told the Eagle he wanted to stay, then led Canada to a win over Finland, and, in the semifinal against Russia, scored two goals in a stunning 3–1 upset win for Canada. For the first time in his career, Lemieux had turned a potential public relations disaster into a major victory. He wasn't all the way home yet but that game was a crucial moment in Lemieux's development.

"That was the first time we saw Mario," says Kasatonov, who would see a lot more of Lemieux two years later. "We didn't get a lot of news in Russia in those days and we didn't know a lot about him. He was just a kid but he was already a great player."

The next season, Lemieux recorded 48 goals and 98 assists for 141 points with the Penguins, moving for the first time into the game's highest echelons. In January of that season, the Penguins visited the Oilers in Edmonton and Lemieux scored a goal and added three assists in a 7–4 Penguins' win. Gretzky, it seemed, was more than aware of the significance of Lemieux's performance and the threat he posed.

"When I first came up, they said I was too small and too slow," Gretzky said after the game. "Now they're saying I'm over the hill. It seems like only yesterday they were saying I couldn't play in this league. Now they're wondering who'll take my place.

"Mario's a great asset to the game. To push me in the scoring race somebody will have to be up around two hundred points. Right now there's a gap of, what, fifty points? He's young yet. Maybe he'll give me a push one of these seasons."

Lemieux also seemed to be aware of what was happening in his young life. "I think I have the talent to be near Gretzky," he said. "If we ever have a Stanley Cup team with great players around me, I could get as many as him. But it's too early for me now. It's too early for me in my second year."

He was right. It wouldn't be until Lemieux's fourth year that he'd overtake Gretzky for the NHL's scoring title.

That spring, Lemieux's image took another knock when he bowed out of the world championships, citing a prolonged bout of bronchitis. Lemieux, however, was seen inhaling deeply on a cigarette during the playoffs in Montreal and that story made the papers. The next season, 1986–87, he again refused Hockey Canada's invitation to the world championships in Vienna. This time it wasn't a health issue. Nor was it the locale of the tournament. Lemieux just didn't feel like it and the grumbling about him, which had quieted after his performance in Prague two years earlier, grew audible again.

This, then, was the Lemieux who showed up in Montreal for the start of Team Canada's training camp. He was a once-in-a-generation talent to be sure but something seemed to be missing, some variable that separated the good from the great; the great from the immortal. He would find that missing something on Team Canada and it seems the whole team, particularly Gretzky, made it their responsibility to show him the way. Keenan, as you might have guessed, has the most interesting take on the relationship that developed between Gretzky and Lemieux, theorizing that, like a great actor, Gretzky shared the secrets of his craft with the one player who was capable of pushing him and his art to greater heights. By the end of the 1986–87 season, the game had almost become boring to Gretzky. He'd concluded a six-year run in which he won six straight scoring titles, averaging 203 points a season over that span. That was impressive enough. But, in that time, the average difference between Gretzky's total and the second-place scorer was 73 points. In 1981–82, Mike Bossy came within 65 points of Gretzky, the closest anyone came during that run. The Oilers had also won their third Stanley Cup in four years in 1987 and only Steve Smith's own goal against Calgary in the 1986 playoffs prevented a fourth.

Then along came Mario, who seemingly could do everything Gretzky could do on the ice and was four inches taller and thirty pounds heavier. Keenan asserts that Gretzky took a long look at Lemieux and made the decision to do everything in his power to help him. "Wayne had two reasons for doing it," Keenan says. "One, he saw Mario's talent and he knew he could make a difference on our team. He wanted to affect Mario's approach to the game as quickly as possible. The other thing is Wayne needed someone to give him a push. Whether it was on a conscious level or a subconscious level, he knew he needed a challenge and he knew Mario had the talent to be the best. From the moment Mario came into the league, Wayne knew what he was up to at every second."

Gretzky, for his part, has dismissed the notion that he had anything to do with Lemieux's breakout at the Canada Cup. Lemieux was always a great player, according to Gretzky, and he didn't need any help ascending to the game's highest level. But in an interview for this book, Gretzky admitted he went out of his way to mentor Lemieux during the tournament for reasons other than Keenan suggests.

"I think it had a lot to do with the history of Canadian hockey," Gretzky says. "I remember hearing about the '76

Canada Cup and how Bobby Orr had taken Lafleur under his wing. In '81, I was the kid and Lafleur was helping me out. It was like Mutt and Jeff.

"Sitting there with Mario, it didn't seem like it had been that long since I was following Lafleur around. It's a special thing to be a part of. It's like a big circle."

Fifteen years later, Lemieux would come out of retirement and help lead Canada to a gold medal at Salt Lake City. "I think that's part of the same thing," says Gretzky, who was executive director of that team.

Still, the two superstars had some practical considerations to iron out. During an earlier tournament game, Gretzky and Lemieux found themselves on a two-on-one when Gretzky, as he'd always done in Edmonton with Kurri, fed Lemieux for a one-timer. This time, however, he was shocked when the puck came back to him, which led to a meeting of the minds.

"I said, 'I want you to be the shooter. You've got a heavier shot and a better release. I'm not used to being the shooter,'" says Gretzky.

At the time, Gretzky was even more pointed in his directive to Lemieux.

"I want him shooting because he's got those awesome wrists," Gretzky said. "He could snap a puck through a refrigerator door."

But Gretzky did a lot more for Lemieux in the Canada Cup than set him up for one-timers. The players and coaches on Team Canada say Gretzky didn't go out of his way to tutor Lemieux and Lemieux didn't attach himself to Gretzky during training camp and the pretournament games. But there was a bond there and while the exchanges tended to be subtle and understated – a quick word here, a nod there – they were noticed by all.

"You could see Gretzky dragging Mario into the fight more and more as the camp went on," says Bob Clarke. "He was so generous on the ice. He did things to bring Mario into it. He wasn't worried about competing with him. And that relationship made that team."

"My observation was they were excited about playing with each other and it was a challenge for both of them," says Larry Murphy. "I think the worst-case scenario for each guy was one of them played great and the other one wasn't so great. They knew they were going to be judged against each other. They weren't going to take that lightly, playing with each other."

"Mario had a lot of respect for Wayne, but the big thing was Wayne had a lot of respect for Mario and he gave it in a kind and generous way," says Hrudey. "There was no hint or sense of, 'Listen kid, I'm still the top dog around here.' Wayne just doesn't have that in him."

But Gretzky wasn't the only one who reached out to Lemieux. Almost from the first day of training camp, the coaching staff seemed to go out of their way to laud Lemieux and his work ethic. "He's a good kid, a nice kid," said Muckler. "He's just really shy and introverted, so a lot of people read him the wrong way."

Said Keenan: "Mario's earned some of the criticism he's had in the past. It's been deserved because at times it looked like he wasn't playing with that much intensity. But I'll tell you this. Mario is not a lazy hockey player."

Lemieux, as mentioned, has always credited his Canada Cup experience as a turning point in his career. He saw the Oilers and the way they conducted themselves on and off the ice. He saw the way they practised and prepared. Mostly he saw the deep and abiding respect Gretzky had for the game, how he never took anything for granted, how he never took a shift off. Lemieux might have been a high-school dropout but he had an intuition about the game and he understood what Gretzky and his teammates were trying to show him. "I learned so much about how the great players work and conduct themselves," Lemieux said. "Remember, I was only twenty-one years old at the time. To be around guys like Wayne and Mark Messier and

Paul Coffey, guys who'd already had so much success and had won Stanley Cups, was a tremendous learning experience.

"They were in their prime and I was just a young guy, learning the game. Being in the Canada Cup and playing with Gretzky gave me a lot of confidence . . . It gave me an opportunity to start my career and really learn what it meant to be a champion and the best in the game."

And maybe the best part about Lemieux's transformation was the startling speed at which it took place. It took him six years to create the image of a hockey slacker, someone who would never fulfill his boundless potential. But in six short weeks he changed the way he was regarded in the hockey world for all time.

"That was the first time I saw Mario play with emotion," says Savard. "He had all this talent and all the moves but he played the same way all the time. Now he had the fire."

"I think a light went on when [Lemieux] played with Gretz," says Hawerchuk. "He looked at this guy [Gretzky], there was nothing to him, he wasn't a great skater or had a great shot. He just had this work ethic that never stopped. I think he realized if he went full-speed every shift like Wayne, he could produce like Wayne."

Says Messier: "I remember watching those two and thinking, 'This is as good as it gets.'"

It also produced a remarkable moment in the game's history. They were the two greatest forwards to ever play the game and, as Murphy says, the only meaningful yardstick by which they were measured was each other. That made them rivals, but it also made them allies. Writing in his memoirs, *Chronicles: Volume One*, Bob Dylan reflected on greatness, what it means to have it, what it means to share it. He was writing about music, but he could have been writing about Lemieux and Gretzky. "To do it," Dylan wrote. "You've got to have power and dominion over the spirits. I had done it once, and once was enough. Someone would come along eventually who would have it again −

someone who could look into things, the truth of things – not metaphorically either – but really see, like seeing into metal and making it melt, see it for what it was and reveal it for what it was with hard words and vicious insight."

Lemieux, like Gretzky, had that vicious insight. Of course it helped that he could shoot the puck through a refrigerator door.

Lemieux's goal fuelled another Canadian rally late in the frame that ended with the sequence described in this book's opening. Gretzky, Lemieux, and Goulet went head-to-head against Larionov's line over the period's final minute and produced a wild flurry in the dying seconds in which Krutov, whose turnover had caused the mess in the first place, slid to deflect Gilmour's shot over the glass. The play ended with Fetisov and Krutov down on the ice, Belosheikin on his knees about twenty feet out of position near the left faceoff circle, Gilmour flat on his stomach in front of the Russian goal, and Lemieux, bent over in frustration, standing all alone by the far post. It almost looked like the final scene from Hamlet.

Keenan, to that point in the game, had been rotating nine forwards and as the third period opened, his team would be fighting fatigue as well as the Soviets. Reusch observed: "We'll see what the six weeks have done for Canada in their conditioning," but if the pace of the game slowed, it wasn't apparent. Messier, who seemed to be engaged in his own private war with Fetisov, led a rush down the left wing, skated through a Fetisov check behind the Russian net, set up Anderson in the high slot, and was stopped by Belosheikin. At the other end, Semenov whistled a snap shot from the slot off the post before Fuhr had to make a reflex save off Priakhin's deflected centring pass.

The Soviets tied the game for the third time in the night moments later on an innocent-looking rush by the Bykov line. Khomutov beat Hartsburg at the blue line, then found Bykov who beat Fuhr with a wicked backhand from the left faceoff dot and from that point, the ice started to tilt toward Fuhr's goal. Semak just missed on a partial breakaway. Fuhr turned away Semenov, who was having an interesting game, before the Russian forward batted in the rebound with a high stick. Stewart coolly waived off the goal without protest from the Russians. Midway through the final frame, the shots on goal were 6–1 for Tikhonov's team. Reusch said: "Canada is clearly tired. They're starting to make mistakes out there. They need a break and then they need some great goaltending."

And damned if they didn't come back again. Keenan started to play Gretzky and Lemieux every other shift with either Goulet or Propp, who hadn't played a lot in the first two periods, on the left side. From a faceoff deep in the Russian end, Gretzky spun away from Larionov behind Belosheikin, found Propp in a prime scoring area, and Gusarov had to take a penalty.

Team Canada's power play had gone 0-for-2 and surrendered a short-handed goal to Krutov to that point in the game but they didn't take long to recapture the lead. Messier beat Krutov on the faceoff. The puck then went from Bourque to Lemieux, back to Bourque whose shot was corralled by Gretzky. Gretzky went back to Bourque, to Lemieux to Bourque to Coffey, back to Lemieux, to Bourque to Coffey, who let fly with a one-timer from the top of the faceoff circle. Belosheikin made the save, but Gretzky was able to push the puck to the far post, where Lemieux, who was almost against the far boards when Coffey took the original shot, swooped in and beat Krutov to the loose puck in the crease, scoring his second of the night. The whole sequence took twenty-two seconds and the Canadians made ten passes before Lemieux's goal. It was his seventh shot of the game.

"I was with him for six weeks and I saw him get better every day," Hawerchuk says of Lemieux. "There were practices where we'd just throw our sticks in the air and start laughing because he was so good. He was going against the best defencemen in the NHL and making them look like juniors."

"Lemieux's coming-out party is what sticks out in my mind about that tournament," says Messier. "I just think he realized he could play with anyone in the world."

Lemieux's goal came with just under ten minutes left in the game and for nine of those minutes, the Canadians did a masterful job of protecting their lead. Sutter, whose ice time had been curtailed through much of the second period, started to appear regularly on a line with Gilmour and Gartner and that line produced some good energy shifts. Messier and Anderson drew the assignment against the Larionov line and didn't surrender a scoring chance against the great Russian trio. Lemieux and Gretzky, meanwhile, remained omnipresent and almost produced the insurance goal on two occasions, the first when Lemieux shook off a check from Fetisov and set up Propp in front of Belosheikin and the second on a two-on-one when Gretzky's saucer pass to Lemieux didn't settle properly and the big winger misfired over the top of the net. All told, the two teams went over five minutes without a single whistle before the Canadians went offside on a three-on-two rush with just under four minutes to play. In that time, the only Soviet threat had been a half-chance from Semenov that Fuhr turned away easily.

"You won't see a better period of hockey to see a team protect a lead," said Reusch. "Canada, almost perfect when it comes to their defence right now." But wouldn't you know it. With just over a minute left in regulation, Gretzky, Gilmour, Bykov, and Kamensky all came together along the right-hand wall in the neutral zone and Kamensky beat the pack to a loose puck just over the centre line. Turning on the attack, the young winger split Gilmour and Lemieux just outside the Canadian blue line, then pushed the puck between Crossman and Rochefort, who were a hair too far apart as they backed into their zone. Rochefort missed the disc, then lunged to bring down Kamensky but was too late. Crossman, moving from the other side, couldn't stop Kamensky either and as he was falling down, the Soviet winger reached out and somehow flipped the puck over Fuhr into the top of the Canadian net.

Kamensky had gone through four Canadian defenders on the play. The goal came with sixty-four seconds left. It was the fourth time the Russians had come back to tie the game. "I didn't realize how fast he was going and he got on me in a hurry," Fuhr says. "I was thinking about poke-checking him. I was thinking about backing in. And I just got stuck in between and he rifled it over my shoulder."

Twenty years later, Keenan remains in awe of Kamensky's goal. "My god, what a play," he says. "It was like he was walking on air," and even at the time he credited Kamensky for a brilliant play rather than finding fault with his players.

"I looked at the tape of that goal," Keenan told the press a day later. "Holy shit. I thought there were four of our players who could have had him and your first reaction is to criticize your own players. But you can't because it was just an unbelievable effort." The reaction on the Team Canada bench, meanwhile, was similar. Messier, according to Hrudey, just turned his head and said: "Wow, that guy is nothing but a pure sniper."

Kamensky's goal marked the second straight game that Canada had surrendered a lead late in the third period, but if they were rattled by the turn of events it didn't show in the first five minutes of overtime. Hrudey, who dressed as the backup for Game 2, remembers most everything about that game and he remembers his teammates' reaction to Kamensky's goal and how they maintained their poise and focus against the crushing pressure applied by the Russians.

"It was something to see," says Hrudey. "There was never any mention that we were facing elimination or what might happen. It was about what they had to do to win the game."

It also helped that Keenan's rigorous training camp had whipped his team into top shape. They didn't exactly line up to thank the coach after the tournament but it's clear that Canada's conditioning played a crucial role in the series and negated the Russians' perceived advantage. Given that they had nine forwards playing against the mighty Russians in a game that went into double overtime, it was a miracle that the Canadians could stand, let alone play at the highest level. But they still pulled Game 2 out in double overtime, suggesting Keenan's team was in better condition than Tikhonov's team, which is why they won this war of attrition.

That's, at least, the way the Canadians see things.

"For some reason we were told they were in better shape than us and their training was superior to ours," says Muckler. "We used to go to their practices and try to find out if they were doing anything differently. We found out they weren't in any better condition than our players."

"We knew it was going to be a battle," says Hawerchuk. "The question was did we have the fortitude to stay the course. There were no surprises. We knew they were good and they knew we were good. It was a question of survival and thank god it wasn't like '72 and we were in shape. If we weren't, we would have lost that series."

Gretzky remained the most dangerous player on the ice in the first overtime, just failing to set up Hawerchuk, then Lemieux on odd-man rushes. The Soviets didn't produce much offence, but about six minutes in, Kasatonov split Coffey and James Patrick, who hadn't played since the second period, with a pass to Krutov, who then found Larionov. Larionov was in alone but instead of shooting, tried to force a pass back to Krutov and the play died with Fuhr smothering the puck in his crease. As the pair skated back to the Russian bench, Krutov could be seen shaking his head and talking to his centreman. "I played a bit in the second period, then Mike shortened the bench and I sat for the whole third period and the first half of overtime," is the way Patrick remembers things. "Then he put me out with Coffey, Paul gets caught and I'm looking at Krutov and Larionov coming down two-on-one. They passed the puck back and forth so many times, I was almost dizzy. I finally lunged at Larionov and the puck hopped over Krutov's stick. I don't think I've ever been so relieved to see a shift end."

Canada responded with a rush by Hawerchuk, who set up Gilmour for a direct shot on Belosheikin. Gretzky and Lemieux then produced a flurry around the Russian net but the scoring forays for both teams became more scattered and the game became tighter. Gretzky, Lemieux, and Goulet created some pressure in the Russian end after a long shift, and Goulet could be seen struggling to get back to the Canadian bench as Gretzky was still buzzing around looking for the puck. Gretzky, in fact, was still on the ice a good thirty seconds later as Coffey's drive from the high slot was deflected over the glass by Fedotov.

"Look at Gretz and how many points he gets at the end of a shift because he's in such great shape," Coffey would say the next day.

Well, maybe he wasn't in the best shape on this night. Midway through the first overtime, there's a stretch when Gretzky is noticeably absent. The problem, as the Great One would later relate, is he'd worked himself to the point of exhaustion, lost control of his bodily functions, and wet himself while he was sitting on the bench.

Keenan learned of the mishap after the game and he still recalls Gretzky calling him over and telling him, "I'm going to need a break for a while."

"I think he'd be the first to tell you he'd never expended so much energy in a game," says Keenan. "He went to a point he'd never been before."

Gretzky now likens his experience to a marathon-runner who becomes incontinent. "You're going so hard and the game is so intense and the crowd is so intense and you just lose control of your muscles," he says. "I remember sitting there thinking, 'I just wet myself.' It was almost an out-of-body experience."

The first overtime ended without further incident (or accidents on the Canadian bench), and the two teams tromped off the ice to ready themselves for another period of extra time. In the Team Canada locker room, Gretzky asked Hrudey to relate his experience with overtime games. That spring, Hrudey had backstopped the Islanders to a 3–2 triple-overtime win over the Capitals and this, in Gretzky's eyes, gave the young goalie some insights into the demands of marathon games. Hrudey, for his part, wondered what Gretzky was thinking.

"Everybody's looking at me and I'm thinking, Right. What am I going to say to this group?" says Hrudey. "I thought for a minute and said, 'Watch for something early,' because that's what happened when we played the Capitals. There'd be these flurries in the early going, then the game would settle into a defensive pattern."

This pleased Gretzky, who singled out Hrudey's between-periods speech to the media after the game.

"That was Wayne's perspective," says Hrudey. "My perspective was here's Kelly Hrudey (soiling himself, or words to that effect)."

In the early going of the second overtime, the Canadians and their nine forwards needed Fuhr to keep them in the game and the series. The Oilers' goalie made solid stops off Krutov, Bykov, and Khmylev. After a strong shift by Gretzky, Lemieux, and Propp, which produced three shots on Belosheikin, Fuhr made another save off Krutov after the relentless Russian outfought Bourque behind the net and walked out in front. "With all the guys we had, we didn't panic," Fuhr says. "I don't think anyone looked around and started to worry. We just knew we had to be better. With the leadership in that room, it was going to happen. My job was to keep it at that point until it did happen."

"I just remember the extreme tension on the bench," says Patrick. "You could feel it. But I also remember the superstars –

Gretzky, Messier – and how calm they were. It's something I remembered my entire career."

Five minutes in, the Canadian rally started on a shift by Messier, Anderson, and Gartner. Gartner had the best chance, hitting the post after Messier set him up in front. Belosheikin then stopped Coffey's point drive but on the ensuing rush, Gretzky hopped over the boards and put the puck in the crease where Propp just missed the empty side. Another Lemieux rush produced a glove save by Belosheikin and the crowd at Copps, which had been quiet, erupted with a prolonged ovation.

After Fuhr made a sharp toe save off Lomakin, and Crossman thwarted a dangerous rush by tackling Kasatonov, Gretzky, Lemieux, and Propp, who'd assumed regular duty on the line, came out for Canada and scored the game-winner. The play started behind the Canada net, where Bourque, with the aid of a Murphy pick, swung away from Kamensky before beating Khomutov in the neutral zone. Bourque fed Gretzky inside the blue line, who found Lemieux in the slot but Lemieux's first shot went wide. Propp then dug out a loose puck and centred to Murphy, who, instead of blasting into the pack, passed to Gretzky by the side of the net. Belosheikin made a remarkable save off Gretzky's first shot but the rebound came right to No. 99, who was able to shovel the puck toward the far post where Lemieux was standing.

The big man waited a split-second, then lifted the puck into the open cage as Gretzky leaped into the air and Copps exploded. Propp's stick was also in the area when the puck was sent across to Lemieux but the scoring play was announced as Lemieux from Gretzky and Murphy. It was Lemieux's third goal of the game and Gretzky's fifth assist.

"It was tough but we had some confidence when we came back in the second overtime," Lemieux told the TV audience after the game. "We wanted to play on Tuesday."

"I'm so happy for everyone," Gretzky said in Team Canada's locker room. "The trainers, coaches, players, fans. I mean, you never know what can happen in three years. This might be our last shot at the Soviets and I wanted there to be a third game so bad, you can't believe it.

"We were so down after they scored late in the third period. I wish the people of Canada could have been in the dressing room to see guys like Brent Sutter and Craig Hartsburg and Kelly Hrudey get us going again, put a smile on our faces and make us believe this was our game and no one was going to take it from us."

Of course, Gretzky had something to do with that, too.

Again, given the circumstances of the game and the level of competition, this is Gretzky's greatest game ever and that statement is not made lightly. The five assists have something to do with it but watching the game, you're almost exhausted watching Gretzky's effort. This was an era before official ice times were kept on the stats sheet, but in a contest that went just over ninety minutes and was played at an almost surreal speed, Gretzky had to have played forty minutes easily. Canada was playing three lines the entire night and even at that there were stretches when he was double-shifted. He played the power play. He killed penalties. He also worked the defensive side of the puck as hard as he worked the offensive side of the puck and there has never been a more dangerous partnership in the history of the game than Gretzky and Lemieux in Game 2 of the Canada Cup final.

"[Gretzky] was so different in terms of his game because he could handle minutes like a top defenceman," says Keenan. "He had stamina but he could also conserve energy because he was so fluid."

"I think it got to a point where they were challenging each other," Hartsburg says of the Gretzky–Lemieux partnership. "It was like who could make the next great play and it was amazing to watch. It just seemed like Wayne would go, 'I've got to do something better.' Then Mario would go, 'I've got to do something better.' And it would go higher and higher."

But this night belonged to Gretzky. The Great One, who complained about being physically and mentally drained before the tournament, who had to be convinced to show up for training camp, had become fully engaged through the six weeks with Team Canada and was playing at the apex of his powers. Keenan describes one incident from the round-robin game against the Americans when Gretzky was involved in play along the boards on the far side of the players' bench when, out of nowhere, he made a ninety-degree turn at the red line, confronted the referee, and said: "They've got too many men on the ice."

"Sure enough, they did," said Keenan. "There wasn't one person in the whole building who knew it. But he did. I got the sense that he knew where all his friends were sitting in the building. That was scary but that's how perceptive he was."

And yet that wasn't the quality that impressed the most about Gretzky.

"It's hard for me to answer that because, to me, he was always great," says GM Savard. "He showed up every night and he competed. He never let up. He had all this talent and the anticipation and the vision but to me, that's what made him great. He worked harder than anyone."

"I can't remember Gretzky ever having a bad practice let alone a bad game," says Clarke. "I've never seen anyone compete like that day after day. That's so unique for any player, let alone a player of his stature. No one would have said a thing if he'd taken a day off. But he always showed up and he always delivered."

Kasatonov was asked what he remembers about Gretzky's performance, if he knew what he was watching at the time.

"No," he said. "But right now I realize the hockey that was played and how lucky I was to be a part of it. I feel honoured and proud to have played against him. It was like a light in my eyes."

Following Game 2, members of the media were suggesting to Gretzky that he'd just played his greatest game. This was met with a predictable response.

"I don't know," he said. "You surround yourself with a great team and you look good individually. I've been on some great teams. I think I played the best hockey I could tonight."

But after the scrum had broken up, Vancouver sports writer Jim Taylor, who'd written an early Gretzky biography, cornered Gretzky alone and said: "I don't care what you say. This was the greatest game you ever played."

"I know," Gretzky responded. "But I couldn't say that."

And twenty years later?

"Yeah, when you take everything into consideration it was unquestionably my best game," Gretzky says.

In hindsight, Tikhonov's decision to start the twenty-one-year-old Belosheikin for Game 2 was, at best, curious. The diminutive Mylnikov, statistically at least, had been the better goalie in the tournament, sporting a 5–0 record to that point, including the win over Canada in Game 1. He would also end the Canada Cup with a 2.96 goals-against average. Belosheikin, meanwhile, was 0–2–1 with a 4.00 goals-against average and had been perforated for five goals by the Swedes in the tournament opener.

But Belosheikin was also one of the rising stars of the national team and the Canada Cup was part of the preparation Tikhonov had mapped out for the young man who was being groomed to succeed Tretiak as Russia's next great goalie. Tikhonov didn't know a lot about the position, and goalies, for the most part, were left to develop on their own in the Russian system. But the coach recognized Belosheikin's natural ability and saw in him the answer to his goaltending problems.

A native of St. Petersburg, Belosheikin emerged as the country's best goaltending prospect at the '84 World Junior

Championship in Nykoping, Sweden, when he backstopped the
Russians to a gold medal and was named to the tournament's all-
star team. Two years later in Hamilton, on a team that included
Kamensky and Semak, he was again named to the tournament
all-star team as the Russians struck gold again with a 7–0 record,
thumping the Canadians 4–1 in the gold-medal game.

At Rendez-Vous the next year, Belosheikin drew the starting
assignment in both games and earned the win in the second
game at Le Colisée. Tretiak had retired in 1984, largely because
he was tired of the crushing demands Tikhonov placed on his
players, and he left a huge vacuum on the national team.
Vladimir Myshkin wasn't the answer. Mylnikov was a marginal
talent. But, in 1987, Belosheikin was considered the real deal, a
lithe acrobat who, one day, was going to provide the kind of
goaltending Tikhonov had been missing in Tretiak's absence.

"He was a young kid, a hard worker," says Nemchinov, who
played with Belosheikin at Red Army. "You saw how he played
and he had so much talent. Maybe he was inexperienced but he
was going to be a great goalie."

There was just one problem. Belosheikin was a drinker and,
while he could beat the best teams in the world, he couldn't beat
the bottle.

It's difficult to accurately assess the impact alcohol had on the
1987 Russian team, but it was a factor, just as it was a factor in
the country's social life. Igor Kuperman, who covered that generation of players, says the problem wasn't as extensive as it was
in the general population and a player like Larionov never
touched anything stronger than a glass of wine. But it was still
an accepted part of Russian culture – Gorbachev often preached
against the dangers of alcohol – and drinking was one of the
ways to ease the boredom of Tikhonov's regimen.

Mogilny, who joined Red Army in 1986 as a seventeen-
year-old, said the national team players were cooped up at the

training centre for weeks at a time, then released for one day of R and R. Given their constraints, it was understandable they didn't spend that day at the library.

"They'd let us loose for one day, and you'd hit the street running," says Mogilny. "You'd try to pack everything you'd been missing into that one day. It's funny now but it wasn't funny at the time. You had no life outside of hockey. That's why so many of those guys have had trouble adjusting to a normal life."

The history of Russian hockey, in fact, is littered with a litany of unexplained deaths and fatal car crashes in which alcohol was a factor. Belosheikin, for his part, had to deal with the pressure of succeeding Tretiak and that, coupled with a predilection for binge drinking, was a tragic combination. He was in and out of Tikhonov's doghouse throughout his short career with the national team and he was suspended in 1986 for his drinking. The Canada Cup would also be Belosheikin's last meaningful appearance for the Russians on the game's biggest stage. At the Winter Olympics in Calgary six months later he was again slated to split the duties with Mylnikov but suffered an injury and didn't dress for any of the games. He received a gold medal but Tikhonov released him from Red Army the following year.

In 1991, after a year of driving cab in St. Petersburg, Belosheikin was selected as a late-round draft choice by the Edmonton Oilers, who sent him to their AHL affiliate in Cape Breton, where he played three games. But, even though he was just twenty-five, he was spent.

"I knew who he was," says Bill Ranford, the Oilers' goalie at the time. "He was struggling mentally and with alcohol. He was trying to turn his life around and Glen [Sather] gave him that chance. But he was just worn out."

Belosheikin returned to St. Petersburg and played for Izhovets in the Russian third division for five more years.

At thirty-three, he hanged himself in his apartment.

"Everyone had forgotten about him by then," says Kuperman.

Nemchinov, who was playing in the NHL, was one of those who'd lost track of his former teammate but he was still stunned to hear the news of his suicide. "He wasn't himself any more," says Nemchinov. "He was a young man and had so much to live for."

"He had his whole life and his whole career ahead of him but he had these problems," says Kasatonov. "We never saw them. They came later but he just couldn't overcome those problems."

Larionov, for his part, says Belosheikin couldn't handle the pressure of succeeding Tretiak. Others who were close to the team suggest his drinking problem had nothing to do with Tretiak, Tikhonov, or the Russian system.

Whatever the case, it was a sad, sad ending to a life that had begun with such promise. "We'd have these young stars come to our team and some could handle the pressure and the outside forces and some couldn't," says Larionov. "He was one of the guys who couldn't. He was supposed to be the next Tretiak and it was too much for him."

CHAPTER 6

Mario Lemieux with 1:26 Remaining

While Team Canada was still celebrating Lemieux's overtime goal, an announcement was made at Copps that the twelve hundred tickets remaining for Game 3 would go on sale the next morning at 9 a.m. The tickets sold in forty minutes as something of a frenzy broke out in Hamilton. An estimated three thousand fans lined up for the ducats. Scalpers reported getting as much as $200 a pair for the deciding game. There were whispers that the price reached $400 a pair.

"This is a unique event, the ultimate in hockey," said one fan who'd driven down from Mississauga and paid $150 for a pair of upper-level seats. "I'd pay just about anything." The atmosphere around Team Canada was equally electric. Clarke had returned to Philadelphia when the finals started and kept in contact with Savard. The players weren't the problem. "It was easy to have confidence in that team," Clarke says. "They'd all won. They were going to figure it out sooner or later." But the normally taciturn Savard, who'd remained with the team, was having trouble staying calm. He had the Russians to deal with. He had the injury-depleted Canadian lineup, which was starting to run on fumes. Eagleson also had the bright idea to dangle $5,000 bonus cheques in front of the Team Canada players before Game 3, a practice that was common at the time with hockey men.

The Habs' GM vetoed Eagleson's plan, feeling the extra incentive was unnecessary, if not insulting, to that group. But, Bill Tuele, the Team Canada PR director, who'd been through four Stanley Cup finals with the Oilers, says he's never seen normally poised, professional hockey men worked into such a state of anxiety. "It was almost painful being around them," he said.

Still, it couldn't have been as painful as reading some of the copy that came out of the off day between Games 2 and 3, as players and coaches outdid themselves trying to capture the emotion of the final and Gretzky's Game-2 performance. "Canada, Soviets try for one more night of magic," read the headline in the *Philadelphia Daily News*. "Hockey now on new level," the *Edmonton Journal* proclaimed. Morrison, the *Toronto Sun* reporter, says the assembled media were dimly aware they were watching something special when the final started. But midway through Game 2, the series took on a life of its own and everyone connected seemed to understand the magnitude of the event, some with more élan than others.

"If the crescendo for Game 3 is the same from the first to third period as it was in [Game 2] then fasten your seat belts," said Team Canada assistant Perron. "This will be a trip into hockey space . . . This is the best thing that has ever happened to the game."

"Maybe I was a little excited but that's what it felt like," Perron now says when his florid quote is called to his attention.

It was also pointed out to Russian assistant coach Dmitriev that the winners' share for the Canada Cup was $6,500 per man and the losers was $5,500.

"When you play at this level," Dmitriev said philosophically. "Rubles don't matter."

Gretzky's performance for the ages, meanwhile, was still a topic of conversation a day later. The Great One had been given the day off to visit his ailing grandmother in Brampton. Mary Gretzky encountered some respiratory problems while watching Game 2 with the Wayner's mother, Phyllis, but she refused to go to the hospital until the contest was decided just before 1 a.m. There were, however, others who were willing to discuss what they'd just seen.

"I've seen [Gretzky] play for seven years and with and without the puck, he was better than I've ever seen him," Coffey said of his Oilers' teammate.

"He is a bit like an invisible man," Dmitriev said of Gretzky. "He appears out of nowhere. He passes to no one. And a goal is scored."

Lemieux also received his share of plaudits for his three-goal effort.

"What's surprised me about Mario here is one word – *intensity*," said Perron. "Even his defensive work is not bad at all and that's very unusual for a guy everyone says can't check their mother."

Keenan, for his part, was still in awe at what he'd seen in Game 2. "You don't have time to marvel at it when you're on the bench because the focus is so intense," he said. "If you get caught up in the last play, you'll lose concentration on the next one. I was so wound up after, I couldn't enjoy the fact we'd scored the overtime goal. I couldn't sleep. I had to take a walk.

"But I watched part of the game on tape this morning. And then I said, 'Holy shit.'"

Keenan also received some good news on the medical front before Game 3. Tocchet, who sat out Game 2 with a nagging injury to his left knee, was cleared to play after he was examined by Flyers' doctors in Philadelphia. Tocchet had provided the team with a huge jolt of energy throughout the tournament and nothing short of reconstructive surgery was going to keep him out of Game 3. As it was, Team Canada's medical staff simply wrapped the knee a little tighter, which enabled him to suit up.

"He didn't give me a shot or anything," Tocchet said of his meeting with Flyers' orthopedist Dr. John Gregg. "He just looked at the knee and I looked at him and said, 'I want to play in this game as much as any one in my life.' [Gregg] looked at me and said, 'I don't blame you kid.'"

Keenan, then, would still be short a couple of forwards, but the Team Canada coach believed his team could draw on the energy of the event and their own stores of adrenalin.

"They've enjoyed this so much," Keenan said. "I'm not worried about fatigue. They want to do this one more time.

"It doesn't matter now. We've got a country behind us. Maybe that'll be the difference. Maybe that will be the fourth line."

But Keenan also ensured his players would be properly focused for the deciding game. While Team Canada players were still peeling off their sweat-soaked gear following the marathon victory in Game 2, Keenan wrote on the greaseboard: "Practice tomorrow, 1 p.m." Gretzky remembers looking up and thinking, 'He can't be serious,' and Keenan had no intention of skating his players the day after Game 2. But he still wanted them around the rink, thinking about hockey, thinking about the challenge that awaited them.

"That was typical of Mike," Gretzky says.

For the Russians, Tikhonov made a rare roster move when he opted to replace Pervukhin, the victim of Lemieux's and Gretzky's second goal in Game 2, with twenty-one-year-old Igor Kravchuk, one of the rising stars of Russian hockey and the man who was being groomed to replace Fetisov. Kravchuk hadn't played in the final, but it was hoped he'd bring mobility and an offensive spark to the blue line. Tikhonov had been concerned about his defence throughout the tournament and inserting the inexperienced Kravchuk for a veteran like Pervukhin showed a great deal of confidence in the youngster.

"I wanted to play," says Kravchuk, who had injured his knee earlier in the tournament. "Of course I was nervous, but, for me, the whole tournament was something special. It was something I'll always remember and everything was fine until the last minute and a half of that game."

Following Stewart's solid refereeing performance in Game 2 – "I was just trying to do my bit for détente," he cracked afterward – Koharski drew the assignment for Game 3. A couple of years ago, the veteran official took his family to the Hockey Hall of Fame in Toronto, where a play-by-play simulator has been installed. As luck would have it, Mario Lemieux's game-winning goal was cued up that day.

"I said to my kids, 'Let me do this. I know everything that happened on this play,'" Koharski says. "And it still gives me chills."

"I've done over twenty Game Sevens and I've done Stanley Cup finals and I've never felt pressure like that in a game," Koharski continues. "It was in my hometown. It was Canada and Russia. I didn't have a lot of experience. But I can also remember details from those games as clear as a bell. It was truly the best hockey ever. I still feel humbled to have been a part of it."

Twenty years later, in fact, the energy, the tension, the passion, and the sheer quality of Game 3 still crackles through the videotape. Game 2 was played at a higher level. The speed and skill and individual brilliance of the stars in that contest has never been equalled. But Game 3 offered something else. Maybe it wasn't as artistically pleasing as the middle act in this piece, but for sheer drama it provided a worthy climax to everything that preceded it. Now, of course, everyone remembers Gretzky dissecting the Russian defence with a perfect pass to Lemieux, who fired a laser over the glove of Russian goalie Sergei Mylnikov. But few remember this game was almost over before it started; that Canada came back from 3–0 and 4–2 deficits and the rally wasn't keyed by Gretzky and Lemieux but rather by players like Tocchet, Sutter, and Hawerchuk, who hadn't been factors to that point in the final; and that Hawerchuk was voted their best player on the night.

Lemieux's goal is rightly entrenched in the game's lore, but for three hours before that, these two giants traded knockout punches while drawing on stores of will and courage that had been virtually exhausted through the first two games. In the end, Game 3 is like the fourteenth round of the Thrilla in Manila when Joe Frazier and Muhammad Ali took each other to a place few fighters have ever been, bringing out the best in each other in the process.

"After that final I said I don't have to coach another game," says Perron, who won a Stanley Cup with Montreal in 1986, won the Canada Cup in 1987, and was out of NHL coaching by the spring of 1988. "This is it. I've seen the best. I didn't have a long coaching career but I had some moments I'll never forget."

"We saw a lot of ourselves in them," says Messier. "When we left that series, we took a lot of things with us. They made us a better team."

The broadcast opened with an upbeat, by his standards anyway, Keenan being interviewed by CTV's Dan Matheson. "It's an all-out effort by two great teams who put everything on the line and take it to the limit," the Team Canada coach said. "It's going to be a fabulous sight for all of us to watch."

And it was. Eventually.

For the opening faceoff Keenan sent out Gretzky, Lemieux, and Messier with Crossman and Coffey against the Green Unit, which seemed like a reasonable choice until Kasatonov hammered Gretzky deep in the Canada end, the loose puck went to Krutov, and Krutov fed Makarov in front. Fuhr was digging the puck out of the net about the same time Gretzky was getting to his feet. Just twenty-six seconds in, the Canadians were down 1–0.

"It wasn't the start we were looking for," Keenan says. "I thought, 'If I don't do something in a hurry, I'm going to get in the car and drive north and they'll never hear from me again.'"

The Team Canada bench boss left Gretzky out for the next shift with Lemieux and Propp to no great effect before setting Tocchet loose on the Russians for the first time. The young Flyers' winger charged around the ice like an enraged rhino for forty-five seconds, taking a wild run at Kamensky, falling spectacularly in the Russian end, and finally nailing Gusarov before returning to the Canadian bench. Toller Cranston he wasn't but Tocchet did give Canada a lift.

Following the early fireworks, Hawerchuk produced a quality scoring chance on a solo rush before Bykov took a penalty for hauling down Lemieux and the Canadians seemed to be reasserting themselves. On the power play, Messier just missed on a Gretzky setup and Mylnikov made a strong stop off Goulet on another Gretzky pass. Gretzky, in fact, stayed out for all two minutes of the power play, which proved to be a problem when Goulet was hauled down in the slot and Gusarov and Nemchinov broke out on a two-on-one against Hartsburg. Gusarov, who was offensively challenged throughout his career, held the puck the length of the ice and, with few other options available, let fly with a wicked slapper from the top of the faceoff circle that beat Fuhr.

Kelly and Reusch were still discussing the relative merits of Gusarov's goal when, a minute later, the magical Makarov took the puck along the boards in the neutral zone, gained the Canadian blue line, performed another dazzling pirouette, and slipped the puck to Fetisov. With the Canadian defenders seemingly mesmerized by Makarov, Fetisov beat Murphy to the outside, then beat Fuhr with a sweet move to his forehand. Eight minutes in, the Canadians were down 3–0. They had allowed four shots on Fuhr. Three of them had gone in. Copps was a morgue.

"Canada's in shock here," said Reusch. "The Russians have scored on everything."

"We couldn't believe it," says Perron. "The game had barely started."

And that's when Keenan made the first of several crucial decisions that would determine the outcome of the game.

On some level this one was easy. As Perron says: "The one thing we knew for certain was Tretiak wasn't there and we had Fuhr. That was our advantage in the final." But if there was ever a time to pull the goalie, this was it. Keenan hadn't fully developed the Captain Hook reputation he'd carry throughout his career, but the Canadians needed something to give them a spark. Their defence was porous. Their stars were flat. The Russians were at their opportunistic best. Yet Keenan stuck with Fuhr while his own goalie Ron Hextall sat on the bench. Fuhr would repay his confidence by turning in a textbook effort the rest of the way.

"I can't recall him having many poor games and when he did he always came back with a strong game," Keenan now says of Fuhr. "It was the same pattern within the game. If he let in a soft goal, he wouldn't let in another one. It was obvious the players had confidence in him, especially the Oilers and they were a big part of that team. I didn't think they needed anything like that to give them a lift."

Well, Fuhr didn't need anything because he was used to playing in high-scoring games. "You just play," he says of his reaction to the game's start. "If you're going to get hooked, you're going to get hooked. You're better off playing and trying to make that next save.

"You knew both teams had firepower and it wasn't going to be low-scoring. You just had to make sure you made one extra save. That was kind of the style we played in Edmonton so it wasn't a big change for me. It was going to come down to the third period, regardless."

And things did turn around quickly for the Canadians. A minute after Fetisov's goal, Kravchuk was sent off for hauling down Gretzky, a penalty the Great One embellished with a professional dive. Midway through the ensuing power play, Canada got a huge break when Makarov's pass for a streaking Krutov hit Koharski and bounced to Anderson, who found Murphy in the slot. Mylnikov came way out of his net to stop Murphy's wrister, but the rebound was left there for Tocchet and the kid from Toronto scored the goal that started the Canadian comeback.

"I shouldn't have been out there but [Keenan] was trying to wake up the team," says Tocchet. "I was terrified. You've got Gretzky and Messier and all those superstars sitting on the bench and there I am. Luckily, I got a goal. You're petrified because you're like, 'Oh my god, those guys are still on the bench.' You're also saying, I don't want to let the team down."

Tocchet's goal got his team back in the game on the scoreboard but, more importantly, it engaged them emotionally and they responded by raising the physical ante to a level unfamiliar to the Russians. Sutter hauled down Bykov, but the Canadians killed off the penalty without surrendering a scoring chance. Hartsburg flattened Khomutov. Messier steamrolled Krutov at the Canadian blue line.

Fuhr even made a save off Makarov and, a couple of minutes after Sutter's return, Tocchet was at it again, chasing down Stelnov all the way behind the Russian goal and kicking a loose puck back the other way, which Sutter picked up and swept out in front of Mylnikov. His half-wraparound was headed wide before it clanged into Propp and Larionov, who were wrestling by the far post. Propp was given credit for the goal. Propp's marker did little to discourage the Canadian assault on the Russians. Gartner, of all people, took a huge run at Gusarov. The TV cameras caught Messier throwing an elbow at Semak's head after Fuhr had made another stop on the Russian forward. Tocchet and Sutter ran Kasatonov behind the Russian net and

Sutter ended up flattening his teammate, who emerged from the collision none the worse for wear.

The period would end on a sour note for the Canadians when Khomutov scored as a penalty to Makarov expired. Keenan's men had actually looked sharp on the power play and just before the goal, Gretzky hit the post on a deflection. But Bourque, who'd been out the whole two minutes, was slow in retreating to his end and Makarov hooked him down as Khomutov roared into the play. The Russian beat Fuhr with a backhand deke. Propp crosschecked him into the boards for his trouble.

So the first period ended with the Soviets leading 4–2 and Canadian fans in a state of confusion about their team. Just about everything that could have gone wrong for them in that period did. The Russians scored in the first minute and the last minute of the frame. They scored four goals on nine shots. The Canadian defence looked vulnerable and, down two goals, they'd have to open it up against the most dangerous offensive team in the world. And if that wasn't enough, Gretzky and Lemieux were almost invisible in the period.

On the other hand, Team Canada could have been buried and it was clear to all concerned the two teams weren't finished scoring. Canada, who'd produced nineteen shots on Mylnikov, had also succeeded in shifting the momentum and the terms of engagement with their physical play. The Russians, as Gretzky had pointed out, were great front-runners and lethal when they could pick teams apart with their speed–and–skill game. But once you scratched that veneer of invincibility, they were a different team and both Tocchet and Hawerchuk now say that's what Canada did with their comeback in the opening twenty minutes.

"I thought they were machines, not very emotional, just machines," says Tocchet. "I thought that was our edge. I didn't see that emotion. For them it was business. We got to enjoy the ride. I don't know if they enjoyed the ride."

"The Russians were unbelievable, but they were so regimented in their system and they never wanted to play outside it," says Hawerchuk. "You could almost see it sometimes. They'd be thinking, 'I better not screw up here or Tikhonov will kill me.' We worried about what we had to do, not what they might do."

That also seemed to represent the Canadians' mindset as they regrouped for the second period. They understood they'd dug themselves a deep hole and they knew they were facing a mighty opponent, but they weren't exactly paralyzed by their predicament. Gilmour remembers the players filing into the locker room and sitting in silence before Anderson broke out into a chorus of "Lions and tigers and bears, oh my," from *The Wizard of Oz*. That eased the tension and it figured if any one of the team would crack a joke at that time, it would be one on the Oilers.

"That was the way those guys competed," Gilmour says. "It was the confidence of the Oilers and it rubbed off on everyone in the room."

Hartsburg, for his part, can recall many of the moments from Game 3, but the one that sticks with him is Keenan's reaction between periods. The Canadians were aware they'd just played an unconscionably sloppy twenty minutes and were justifiably concerned about the reaction of their volatile head coach. But when the heat was at its highest, Keenan breezed into the Canadian locker room like he had the Russians exactly where he wanted them and said: "Gentlemen, you are about to become part of the greatest comeback in Canadian hockey history."

"And that was it," says Hartsburg. "We were waiting for this big explosion and it calmed everyone down. We stopped worrying about being behind. I'll never forget that. To me that was the best thing Mike did the whole series."

Maybe, but what he did on the ice in the second period was just as important.

Gretzky didn't disappear entirely – early in the second he broke in with Tocchet on a two-on-one, fed the Flyers' winger the exact same saucer pass on which Lemieux had scored in Game 2, and Tocchet fanned completely – but neither was he as visible as he'd been in the first two contests. Keenan, instead, started rolling three and sometimes four lines evenly, splitting up Gretzky and Lemieux for the first half of the frame. The result was the Canadians kept up the hitting – Gartner took out Makarov with a knee; Gusarov kneed Hawerchuk going up the middle, and Rochefort flattened Gusarov in retaliation; Hartsburg hammered Yuri Khmylev in open ice – and players like Hawerchuk, Sutter, and Tocchet started getting more and more ice time.

Keenan now says there was a good reason for that. Earlier in the game, an ashen Gretzky had turned to the coach and said, "I'm exhausted. I need a rest," which was a little like a fat guy saying, "I'm full. No dessert for me." Keenan immediately understood he had to change things up, which is when the role-players started coming over the boards. That's also when the complexion of the game changed.

"[Gretzky] had incredible stamina but he was spent," Keenan says. "I knew he was drawing on the last reserves of his energy. We needed a different look at that point. We had the players who could play a skill game but they could also shift gears and play a different style if they had to. That's what happened in Game 3."

Sutter hadn't played much in the first game and during the off-day practice between Games 1 and 2, he asked Perron about his ice time. Perron told him, "You know Mike, he always has a plan. Just work hard in practice."

"Who changed the momentum in the third game?" Perron now asks. "It was Sutter." With some help from others.

"Guys got put in positions where they had to respond," Sutter said. "We were also playing with guys who know how to win championships and we fed off that. Hopefully [the superstars] pushed us and we pushed them. But that's part of being a team."

Actually, it was the superstars who started the second Canadian comeback. Shortly after Krutov barely misfired on a two-on-one with Makarov, Bykov took a penalty for upending Lemieux by the side of the Russian net and Keenan put out the unlikely trio of Gretzky, Lemieux, and Tocchet on the power play with Murphy and Bourque on the points. Gretzky took a look at his new linemate and offered a few words of inspiration. "I was going out there and Wayne said under his breath, 'Don't take a penalty,'" Tocchet says laughing. "I swear he saw everything." And a minute into the power play, Gretzky certainly saw Murphy standing on the left faceoff dot by himself for the third Canadian goal.

Lemieux had started the play by outworking Makarov and Kasatonov behind the Russian net and feeding Gretzky in his office, who relayed to Murphy. His one-timer beat Mylnikov, and the crowd and the game were re-energized.

Less than two minutes later, and following another robust shift by Tocchet, Hawerchuk set up shop behind the Russian net, took a pass from Crossman, and found Sutter in almost the same spot Murphy had just scored from. This time the Islanders' centre snapped a one-timer under the crossbar.

Now all of Keenan's moves were starting to pay off. Fuhr made a huge stop off Krutov on yet another two-on-one with Makarov, then followed that up with another two-on-one save off Khmylev. The play went the other way with Lemieux feeding Gretzky this time on a two-on-one and Mylnikov making the save. On a Canadian power play, Fetisov took a sure goal away from Murphy, who was becoming more of a factor, when he slid to block a shot with Mylnikov down and out. A minute later Murphy and Hawerchuk broke out of the Team Canada zone together and Hawerchuk unloaded a slapper from the left wing that Mylnikov stopped. Kasatonov, however, was a little late getting to the rebound and Sutter barged in on the forecheck. His hit produced a loose puck that Hawerchuk, who'd been following the play, collected. Mylnikov stopped his first attempt at a wraparound but the Jets' centre hung tough and poked the rebound under the falling Russian goalie as Copps went crazy.

"We had so much energy," Hawerchuk says of his line's play in that period. "It was open the door and let us loose kind of thing. We were going to go out and act like we were crazed to get back into the game. I think we surprised them."

Alas, the Canadian rally died there when Bourque took back-to-back penalties to close the period, both of which his teammates killed off efficiently. Still, it was an amazing performance by Team Canada, erasing a 4–2 lead against the mighty Russians, scoring three goals in just over six minutes with Fuhr stopping everything he faced. It was also an amazing performance by Keenan, who orchestrated the comeback by using twenty-two different line combinations in the first two periods and helped spark the offence through the inspired use of his supporting cast. It could be that the Flyers' coach had driven his players crazy in the runup to the final with his demanding and erratic ways, but when the stakes were at their highest, it was clear that Canada's greatest edge was behind the bench.

"Our energy level wasn't where it had been and Mike saw it right away," says Gretzky. "That's when he started playing those other guys and, before you know it, we were right back in the game and our line was feeling re-energized. That changed the game. It was the best game Mike ever coached."

"Mike's one of those coaches you either like or hate but when the game is on the line, you want him on your side," says Hawerchuk. "He knows who's going that night and he knows how to motivate the guys who aren't going."

Keenan's contribution to the Canadian victory, in fact, has been under-reported in hockey history and that's a gross oversight. In the three games of the Canada Cup final, he was facing one of the best-ever teams with reduced numbers yet managed to camouflage his team's weakness through creative juggling of his forwards. His blue line, with the notable exception of Bourque and Coffey, was undistinguished, but he kept the Russians off balance by mixing up the pairings from shift to shift. He also had an uncanny instinct for which player was hot during any given point in the game and he even managed to optimize the effectiveness of Gretzky and Lemieux by double-shifting them judiciously.

It helped that he had Messier to counteract Larionov. Like Keenan's role behind the bench, Messier's checking job on Larionov has been under-reported by hockey historians, but it's impossible to underestimate its importance to Team Canada's win. Messier, one of the greatest centres in the game's history, sacrificed his offence to concentrate on Larionov and the Russian was held pointless in the final. True, the Canadians couldn't shut down Makarov or Krutov as efficiently but Messier's line, which usually featured Anderson and Gartner, at least produced a push against the Green Unit. Coupled with the production of Gretzky and Lemieux, that was all they needed.

"You look at those three players and they could skate with Larionov's line," says Tom Watt, Keenan's assistant who worked the press box. "I don't think that happened too often to them. I also think Mark scared them."

"Maybe I should have been a checking centre," Messier cracks, before adding, "When you're playing on a good team, you have to identify your role. Wayne and Mario were going to lead us offensively and we needed to make our contribution in another way. It didn't matter what the role is."

But Keenan was also shrewd enough to exploit the edge Messier's work gave him. With Larionov accounted for, Keenan could manipulate Gretzky and Lemieux so the bulk of their ice time was spent against the Russians' second and fourth lines because Tikhonov was married to a four-line rotation. While his

stars got their extra ice time on special teams, he made no
attempt to get Larionov away from Messier or assign checkers
to Gretzky and Lemieux. Keenan, of course, ate this up. Watt
kept track of the Russian lines and would tell Keenan who was
due up next. Keenan would then get the matchup he wanted.

"That was their philosophy and we were able to exploit it,"
says Keenan. "I thought it was the one advantage we had going
into the tournament. They were predictable. We didn't want to
be predictable."

And that was never a problem with Keenan. "I had a pretty
good run that lasted through New York," he says. (Keenan's stint
with the Rangers lasted into the mid-nineties.) "I was confident
enough in myself but that group brought out a lot of confidence
as well. You look at the coaching staff and they'd won everywhere they'd been. I think we fed off each other."

Hawerchuk, meanwhile, chose Game 3 to play the best
hockey of his life, and it was in keeping with his Hall of Fame
career that his signature performance was overshadowed by
Gretzky and Lemieux.

The Jets' centre broke into the NHL two years after Gretzky
and in his first seven seasons in Winnipeg, he averaged 107
points a year, helping transform a dreadful Jets team into a
respectable outfit. His first season, he recorded 105 points and
was named rookie-of-the-year as the Jets, who recorded nine
wins and 32 points the previous season, made the playoffs with
an 80-point campaign. It was the largest single-season improve-
ment in NHL history. The problem was the Jets never took the
next step after Hawerchuk's rookie season. His supporting cast
in Winnipeg didn't quite measure up to Gretzky's in Edmonton.
No one's did. Hawerchuk's linemates the first couple of years
were Paul MacLean and the immortal Larry Hopkins and he
helped turn MacLean into a forty-goal scorer. Before Lemieux
came along and Messier matured, in fact, Hawerchuk was likely
the second-best centre in the NHL and there was a fair bit of

Gretzky in his game. He wasn't exactly Brian Boitano on his skates but he was deceptively fast and had great lateral movement. He also had the genius passer gene that Gretzky possessed and the vision and creativity to complement it.

He even had the artistic temperament to go along with his game.

One of the great stories to emerge from Hawerchuk's early years with the Jets concerned his relationship with Watt, who often harangued his star centre on the merits of a strong two-way game. Hawerchuk didn't always see things the same way and the feud came to a head when Watt placed his coach-of-the-year trophy in Hawerchuk's locker, suggesting if you want to coach the team, go ahead but here's where the bar is set.

"If you ask Dale, I think he'd tell you we helped him out and gave him some direction when he was young," says Watt.

"It happened to me and it happened to other players," says Hawerchuk. "I always tried to do whatever the team needed most."

In 1984–85, Hawerchuk enjoyed his best season, ripping off 130 points as the Jets finished with 96 points. But that year, with Hawerchuk injured, they were again ousted by Gretzky's Oilers and it seemed both the team and the player would never measure up to the impossible standard set in Edmonton. This bothered Hawerchuk. It bothered him immensely. He knew playing in Winnipeg was like playing on the dark side of the moon but he still longed to be taken seriously by his peers.

It was with some irony, then, that after piling up all those points in Winnipeg as a first-line centre, Hawerchuk played his most significant hockey as a grinder for his former Junior-B coach. And he had no problem with playing out of character. Like a lot of his colleagues on Team Canada, he was committed to doing whatever it took to beat the Russians. In this case it was playing like a madman when he'd always adopted a more cerebral approach to the game.

"He was willing to do anything for that team," says Keenan. "You look at its makeup and you see players like Dale, and Brent Sutter who were essentially role players but they made that team. I'm not sure there was another group of players who'd accept that role and still contribute the way those guys contributed."

"It was a chance to prove to others and myself what kind of player I was," Hawerchuk says. "Nobody seemed to know what we were doing in Winnipeg. We were off the map there and a lot of people thought I was just a good player on an average team. Then I had the opportunity to show I could play with these guys but also show I enjoyed that kind of hockey.

"I got so much pleasure out of that kind of game where you're pushing your skill level and pushing yourself physically. What could be better than that? To be a part of that series is something you hold on to forever."

In the second period of Game 3, Koharski handed out five penalties, three to Canada, two to the Russians. It was the highest number of penalties called in one frame during the final contest, but, if the post-lockout standard enforced by the NHL was applied, there would have been a penalty every five seconds. The stickwork in the game, and all three games of the final for that matter, is astonishing. "There might have been thirty thousand penalties," says Tocchet. "There was a lot of chopping and hacking." On virtually every rush, the first instinct of the defenceman is to impede the attacking forward with his stick. Not to be outdone, the forechecking forward's first move is to engage the defenceman with his stick. The neutral zone? Forget about it. Players had to fight their way through a maze of arms and sticks. Anderson and Messier, it seems, didn't throw a hit in the series when their sticks weren't around a Russian's neck.

But, for all that, the hockey is still magnificent. There is space all over the ice for the skill players to shine. The speed of the game is awesome. The flow is uninterrupted. No lead was safe in the final. Following the 2004-5 lockout, the NHL reinterpreted its rulebook and essentially changed the way the game had been played for fifty years to reintroduce some excitement to the ice and it had to be done because the hockey had become unwatchable. But in the '87 Canada Cup final, where hooking and holding and obstruction are a given, the game was played at its highest level. Why?

It's an interesting question to consider, given the NHL's devolution in the late 1990s and the subsequent restructuring of the game. If you're wondering what went wrong, much is revealed in this series. For starters, there is a fundamental difference in the players' approach to the game. A lot of that, admittedly, has to do with their skill level. Canada had Gretzky, Lemieux, and Messier down the middle but they also had natural centreman Hawerchuk, Gilmour, and Sutter, who could all handle the puck and make plays at top speed. The Russians' artistry, meanwhile, needs no further description here.

But it also goes deeper than that. There is no evidence of a system or regimentation on either team. Players are given the freedom to attack and use their instincts. The dump-in is used only as a last resort and defencemen are loath to give the puck away. The result is a possession game predicated on skill and team play. Is it high risk? One supposes. You see players trying things in the three games of the final you just don't see in today's game. Defencemen are always up on the rush. Passes are going through the middle of the ice. Players are all over the place, overlapping and crossing over, creating space for themselves and their teammates. When the puck is turned over, there's also more space for the opposing team because no one has retreated into the neutral zone and no one seems overly concerned about holding his position. There are odd-man rushes. There are breakaways. But it's also the farthest you can get from river hockey.

Most of this is a testament to the players on the two teams who battled like Huns and Visigoths through the three games without taking a backward step. "The passion in those games was incredible," says Keenan. "Players would fight for their space. They thought that was part of the game. If there was a tug or a hook, they'd battle through it and if they were going into the prime territory on the ice, they knew there was a price to be paid. It took courageous athletes to play that game."

"Their skill was unbelievable," Hartsburg says of the Russians. "But the most impressive thing to us was they were willing to pay the price. You could whack them, you could chop them, you could hit them. And they'd give it right back. There was no intimidation factor at all. By the end of the series we'd both tried to intimidate each other and I think we both just gave up and played."

But there is also a fundamental difference in the way the game is coached. The Canadians and Russians both had leads throughout the final three games but there is never a suggestion of changing the game plan to protect that lead and there is never, ever the hint of stringing four players along the blue line or attempting a trap. Both teams continued to play. Both teams continued to attack. Maybe the rushes weren't all choreographed by Fosse but there was always speed and flow to the game. "We never had a system or a trap or told them they had to play this way," says Perron. "There were just a few assignments that had to be carried out. Mike's style never changed. It was pressure, pressure, pressure. The players loved it."

So did the fans. Now there's a concept. But there were other factors that contributed to the quality of the game. In looking at the rosters, the size of the players is striking. After Lemieux, Canada's biggest forwards were Tocchet at 6 feet and 215 pounds and Messier who went 6 foot 1 and weighed about 205 pounds. The Moose jokes that he came into the league as a power forward and fifteen years later was shocked to learn he'd become a shifty centre. But that also says a lot about the way the game changed over his career.

The Canadian blue line, meanwhile, had a bit of size but Rochefort was by far the biggest defenceman at 6 foot 2, 220 pounds. None of the rest – Bourque, Coffey, Crossman, Hartsburg, Patrick, or Murphy – were exactly behemoths.

As for the Russians, their team would be laughed at in today's NHL. Krutov was a tank, but he also stood 5 foot 9 and weighed 190 pounds and he qualified as the power forward of the group. Priakhin was their biggest forward but he rarely played. Of their top six forwards, only Kamensky was over six feet tall and none of them weighed more than 200 pounds.

Their blue line was bigger and no one played tougher than Fetisov or Kasatonov. But they'd also be classified as undersized by today's standards.

Add it all up and there were smaller players who played a more skilled game without the constraints of a system. There was more room on the ice and more flow to the game, yet the play was still physical and highly competitive. The NHL would sell its soul to get that game back. Come to think of it, it has.

The goaltending, finally, is the other big difference between today's game and the game of twenty years ago. For starters, both Fuhr and his Russian counterparts Mylnikov and Belosheikin were average in size and their girth was not augmented by the freakishly large, Michelin-man equipment that came into vogue about ten years later. Their style of play was also radically different than the goalies' of the next generation. Again, you seldom saw Fuhr or the Russians drop into a butterfly or play for any length of time on their knees. They stood up more and relied on their reflexes. But they also moved around their crease and the area in front of their net. Maybe it isn't the most efficient way to play the position, but it's certainly more exciting when the goalies are up and down and scrambling to get back into position.

Fuhr's preferred style of play also brings a new appreciation for his athleticism. In addition to his other attributes, it is clear that he's a phenomenal skater, as nimble on his goalie blades as some of the forwards in the series are on theirs.

Finally, the expectations on the goalies were completely different in 1987 than they'd become in the dead-puck era of the NHL. Hrudey now says the benchmark for goalies at that time was a .885 save percentage. Today, that number would have a keeper packing for the minors faster than you can say Wilkes-Barre. In Fuhr's ten years with the Oilers, he never recorded a save percentage higher than .900 or a goals-against average of less than 3.00. His best season with the Oilers was 1987–88, when he played seventy-five games with a 40–24–9 win-loss record coupled with a .881 save percentage and a 3.43 goals-against average. His role on the team, therefore, wasn't to completely shut down the opposition. It was to make one more save than the goalie at the other end, and that's what he provided in the Canada Cup.

The third period of Game 3 is remembered as the setting for Lemieux's series-winning goal and that play – which started with a faceoff in the Canadian end and took all of ten seconds for Gretzky and Lemieux to go the length of the ice – has justifiably earned its place in the game's history. But the eighteen minutes and thirty-four seconds that preceded it – in which the Soviets tied the game after Canada, behind a rejuvenated Gretzky, had carried most of the play – weren't too shabby either.

Canada killed off the remainder of Bourque's penalty to open the third frame before Gretzky almost engineered a two-goal lead with a typical piece of work. The sequence started with Gusarov handing the puck to Lemieux in the Russian end and Lemieux finding Gretzky, who materialized out of nowhere. No. 99 carried around the Russian net before Mylnikov kicked his backhand out to the high slot, where Gretzky, who'd never stopped moving, came out of the pack with the puck and spun away from traffic. He then dished to Coffey, who'd steamed into the slot, and Mylnikov made his best save of the game off Coffey's forehand deke. Seconds later, Gretzky was back again on a three-on-two rush, setting up Propp, who just missed with a one-timer.

Messier, who grew up with Gretzky and had played with him for eight seasons before the tournament, was asked what he remembers about his teammate's performance against the Soviets. "Wayne marvelled at the skill of the Russian players," Messier says. "But they marvelled at Wayne. I think [before '87] they thought their five were the most skilled players in the world. I don't think they expected to see what they saw out of Wayne."

On his next shift, which the TV crew timed out at two minutes in length, Gretzky had Mylnikov down and out but couldn't beat him with a backhander. Lemieux had a chance from the slot but couldn't convert. During a stoppage in play with eight minutes and thirty-two seconds left in regulation, Reusch said: "The game is being played for a good part down in the Soviet end . . . I can't stress how confidently Canada is playing in the third period." Kelly noted the Canadians were outshooting the Russians 10–4 in the final stanza. And that's, of course, when the Russians tied the game.

The trouble started when Tocchet, Sutter, and Hawerchuk, who'd been Canada's three best forwards to that point in the game, stayed out too long for a shift and the Russians counter-attacked with Semak and Lomakin. Semak missed Lomakin with his first pass, but the Russian forward chased down the puck, moved behind the Canadian net, and, with Hawerchuk and Coffey both going to Semenov, he fed a nifty pass to Semak in front, who beat Fuhr with a one-timer.

"So what else is new," Reusch said, as Lomakin bussed Semak on the cheek. "Here we are, 7:39 left in regulation time and a 5–5 tie."

"It just seemed like it was destined to end that way," says Hawerchuk. "We could have done without the drama but since the first period we'd been playing well. It didn't really affect our confidence."

Maybe, but the next couple of minutes after Semak's goal was a nervous time for the Canadians. Makarov walked around Murphy, and Fuhr had to make a save from in tight. Kamensky almost reprised his Game 2 goal when he split the Canadian defence but couldn't control the puck.

Then a Gretzky–Lemieux shift seemed to restore the Canadian equilibrium. With just over four minutes left, Hawerchuk also produced a half-chance on a solo rush and Mylnikov made a blocker save. With two and a half minutes left, Tikhonov called a timeout to give the Larionov line a rest, but Keenan again sent out Messier, Anderson, and Gartner, the Russians didn't produce a thing, and Gretzky and Lemieux were given an invaluable breather.

They'd just come out with Propp, in fact, when Coffey uncharacteristically iced the puck with a minute and thirty-six seconds left. Under normal circumstances, Messier would have taken the draw in the Canadian end but he'd just finished a long shift chasing Larionov around the ice. Keenan instead opted for Hawerchuk, who replaced Propp on the line, reasoning that either Gretzky or Lemieux, both natural centremen, could take the draw if Hawerchuk was booted out of the faceoff circle.

The Canadians lined up five across with Gretzky outside of Murphy and Lemieux on the right side of the faceoff circle and Crossman on the left side. Tikhonov countered with Bykov, Khomutov, and Kamensky, with, curiously, the young defensive tandem of Kravchuk and Stelnov behind them.

"All I thought was I'm not going to lose this cleanly," says Hawerchuk. "I didn't care if all I did was tie him up. I'm not going to lose it. Then the puck just seemed to go in the right place and after Kravchuk pinched, it all happened pretty fast."

That's an understatement. The astounding part of Lemieux's game-winning goal wasn't the pass by Gretzky or the shot by

Le Magnifique but rather the speed with which the Canadians moved the puck from the faceoff circle to the Russian end. Hawerchuk didn't win the draw, but he did tie up Bykov and the puck squirted into an open spot behind the Russian centre. Kamensky and Bykov then started the Russian comedy of errors by colliding as they went for the loose puck about the time Lemieux arrived on the scene. Lemieux poked the disc into space then, with Kravchuk inexplicably moving forward, chipped it by the twenty-one-year-old Russian defenceman and the Canadians were off. "I didn't realize his reach was so long," Kravchuk says of Lemieux. "I thought I was going to get to the puck first. When I saw him get to the puck and I realized I was too late, I tried to hit him but he was too big. Two other guys fell down. Everything went wrong in that one shift."

And it would only get worse for the Russians. Gretzky and Murphy both read the play the same way and jumped ahead while Lemieux was leaping around Kravchuk. Lemieux hit Gretzky with a backhand pass and the Great One led a three-on-one against Stelnov over the Russian blue line as Murphy drove wide. Gretzky held the puck, looked at Lemieux, who'd beaten the Russians down the ice; looked at Murphy, who was by the far post by this time; then dropped a pass to Lemieux, who took one strike and zipped a wrister, top shelf, over Mylnikov's glove hand. Gretzky and Lemieux embraced behind the Russian net. They were joined by Murphy, then Hawerchuk, who jumped on to the pile as Copps erupted.

"You see the puck go in the net and the red light come on, it's like someone threw a bucket of cold water on you," says Kravchuk.

"When I saw Gretzky and Lemieux go down the wing, I understood it was the end of the game," Dmitriev said after the game.

The play had taken ten seconds from the drop of the puck in the Canadian end to Lemieux's shot. Here was Kelly's famous call:

"Hawerchuk will draw the assignment against Bykov. Hawerchuk wins it and here's Lemieux poking it to centre. (Kelly's voice starts to rise) Lemieux ahead to Gretzky. Has Murphy with him on a two-on-one. To Lemieux. In on goal. (pause) He shoots! He scores!! Mario Lemieux with 1:26 remaining."

A full thirty seconds of crowd noise followed with Reusch trying to describe the rush. Kelly then said: "What did I say earlier about Gretzky loading the gun and Lemieux pulling the trigger? There it was in living colour."

So how did it happen so quickly? How did the Russians manage to give the two greatest forwards in the game's history the length of the ice to work with in the final ninety seconds of a tied game? It started, as mentioned, with Bykov and Kamensky colliding in the Canadian end and Kravchuk's ill-advised pinch. But that was only the beginning of the Russians' troubles. Bykov had put his head down and might have gotten back in the play, but Hawerchuk gave him a little tug and the Russian centre fell spectacularly. Koharski, who'd put his whistle away long before Lemieux's goal, saw the hook and was unimpressed.

"The Russian player quit on the play," Koharski says. "Tikhonov wasn't too happy about it, but the guy had no chance to get back into the play."

Koharski was asked where he was when Lemieux scored.

"I weighed 230 pounds," he answers. "Do you think I was ahead of the play going up the ice?"

Stelnov, meanwhile, made a mess of things as the lone man back. His only chance was to stay in the middle of the ice and force Gretzky, who was at a sharp angle, into shooting. Instead, the Russian defenceman made an awkward lunge at the Team Canada captain and fell as Gretzky was slipping the puck to Lemieux. That opened up the entire slot for the Penguins' sniper and he didn't miss.

"Before the game, Igor Dmitriev said he was watching

Lemieux in the warmups and he saw him put nine out of ten shots in the top corner over the goalie's shoulder," says Kravchuk. "I guess if he was going to get his chance that's where he was going. He got his chance."

The other question about the most famous rush in hockey history concerns Gretzky's options. He can't be second-guessed for picking out Lemieux, but Murphy was all alone at the far post and seemingly had a gimme if Gretzky had gone that route.

"I actually thought Wayne was going to pass to Larry Murphy," says Tocchet. "Wayne's probably had a million assists from that saucer pass to the guy off the far post for a tap-in. But he went to the shooter and I've seen Mario make that shot a million times. What can you say. It was a laser."

Hawerchuk, who trailed the play all the way up the ice, saw the same thing.

"I couldn't believe he didn't slide it over to Murph. It looked like he had a tap-in. But maybe Wayne thought too many things can go wrong if I make that pass and when you look at the goalie, it's like he's leaning toward Murph and he never gets his glove up. You'd have to ask Wayne, but he probably thought about all of this."

Gretzky was asked about the pass. Turns out he did think about all this.

"I've always kidded Murphy that if I had that play a thousand times, I wouldn't pass it to him a thousand times," says Gretzky. "He made that play by driving to the net and that created that gap for Mario to shoot. I was looking at Murphy all the way but my focus was always on Mario. He was going to get the puck."

And Lemieux's shot?

"You almost feel sorry for the goalie," Gretzky says. "It wasn't even close."

Murphy, in fact, did make the play with a shrewd read off the faceoff in the Canadian end. But given the circumstances, wasn't it a little risky?

"I turned out to be a decoy, but it affected the coverage," Murphy says. "You look at a lot of things. We had good control. You look at who's got the puck. It doesn't look like the play's going to be broken up. It's a calculated risk. That's the way I played. It was a game of percentages."

Murphy laughs when asked if he'd ever thought how things could have turned out for him on that rush.

"[Gretzky's] play was to Lemieux, but Lemieux's play was to me. I was that close to being a hero. I've never forgiven him for that. He just went ahead and shot it in the net."

There was still a minute and twenty-six seconds left in the game after Lemieux's goal, which, in theory, should have given the Russians enough time to at least make things interesting. The problem was Tikhonov seemed to lose his mind the second Lemieux's shot beat Mylnikov. The television cameras caught him berating the luckless Kravchuk a good thirty seconds after the Canadians had taken the lead. With the delay following the goal, he had plenty of time to get the Larionov line on the ice. Instead he put out his fourth line of Nemchinov, Khmylev, and Priakhin, with Gusarov and Fedotov on the blue line. The Canadians, in fact, almost scored right off the faceoff with Messier, Anderson, and Gartner charging the Russian goal. The Green Unit finally came out with Fetisov and Kasatonov with about forty-five seconds left, but Tikhonov, as per Russian custom, never did pull Mylnikov. Messier, meanwhile, stayed out for the entire eighty-six seconds, blocked a couple of Fetisov's shots from the blue line, then almost took off Krutov's head at the Russian blue line with ten seconds left. The Russians didn't produce a shot on Fuhr after Lemieux's goal.

"It was typical of Russian coaches in that era," says Kravchuk. "They yelled a lot. After the game he came back and said, 'I know you're young and you made a mistake but, overall, you had a good tournament.' That made me feel a little better."

Following Lemieux's goal, Eagleson appeared by the Canadian

team bench and could be seen brushing a tear from his eye. He was also on the ice with the team after the final horn sounded.

"I think they were tears of joy and relief," Eagleson now says. "We had survived a semi-mutiny of the players and a 3–0 deficit after ten minutes. I also told Mike to play five defencemen if necessary for the last ninety seconds. I reminded him that we had a one-goal lead in Game 1 of the finals with two or three minutes to go and let the Russians tie it and win in overtime."

There would be no such drama this time. After a brief on-ice celebration in the Canadian end, the two teams lined up on their respective blue lines for the postgame presentations. Hawerchuk was named player of the game for Canada and received a set of commemorative coins for the 1988 Winter Olympics in Calgary. Fetisov won the same award for the Russians. A beaming Eagleson then came out and presented the Canada Cup trophy to Gretzky, followed by a photo-op at centre ice, a victory lap around Copps, and a stirring rendition of *O Canada* sung by Michael Burgess. And that was it.

"If that doesn't bring a tear to your eye, nothing will," said Kelly as Gretzky skated off the ice with the trophy.

Only a year and a half after Game 3, Kelly would lose his battle with cancer, but his call of Lemieux's marvellous goal remains the single most memorable moment from the '87 Canada Cup and captures the magic of Kelly's style. It is simple. There are no wasted words. But the tone of his magnificent Irish tenor rises in perfect measure to the rush up the ice, climaxing with the classic, "He shoots! He scores!! Mario Lemieux with 1:26 remaining."

"That call was all about Dan Kelly as a broadcaster," says his son John Kelly, who followed his father into broadcasting. "It starts with the faceoff and he builds up the tension and the drama just with the inflection in his voice. I'm very proud of that. It gives me a chill every time I hear it. That call was so him."

For a generation of American hockey fans, Kelly was the voice of hockey in the States, first as the play-by-play man for the St. Louis Blues on KMOX radio, then on broadcasts for CBS and the USA Network. He called Bobby Orr's famous overtime goal in Game 4 of the 1970 Stanley Cup for CBS. He worked playoff games throughout the 1970s and 1980s. Brian Sutter, the former Blues' player and coach, remembers listening to Kelly's work on the mighty KMOX as a boy growing up in Viking, Alberta. He also worked the Canada Cups for CTV where he partnered up with Reusch, the veteran Montreal broadcaster, and together they did a first-class job of presenting the epic three-game final in 1987.

"Johnny Esaw [the head of CTV Sports] was tight with Eagleson," Reusch says. "That's another thing the Players' Association should have looked into. How the television rights were sold."

"[Kelly] was a perfectionist," Reusch continues. "But he was hard on himself, not on the people around him. He never missed a pregame skate. He was always taking notes. You couldn't talk to him when he was getting prepared.

"He was one of those guys who liked to drive it, keep up the energy in the game. He did it all with the inflection of his voice. Danny Gallivan was the best I ever saw, but Dan was pretty close."

A native of Ottawa, Kelly had worked as the host of *Hockey Night in Canada* throughout the 1960s. He longed to do play-by-play, but the legendary Gallivan held that franchise in Montreal. When Scotty Bowman took over as coach of the Blues in the first year of expansion, he recommended Kelly to KMOX. Jack Buck, another Hall-of-Famer, had worked the Blues' first year, but Kelly succeeded him in year two and, over the next twenty years, he become synonymous with the Blues.

"In sports we talk a lot about franchise players," said former Blues chairman Michael Shanahan. "Dan Kelly was a franchise broadcaster."

His two sons would follow him into the business. John Kelly worked in the minors for six years before graduation to back up

Marv Albert on Rangers' games. He succeeded his father for three years in St. Louis and spent nine years in Colorado before returning to the Blues. Dan Kelly, Jr., was barely in his teens during the '87 Canada Cup but would also work for the Blues in the late 1990s. He now works for the Chicago Blackhawks.

Shortly before Dan Kelly passed away, the family gathered together and watched, of all things, a videotape of Game 1 of the '87 Canada Cup. Someone remembered the Russians had won the game in overtime, but a discussion arose over who scored the game-winning goal. A call soon went out to the back bedroom where a heavily medicated Kelly was resting. "Dad, do you remember who scored in overtime in the first game?" the questioner asked. Dan Kelly rolled over and said, "Semak," without hesitation, then turned away.

It was one of the last things Dan Kelly, Jr., remembers his father saying.

The first thing Keenan saw when he walked into the Team Canada dressing room following the trophy presentation was Gilmour, still in his hockey gear, dancing on the team's portable stereo. That boombox had played two songs incessantly throughout the team's stay in Hamilton: "If I Should Stumble Catch My Fall" by Billy Idol and "The Greatest Love of All" by Whitney Houston.

For the first time in a week, Keenan could honestly say he wasn't sick of hearing them. "I still haven't figured out what those two songs have in common," Keenan says. "But I'll always remember Dougie dancing on that jukebox."

Still, by the time the TV cameras were allowed into the Canadian dressing room, they found a celebration that was happy but not exactly unrestrained. Matheson, the host, interviewed Keenan, who tried to remain businesslike as he was being sprayed by champagne. Keenan still broke into giggles a couple of times.

"It's hard to capture the feeling right now," the coach said. "It was a tough battle. You have to be proud of these guys and our team representing Canada."

What brought his team back? Matheson asked.

"I think it was just composure and a sense of confidence and they've had that throughout the tournament," Keenan said.

Gretzky then came on and described the game-winning goal before he was asked what made the difference in the tournament.

"I'm not trying to be critical of their team," he said as Anderson dumped champagne on his head. "I'm just trying to praise Canadians. Since '72, Canadians have been winning on guts and pride and desire. We don't get a lot of time to get a system down. We won this tournament on sheer hard work and pride. We played six games with three, three-and-a-half lines, we had a lot of injuries and nobody complained. We had a great time. It was a special win. It's my grandmother's birthday today. Happy birthday."

The broadcast ended with a quick Fuhr interview and some closing comments by Kelly and Reusch. The scribes then worked the room, producing at least one memorable quote for the next day's papers.

"If you saw an NHL game tomorrow, I think you'd realize the level of this game," Bourque said. "What you saw tonight was like nothing I've ever seen."

But the overall mood among the Canadians was subdued given the magnitude of what they'd just accomplished. Keenan remembers the same thing. "They celebrated, but there was an inner peace there, a quiet sense of what they'd just accomplished," says Keenan.

"I think it was because our team had so much respect for every member of the other team," says Patrick. "After that series, you saw them in a different light."

"It was a quiet happiness," says Hawerchuk.

Gretzky, for his part, received the five days off he'd negotiated back in the summer before he had to report to the Oilers. He needed them.

"The mental fatigue and physical fatigue were extraordinary," says Gretzky. "We'd battled and battled to the point where we got that one goal to win the thing and we were drained. I think that's what you saw [in the Team Canada locker room]."

Koharski, meanwhile, showered and changed while the celebration was still going on. As he was leaving the officials' room, he noticed a box of pucks that he scooped up and took to a nearby bar. There, he proceeded to give away every puck as the establishment held a series of contests in celebration of Canada's win.

"I always thought I should have saved those pucks," Koharski says. "They could have paid for my retirement."

In the quiet of the Russian dressing room, Slava Fetisov stood up and said, "Maybe it's good we lost this one. Maybe it means we're going to win the Olympics."

"He was looking into the water," says Kravchuk. "That's the Russian expression."

And six months later, in their last great feat together, the Russians demolished the field in Calgary and won the gold medal. A year and a half after their loss in Hamilton, Larionov, Krutov, Makarov, Fetisov, and Kasatonov would be playing with and against their Canadian rivals in the NHL.

"It wasn't like 1980 when we lost to the Americans," Larionov says of his team's defeat in Game 3. "That was a big shock. It was devastating. This was disappointing, but the Canada Cup wasn't the most important thing to us."

Maybe, but for the players on Team Canada, that victory meant everything. They'd started almost two months before, sacrificing most of their summer for the honour of wearing the Maple Leaf and they came to believe in each other and their cause. For the Russians, the series meant a chance to test themselves against the best players in the world and that was not insignificant. But it wasn't the all-consuming mission it would become for the Canadian players, which is why the experience still holds a cherished place in their hearts.

"If you lose you feel like you've let the whole country down," says Hartsburg. "I was part of '81 and I know the emotion after that was sickening. By the end everyone had to scrape and scratch for everything we got. We were a great team but we were playing a great team and that's why it was special."

"We weren't doing it for the money," Messier says. "We were doing it for pride and our country and that made the stakes even higher. We had to win. We didn't have much choice."

There were, of course, a number of individual reasons why the Canadians won: Fuhr's goaltending in crunch time; Keenan's expert manipulation of his bench; the offensive production from Gretzky and Lemieux; Messier's checking job on Larionov and the contributions of lesser lights Hawerchuk, Tocchet, and Sutter in Game 3.

But, for all that, the Canadians believe they defeated their arch-rivals because of less tangible reasons, because of those vague, hard-to-define qualities that the country's hockey players believe is their birthright. It's an arrogant presumption, of course, because the Russians demonstrated their own brand of perseverance and resilience in the series and, in the end, the deciding factor wasn't Canadian heart or will but one shot by Lemieux.

But that's not the way the players remember it. They talk about the team building that started with those lunches at Chez Paree. They talk about the leadership of Gretzky and Messier and how the two great Oilers weren't going to allow any internal divisions in the locker room. They talk about players like Sutter, Hawerchuk, and Gilmour who epitomized the best of the Canadian game.

"I heard the stories about the Islanders and the Oilers [in '84]," says Tocchet. "I don't know what happened then but, from the first day of camp, we were a team."

"Those guys still can't believe they lost that series," says Hawerchuk. "I remember talking to Igor Kravchuk years afterward and he was still moaning about it. They thought they had us buried three or four times."

Hawerchuk was asked if he believed Canadian heart and fortitude was the difference in the '87 series.

"It sure seems to add up that way," he says. "It's a great resource to call on."

Then again, so's Gretzky.

"You always have a bond with the players you've won with," says Sutter in a rare display of emotion. "You never forget those guys. You never forget the things you've accomplished. If I ever needed something, I knew I could call Wayne Gretzky. It will be a long, long time before another Wayne Gretzky comes along. There's only one Wayne Gretzky."

CHAPTER 7

Gretzky, Eagleson, Tikhonov

D uring their six weeks together with Team Canada, Paul Coffey often prodded Kelly Hrudey for information about the New York Islanders' payroll, specifically the contract of all-star defenceman Denis Potvin. Hrudey understood the underlying message, that Coffey felt he was underpaid. But he didn't understand the depth of Coffey's feelings until the conclusion of the Canada Cup when the Oilers' defenceman headed to his parents' house in Toronto and refused to report back to Edmonton.

Coffey's holdout would last for two months, dissolve into a juvenile war of words precipitated by Oilers' owner Peter Pocklington, and end with a huge seven-player trade with the Pittsburgh Penguins. At the time most of the Oilers thought Coffey, who seemed to pay more attention to these matters than they did, was simply trying for a big payday. They didn't understand the same fate awaited all of them.

"We didn't think it was a big deal," says Messier. "It was Paul's thing."

"I didn't recognize the breakup at that time," says Muckler. "We thought that was for other reasons."

But it was the same reason all the Oilers would leave. Money. The numbers now seem quaint compared to today's salaries, but Coffey was painfully aware Potvin was making US$520,000 (about CAD$700,000) and Bourque was pulling in US$380,000. Coffey, who was making about CAD$320,000, was originally looking for a deal in the $800,000 range, which caused great hysteria among the Oilers' brass. Sather said: "He's dreaming." Pocklington, however, did his general manager one better, calling Coffey a "little shit" and saying the defenceman "has no balls."

At that point, Coffey was as good as gone from Edmonton even though both sides tried to resurrect contract negotiations.

"It's impossible for me to go back and put on that hockey sweater again," Coffey said. "I don't know how you can win two Norris Trophies, play in two Canada Cups, and win three Stanley Cups and have no guts."

"Paul and I had talked about it during the series and he said he was finished as an Oiler," says Gretzky. "I'd played with Paul since he was thirteen. I knew how good he was and what he meant to our team. Selfishly, I was thinking, we can't lose this guy. We can't replace this guy."

Sather, who would be left to clean up a number of Pocklington's messes in the ensuing years, tried to play the conciliator.

"I don't think [Pocklington] meant it that way," said the Oilers' GM and there was a point where he'd almost worked out a deal with Coffey before Pocklington screwed that up, too. Coffey might have accepted a six-year, CAD$3-million offer, but Pocklington insisted a parcel of land be made part of the deal. The idea was Pocklington would buy an undetermined piece of land, and guarantee it for $1 million down the road. Some beads and coloured glass were also thought to be part of the deal.

Coffey's agent, Gus Badali, studied the matter and said his client wasn't interested in "swampland."

With the season almost two months old, Coffey was finally dealt to the Penguins along with Dave Hunter and Wayne Van Dorp for forwards Craig Simpson and Dave Hannan and defencemen Moe Mantha and Chris Joseph. "It's too bad it had to come to this, but I still think I did the right thing," said Coffey, who signed a new deal for US$425,000 with the Penguins.

"We set him up as an example," said Sather. "We weren't going to be blackmailed by anyone."

Sather, of course, would have to set other examples over the next five years as the most talented team in hockey history was sold off like items in an estate sale. In the 1987–88 season, the Oilers won their fourth Stanley Cup, sweeping the Boston Bruins in four games in the final. Gretzky recorded 40 goals and 149 points in 64 games in the regular season as Lemieux ended his streak of eight straight Hart Trophies and seven straight Art Rosses with a monster 70-goal, 168-point campaign. But in the playoffs that spring, Gretzky exploded, counting 12 goals and 43 points in 19 post-season games as he carted off his second Conn Smythe.

That summer he married Janet Jones in Edmonton in the closest Canada has ever come to a royal wedding. Five days later, when Gretzky was on his honeymoon, L.A. Kings owner Bruce McNall called to inform Gretzky that Pocklington had given the Kings permission to talk to him.

He would be traded twenty-five days after his wedding.

"I just assumed I'd be an Oiler for life," says Gretzky. "I pictured myself like Gordie Howe or Rocket Richard, playing my whole career for one team, then joining the organization. I didn't have an inkling what was going on."

Gretzky says the first he ever heard about a trade was the day after the Oilers won their fourth Stanley Cup in five years. After partying all night, he got a call from Nelson Skalbania, the man who'd signed him to his first pro contract with the WHA's

The Soviets prepare for Team Canada

Doug MacLellan/Hockey Hall of Fame

Oiler teammates converge for Canada

Gretzky and Coffey renew acquaintances

Canada scores past Belosheikin . . .

. . . and Sutter celebrates

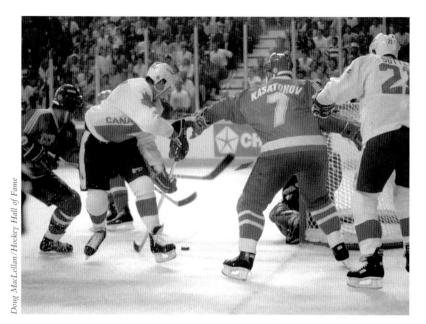

Canada converges on the Soviet net . . .

. . . and Sutter ends up celebrating again

Gretzky to Lemieux

Lemieux scores with 1:26 left to play

A tired captain prepares to receive the prize

Oilers unite to celebrate Canada

1987 Canada Cup champions

Canada celebrates

Indianapolis Racers and Pocklington's former partner with the WHA Oilers. Skalbania was trying to broker a deal for the Griffith family, owners of the Vancouver Canucks, and wanted to know what it would take to get Gretzky to Vancouver. Gretzky, who was sipping on champagne and orange juice in an attempt to quiet the pounding in his head, was more than a little confused.

"I wasn't thinking very clearly and I had a hard time understanding what was going on," Gretzky says.

Twenty years after the fact, things are a little clearer. The trade wasn't a trade in the traditional hockey sense so much as it was a sale. The Alberta economy, if you can imagine such a thing, had tanked in the early 1980s and a couple of Pocklington's businesses had gone bankrupt. The Oilers' owner began to sell off some of his assets, including his art collection. About the same time he also explored the idea of taking the Oilers public and approached his most valuable asset, Gretzky, about reworking his personal-services deal with Pocklington so that the new contract could be rolled in with the new public company. Gretzky asked for a new five-year deal at the conclusion of which he would become an unrestricted free agent. For the first time, Pocklington had to consider the possibility of losing Gretzky without getting anything in return.

Dr. Jerry Buss, who predated McNall as the Kings' owner, also got in Pocklington's ear, telling him Gretzky was a depreciating asset and wasn't worth $15 million in Edmonton, where the building was consistently sold out. In Los Angeles, however, where the Kings struggled with attendance, he would be worth that kind of dough. Buss would persist with his sales pitch and while he never closed the deal with the Oilers, he succeeded in opening Pocklington's mind to the possibility of selling Gretzky.

The perfect storm was building. Shortly after he received the call from Skalbania, Gretzky says he talked with his father, who admitted he'd heard the rumblings but didn't want to say anything during the Oilers' playoff run. Gretzky then met with Pocklington to renegotiate his deal for the umpteenth time, but now he asked for a no-trade clause. Pocklington refused it, which sent a clear message to Gretzky. A few days later the Oilers' owner talked with Detroit and the Rangers about the possibility of trading Gretzky. He also had a conversation with McNall, the Kings' new owner. McNall initially thought Pocklington was talking about dealing his crown jewel the following off-season, but the talks mushroomed from the conceptual stage to serious negotiations over a space of weeks. In the end, Gretzky was moved to the Kings on August 9, 1988, with Marty McSorley and Mike Krushelnyski for Jimmy Carson, Martin Gelinas, three first-round picks, and, the most important component of the deal, $15 million. The two owners worked out the biggest trade in hockey history. Sather wasn't called in until the negotiations were well underway and he made a late push to include Luc Robitaille in the package for Carson.

"It was almost surreal," says Gretzky. "I think the two people that knew the least about it were me and Glen Sather. Everybody else was talking about it, but no one was saying anything to me."

As was the case with Coffey, the Gretzky deal ended in bitter acrimony. Prior to the announcing of the trade, Gretzky was in McNall's office in Los Angeles when Pocklington called. Unbeknownst to Pocklington, the Kings' owner put him on the speaker phone and Gretzky listened as his boss went on in great detail about Gretzky's selfishness and Walter's meddling ways. After the trade, and Gretzky's teary press conference in Edmonton, Pocklington also claimed Gretzky had an ego the size of Manhattan and accused him of faking his tears during his farewell press conference in Edmonton. Then Janet got into the act, phoning the *Edmonton Sun* and unloading on Pocklington. Among other things, she noted Pocklington didn't have the decency to call Gretzky and tell him the Oilers were going to trade him; that McNall had told her it was

Pocklington's idea to blame the trade on her; that she and Wayne were expecting to live in Edmonton while he played out his career; and that Pocklington's sole motivation for trading Gretzky was the money.

"It got a little heated there for a while," Gretzky says. "I'm sure everybody wishes we could have got through it more calmly."

Gretzky now says Pocklington was simply making a business decision. He even shoulders the responsibility for leaving Edmonton, claiming he could have signed the contract extension but wanted to test the open market once in his career. Part of that extension, he says, without a trace of irony in his voice, was a parcel of land in northern Canada. It's typical of Gretzky, who's avoided controversy the way Superman avoided kryptonite, and when interviewed for this book, he even had something nice to say about Eagleson. But the idea that he left Edmonton to sell himself as a free agent is, at best, disingenuous.

By 1991, Messier, Anderson, and Fuhr had all left Edmonton, under circumstances similar to Gretzky's. Under Eagleson's rule, in an artificially suppressed marketplace, Pocklington had a chance to keep the team together. But as Eagleson's grip on the game loosened, the marketplace changed and Pocklington, in his reduced financial state, couldn't keep up. The Oilers won another Stanley Cup in 1990 with a team built around Messier, Kurri, Anderson, a veteran defensive corps, and Bill Ranford in goal. But by 1991–92, Messier was traded to New York and Anderson and Fuhr were both dealt to Toronto. The Oilers survived for a while on the first generation of trades for their stars, but the franchise didn't revitalize itself until Pocklington sold to a local group and Lowe took over as general manager.

"Now that I'm on the business side of the game, I understand why he did it," Gretzky says.

That's more than hockey fans in Edmonton can say.

In the off day between Games 3 and 4 of the 1988 Stanley Cup final, Russ Conway was walking back to his car in downtown Boston after an NHL luncheon when a stretch limo pulled up and Ace Bailey, the former Bruin who was scouting for the Oilers, alighted. Bailey, who'd gotten to know the veteran newspaperman during his playing days in the 1970s, said he was going to meet up with Gretzky and invited Conway along. A couple of blocks later, they encountered the Great One, whose Oilers were meeting the Bruins in the final, and they repaired to a sports bar in the Marriott Hotel on Copley Square. There, the topic of conversation quickly turned to Bobby Orr's departure from the Bruins.

Gretzky believed the great defenceman was unloaded by the Bruins because owner Jeremy Jacobs didn't want to pay his salary. He compared his situation to Orr's and told Conway he thought Pocklington would dump him that summer — suggesting his eventual fate wasn't a complete surprise — because he was getting too expensive. Conway wondered aloud how much money Gretzky had made for the Oilers' owner, and Gretzky said no one would ever know because of Pocklington's creative accounting practices. Gretzky then said it was like Eagleson and the Canada Cups. No one knew how much money the tournament generated because no one had seen an independently audited financial statement.

"Gretzky says there's something really wrong," Conway says. "There's no accounting. No one knows where the money goes. I remembered that.

"That was a private setting. Ace was a friend of mine and Wayne loved Ace. They knew I cared about the players. It just evolved from there."

Two years later, Conway was attending a twentieth-anniversary reunion of the Bruins' 1970 Stanley Cup team when the conversation again turned to the subject of Eagleson. Again, Conway was stunned at what he heard. Don Awrey, the hard-rock defenceman whose career lasted sixteen seasons, talked about his US$10,000 pension. Dallas Smith talked about how Eagleson manipulated Orr's signing with the Blackhawks. Gerry Cheevers talked about Eagleson negotiating a $1,500 raise for the Bruins' goalie, then sending Cheevers a $3,000 bill for his services. Terry O'Reilly, the former Bruins' player rep, talked about challenging Eagleson on the one-third buyout clause the PA chief had allowed in the standard player's contract and being insulted by the Eagle.

There were other voices in and around the Bruins – Phil Esposito, Brad Park, Steve Kasper – with similar stories. Conway took it all in, then resolved to do something about it. He met with Dan Warner, the editor of the Lawrence *Eagle-Tribune*, and Irving Rogers, the paper's publisher, and said he'd like to look into Eagleson. When asked how long he thought it would take, he said, six months.

Seven years later, he was still at it.

"It was one thing after another," Conway says. "Guys talking about their pensions. Guys talking about disability insurance. It all started to fall together. It was amazing. There were all these hockey players, tough guys who wouldn't take a backward step on the ice, who Al had intimidated completely. But they'd had enough."

Conway wasn't the only person looking into Eagleson. In Toronto, former Leafs' defenceman Carl Brewer was investigating the NHL's pension plan. Agents Winter and Salcer had procured the services of former NFL players' union head Ed Garvey to examine the NHL Players' Association. But Conway's work was, by far, the most exhaustive.

It helped, he admits freely, that he worked for a privately owned newspaper that encouraged his cause both philosophically and financially and was vitally interested in this sort of journalism. Conway was the paper's sports editor and he was working on a story that had only peripheral ties to the Boston area. Nevertheless he was given all the resources he needed to do the job properly. He flew to London to chase down leads. He flew to Bermuda. He spent a considerable amount of time in Canada. He started with disability insurance claims and the work was dry, tedious, and uninteresting.

But he also discovered that once he got involved in Eagleson's world, an astonishing number of people were willing to help him out. Prior to his investigation, Conway had been like most journalists when it came to Eagleson: he regarded him as a valuable resource who'd supply inside information and he was more than aware of the power Eagleson held in the hockey world. But as he delved deeper, a far different picture emerged.

"I always asked the same question: 'Have you got documents?'" Conway says. "Everyone had a story, but they had to have the documents to go with them and, because it was insurance, there was a paper trail. There were always questions and innuendo around Al but nothing could be proven.

"Every time we published stories, it would open up all these other doors. People were just fed up. And I'm talking about people at the most sensitive levels. Al could be charming one minute, then the next minute he'd treat you like dirt and he treated too many people like dirt."

The documents and other materials Conway amassed filled six filing cabinets, four-rows deep. He interviewed about six hundred people during the course of his probe and enlisted the aid of CPA's lawyers, professionals with expertise in real estate, pensions, and insurance to help him wade through the morass of information he uncovered. He copied $380 worth of documents at the Ontario pension appeal board one afternoon. Turning in monthly expense reports became too onerous so he would simply turn in an annual accounting of his expenditures. His phone bills regularly topped $5,000.

It's assumed that Bobby Orr, Eagleson's aggrieved former client, helped orchestrate Conway's work and was his primary source throughout the investigation. But, while it's reasonable to assume Orr helped out Conway, it also does the newspaperman a disservice to suggest the reams and reams of information he uncovered were served to him on a platter. What makes Conway's work so complete and so damning is the extent of documentation and that was assembled through tireless reporting, not by taking dictation.

"He underestimated me," Conway says. "He never thought anyone would take the time to follow the paper trail all over the world. And for a brilliant man, he left a huge paper trail."

Not long after his probe began, Conway turned his attention to Hockey Canada and the business of the Canada Cups. In 1987 there were suspicions about Eagleson but, like most everything involving Eagleson, nothing was sticking. Hrudey says there were stories about the star players getting cash payments but, "It was just talk." There was also talk about the coaches receiving fifteen thousand dollars in cash as a bonus after Team Canada's win. "I heard that one," Perron says, without elaborating further. Hawerchuk says Eagleson wasn't the most popular figure, "But I wouldn't say there was a lot of talk about him lining his pockets."

Conway would change that. He started by trying to obtain Hockey Canada's financials and ran into the same roadblock many of the players encountered. Hockey Canada was a public, non-profit organization. It received millions in federal funding. The Canada Cups were run under its name. Yet the accounting for this hugely popular, hugely profitable event was a deep, dark secret.

Eagleson maintained that his business dealings in international hockey ran through Hockey Canada and were therefore independent of his position as head of the players' union. That he used members of the Players' Association to put on this event apparently didn't occur to him. He also, as mentioned earlier, said he never profited from his work in the Canada Cups, but as Conway began to wade through the labyrinth of deals and agreements Eagleson set up, he found that was a lie. After examining all the information, Conway concluded that somewhere around $1.5 million had been paid in fees, bonuses, and expenses from international hockey to Eagleson and companies and people close to Eagleson.

The first collection of stories was published in the *Eagle-Tribune* beginning in September 1991 and they detailed, among other things, the rinkboard advertising scam, the depths of which are mind-boggling. Eagleson told Labatt, who'd paid $4.2 million for the 1991 tournament's advertising rights, that the endboards were excluded from the deal because they belonged to the IIHF. He then told the Zurich-based agency that bought the European TV and rinkboard rights that the endboards were excluded because they belonged to Labatt. The rights then went to All Canada Sports Promotions, which was run by long-time Eagleson crony Irving Ungerman.

Conway not only uncovered this, he uncovered that $400,000 was paid to All Canada Sports. Conway had cheques going through Toronto bank accounts. He had cheques going through Zurich bank accounts. When Eagleson panicked and tried to cover his tracks, Conway uncovered the cover-up. As with his work on disability insurance, he learned a number of people who Eagleson had crossed were more than happy to help him. "I had faxes sent to me by people in his office within fifteen minutes of Al sending them," Conway says.

And he didn't have to solicit the help. Once the series ran, brown envelopes would appear at Conway's house stuffed with documents. Conway says a member of Eagleson's family was supplying information on the head of the PA. For the 1987 Canada Cup, Conway reported extensively on Eagleson's airline-ticket scam outlined earlier. But he also concluded the crooked endboard scheme wasn't invented solely for the 1991 Canada Cup, noting All Canada Sports was involved in the sale of endboards for the 1984 and 1987 tournaments.

The underlying outrage to all this, of course, was that Eagleson had built the Canada Cup on the labours of Players' Association members. He told them they were helping their fellow union members by contributing greatly to their pensions. He told them they were helping the game in Canada by contributing greatly to Hockey Canada. Those players, the greatest players in the world, gave their services to Eagleson virtually freely for almost two months in 1987. And he betrayed their trust.

"The first time I heard about the Canada Cup stuff was when Russ Conway's book came out," says Ray Ferraro, a former Eagleson client who'd played in the world championships in the 1980s. "I remember reading it once and having to go over it again to really understand what Al had been doing."

In all, the *Eagle-Tribune* would print Conway's work in eight different series between 1991 and 1998. His newspaper reports also became the basis for his book, *Game Misconduct*, which was published in 1995. When it came out, NHLPA chief Bob Goodenow, the man who'd succeeded Eagleson, ordered more than six hundred copies of the book and distributed them to each player in the NHL.

"You don't have to be a sports fan to appreciate pensions being stolen or insurance money being stolen," Conway says. "And a lot of those people had become friends of mine."

As for Eagleson's role in international hockey, Conway says: "My reaction was how can you do this to people who are playing for peanuts who think they're playing for the honour of their country. What he did was despicable. He turned out to be a conniving, lying cheater."

Winter, meanwhile, was attacking Eagleson on another front. About a year after the 1987 Canada Cup, Winter, Ron Salcer, and Jim Fox attended a seminar in Malibu put on by former NFL Players' Association head Ed Garvey. Garvey had been the first executive director of the football players' union and presided over it during a particularly tumultuous time in the league's history. He'd just concluded an unsuccessful campaign for a Senate seat in Wisconsin when Salcer called and asked if Garvey would be interested in taking a look at the NHL Players' Association.

"We met with each team and asked, 'Do you have a problem with the way things are being run?'" Winter says. "Over-whelmingly, they did. We asked for one hundred dollars from each player so we could keep Garvey on a retainer. At first we were seen as a minor annoyance which would go away if you ignored it."

But they didn't go away. Garvey was the perfect man to take on Eagleson. He was fully conversant with U.S. and Canada labour laws. Over his career, he'd taken on figures far more powerful than Eagleson. He was also aware of the Eagle's hold on the players and some of his more dubious methods.

He even had some first-hand experience with the man. While Garvey was with the NFL, Eagleson had called him in Chicago and invited him to dinner and a Blackhawks game. Between periods, Eagleson took Garvey to a cocktail reception held inside one of the suites at Chicago Stadium and there the two men rubbed elbows with NHL president Clarence Campbell, Blackhawks owner Bill Wirtz, and other NHL powerbrokers.

"It was so obvious they were colleagues," says Garvey. "I thought that was odd."

Garvey would spend a year poking around the affairs of the Players' Association and he would encounter much stranger things. His first meeting was with L.A. Kings players at their practice facility and he was expecting two or three players to attend. Instead, the whole team, including Gretzky, showed up and listened intently for three hours while Garvey explained what a union was supposed to do for its membership. At the end, Kelly Hrudey said: "If I would have raised any of these points [at a PA meeting], I would have been told to shut up."

"What surprised me was the level of intimidation among the players," Garvey says. "Al was the classic bully. But it was still unbelievable. I thought, what is this? Has everyone gone to sleep?"

Garvey soon started publishing his own newsletter, *The Players Voice*, in response to Eagleson's publication *Goals* and began hammering away at Eagleson. He wrote about Eagleson's uncomfortably close relationship with NHL president John Ziegler. He wrote about Eagleson's own contract, which called for a two-hundred-thousand-dollar annual salary paid in U.S. funds, even though the PA was operated out of Toronto.

At first, Eagleson ignored the insurrectionists, but when it became clear they were preparing for a fight, he fired back, starting a smear campaign against Garvey and claiming Winter and Salcer were trying to steal his clients. At one point, Eagleson called Garvey and said: "I've got you in my sights."

"Just make sure you shoot straight," Garvey answered.

The whole thing came to a head at a Players' Association meeting in Palm Beach at the sumptuous Breakers Hotel during the summer of 1989. There, Garvey and his group, which now numbered around seventy, rented rooms in a hotel owned by former Penguins goalie Denis Herron, then rented an old school bus and drove to The Breakers. And there, they stormed The Bastille.

"My regret is we didn't have videotape of that old school bus pulling up to The Breakers and all the players piling out," says Garvey.

What followed was interesting enough. Garvey, Salcer, Winter, and three other Ontario lawyers – John Agro, Bill Dermody, and David Dempster – had prepared a fifty-five-page document entitled, "Confidential Report to NHLPA Members," and it outlined the case against Eagleson in plain and powerful language.

"If any other union leader did what Alan Eagleson has done over the past 22 years, the news media would be screaming for an investigation," it read. "The conflicts of interests are shocking but even more shocking is a pattern of sweetheart agreements with the NHL over all these years."

It went on, "No benefits of any significance were achieved in the entire decade of the '80s through collective bargaining . . . Alan Eagleson might well be the most overpaid executive in the labour movement in North America . . . Alan Eagleson refused to provide information that is required by law to be made available to all union members."

Armed with Garvey's indictment of Eagleson, the dissident faction invited themselves to sit in with Eagleson at the PA meeting. Garvey then moved in behind a microphone and proceeded to "cross-examine" Eagleson for an hour. After the meeting, the Kings' Marty McSorley went up to Garvey and said, "Thank you for giving us our union back." If there was a turning point in the players' battle with their union chief, this was it.

"I certainly thought so," Garvey says when asked if this was the beginning of Eagleson's end. "It's one thing to go across the ice and give the finger to the Russians. It's another to start screwing around with union money."

Garvey, according to eyewitness accounts, didn't resort to showboat tactics in his confrontation with Eagleson. He simply asked his questions calmly and responded just as calmly when Eagleson launched his inevitable counterattack. The Eagle had finally met his match.

Garvey's lead was also followed by many of the players in attendance. Jim Fox recalls one of the most telling moments in the meeting occurred when Jim Korn, a journeyman with the New Jersey Devils, asked Eagleson about his practice of lending out Players' Association money for his friend's mortgages. At other times, Eagleson would go into one of his tirades and the player would back down. But Korn was part of a new breed of NHL player, university-educated at Providence College and more worldly than his forebears.

"This time Jim asked his question and Eagleson started in on him," Fox says. "'You're just a big goon. You shouldn't even be in the league.' That was true. Jim was a marginal player but that didn't mean he didn't have a right to ask that question. He just repeated it very calmly and Eagleson didn't have an answer."

That day the NHLPA executive and the player reps voted on whether to retain Eagleson on new terms or fire him outright. Eagleson survived, largely because he'd stacked the executive with his cronies. But his power base started to crack at that meeting and within a couple of years it would crumble around him.

In January of 1990, Winter filed a fifty-page complaint against Eagleson with the Law Society of Upper Canada. A year later, the FBI started investigating Eagleson. In September of the same year, Conway's first series of articles ran in the *Eagle-Tribune*. A grand jury was struck in the States soon after, and Conway turned over much of his research.

"I believed we were the eyewitness to a crime," says Conway. "I thought we should co-operate."

In late 1991, Eagleson was replaced as head of the Players' Association by Bob Goodenow. In March 1993, he resigned from Hockey Canada. In January 1998, he pleaded guilty to three charges of mail fraud in a packed Boston courthouse and was fined CAD$1 million. Three charges of racketeering were dropped as part of the plea bargain.

"You have defrauded and stolen from hard-working professional athletes," Judge Nathaniel Gorton said in passing the sentence.

The next day, Eagleson pleaded guilty to three charges of fraud and theft in another packed courthouse in Toronto and was sentenced to eighteen months in jail. He wore his Order of Canada pin to his sentencing hearing in Toronto, where some thirty character references were read in court, including one from former prime minister John Turner. Shortly thereafter he was asked to resign from the Order. He was also expelled from the Hockey Hall of Fame.

Garvey attended the court hearing in Boston at the invitation of Bobby Orr and still remembers the mixed emotions of that day. "It was part happiness, part sadness about what had happened to the game and part embarrassment that they'd let it happen," says Garvey.

The plane had barely set down in Moscow following the Russians' loss in Hamilton when Larionov, in an interview with *Football-Hockey* magazine, fired the opening shots in the battle against Tikhonov. Among other things, Larionov openly questioned the Russian system and the impossible demands it placed on its players. There had been murmurs about the players' dissatisfaction before, and Larionov's unhappiness wasn't exactly a secret. But this was the first time a Russian player had the stones to go public with their grievances, and it sent shockwaves throughout Russia.

"I'm tired of the training regimen, of the endless separation from home, when necessary and when not necessary," he wrote. "I have a seven-month-old daughter, Elena, who my wife is alone to take care of. I can do nothing worthwhile to help.

"After eleven months of training without a break, after all the games, after the travel, we had one month's break and then immediately had to come back for intensive work for the Canada Cup. We were never really able to get away from hockey."

Tikhonov, understandably, was thrilled by this development. In the first practice after the article came out, he assembled his team and said he thought he was working with hockey players, but he'd learned there was a writer in their midst. "Larionov, for example, is a Boris Pasternak," said the jovial coach. But if he thought Larionov's broadside was an isolated incident, he was sadly mistaken.

The long-buried resentment erupted into open warfare following the 1988 Winter Olympics in Calgary. In the runup to the Games, the federation had implied that all five members of the Green Unit would be released to play in the NHL if they brought him the gold medal. The Russians flexed their muscles one last time – "Our last hurrah," says Larionov – and buried the field in Calgary en route to gold.

It was even hoped that Tikhonov would retire after the Games, but, shortly after returning home, Tikhonov issued a statement: "Four years from now we want to emerge victorious from the Albertville Winter Games and we have started training for them five days after Calgary."

That was it. For the next year and a half, until Fetisov, Larionov, Krutov, Makarov, and others were finally released to play in North America, Tikhonov and his players engaged in a bitter fight that was unlike anything the Russian people had ever seen. Krutov, of all players, aired his grievances to Tikhonov and, when he was rebuffed, quit the national team for a couple of days. Fetisov became enraged when his way to New Jersey was blocked. In the fall of 1988, Larionov again popped off in the Russian media, revealing how his travel visa had been taken away from him, about the drugs prescribed at Archangel, about Tikhonov's unholy methods.

"It's time to speak boldly about the style of leadership in our hockey associations," he said. "What has been created is a personality cult where military discipline and unquestioning subordination is substituted for democracy."

And your point is? Tikhonov seemed to respond. He held Larionov out of the Izvestia tournament, claiming he was unfit to play, but Fetisov, Krutov, and Makarov confronted him and the autocratic coach backed down, sort of, saying Larionov wouldn't play at Izvestia but would take part in the upcoming tour of NHL clubs.

During that tour, Red Army met the Devils at The Meadowlands and Fetisov was cheered wildly by the New Jersey crowd. "If Tikhonov wanted it, I think this thing would be resolved quickly. He's all talk and no action," Fetisov told the *Washington Post* after the game.

Upon returning home, he then quit Red Army, saying: "I don't want to play on Tikhonov's team. I'm tired of Tikhonov's dictatorial regime."

Tikhonov fired back, saying Fetisov had gotten drunk in Kiev and had beaten up a Second World War veteran. Fetisov, meanwhile, had quit the Red Army team but hadn't quit the Red Army and drove to his desk job each morning in his big, blue Mercedes.

The final battle was fought over the world championship in Stockholm in the spring of 1989. Fetisov was still boycotting Red Army but he wanted to play in the world championship. Tikhonov, predictably, took a contrary view. But this time, in a stunning move, Larionov, Krutov, Makarov, Kamensky, Bykov, and Khomutov appeared on television in Russia and issued an ultimatum: Fetisov plays or we don't. Tikhonov initially tried to bluff his way through, saying anyone could be replaced. But he'd been beaten. Fetisov not only returned to the national team, he was named captain and led the Russians to a perfect 10–0 record and their twenty-first world championship. "I think I will be in the USA by August," Fetisov said.

But he wasn't the first.

For reasons which are still unclear, the Russian federation had granted Sergei Priakhin his release in February 1989, a couple of months before the world championship. Priakhin had seen fourth-line duty during the 1987 Canada Cup as a checking winger and the Calgary Flames had taken him in the twelfth round of the 1988 draft. But the Flames, who'd also drafted Makarov, weren't particularly interested in Priakhin and were shocked when he landed on their doorstep.

"We were trying to get our foot in the door and negotiating with the Russians," says then Flames GM Cliff Fletcher. "[Priakhin] had no idea he was going to play for us. His club team [Soviet Wings] were touring in North America. He showed up in Calgary with the clothes on his back and that was about all."

Dave King's national team was playing the Wings as part of that tour when Priakhin was released. One day, King received a call from Fletcher and asked if their new forward could fly back to Calgary with the nationals.

"I remember he had this little tote bag that had room for a shaving kit, a change of underwear, and maybe a shirt," says King. "And that was his luggage. He had no idea he was going to be released. In the middle of this tour, they told him, 'You're going to play for Calgary.' Two nights later I was watching him on TV. It was amazing."

Priakhin played two games for the Flames in the regular season, then took a seat in the press box to watch their Stanley Cup run that spring. He played parts of two more seasons in Calgary before returning to Europe and his NHL career totals read three goals and eight assists in forty-six games.

For Russian hockey, the more important development took place following the world championship in Stockholm. Tikhonov had identified Alexander Mogilny as one of the players he'd build the new national team around. Mogilny was eighteen when he joined Red Army in 1986–87 and promptly ripped off fifteen goals in twenty-eight games. Along with Pavel Bure and Sergei Fedorov, he would play on the new first line that would replace the KLM line, and Mogilny, who was oblivious to the intrigues surrounding Larionov and Fetisov, believed he was looking at a long spell of playing for Tikhonov.

"It was hard to believe it was going to happen," Mogilny says. "The politics were changing but you didn't know what way it was going. Nobody could anticipate what the future would look like. I don't remember guys talking about it a lot. Why would you consider something that was impossible?"

But two years later it would suddenly be possible. Mogilny, who shared Larionov's independent streak, won gold in Calgary but suffered through a difficult season under Tikhonov. He'd also seen the manner in which the great veterans on the team were treated and decided that wasn't going to happen to him. Mogilny had been drafted by the Buffalo Sabres in 1988 and his initial contact with the club came at the World Junior Championship in Anchorage in January of 1989. Four months later, following the celebration after the World Championship in Stockholm, he stole away from Tikhonov and his countrymen and made his way to Buffalo.

"It was brutal," Mogilny says. "I didn't like the way the older players were treated after everything they'd done for hockey. There was nothing about the person. It was just about the job and it lasted eleven months of the year.

"We got some goodies every Christmas. We got to travel and we got paid fifty dollars a month. You could buy a VCR, bring it back, and hopefully sell it. But that was the better life they promised and I didn't think it was that great."

Now, it was one thing for Tikhonov to lose players like Fetisov and Larionov when it was perceived they were at the end of their careers. It was another to lose a young star like Mogilny, and his defection rocked the Russian system to its foundation. Fletcher, who'd been trying to liberate Makarov for a couple of years, noticed a change in the Russians' attitude in the wake of Mogilny's departure. The long-time hockey man still believes it was the threat of losing more players that opened up the pipeline to Russia. "After the first defection took place, they started to realize they were going to have problems keeping their players," Fletcher says. "They were hard negotiators. They certainly weren't interested in doing any favours for the NHL. But they wanted to protect their system and they were a lot more concerned about the threat of defection than money. The floodgates opened pretty quickly after that."

Still, the money helped. As part of perestroika (restructuring), Gorbachev wanted InterSport, the governing agency for Russian sports, to become self-sufficient. The easiest way to reach that goal was to negotiate the release of star players and that practice had started with soccer players. Pat Quinn, the Canucks GM who was trying to pry loose Larionov, travelled to Russia with Fletcher in the summer of 1989 and, like Fletcher, noted the change in atmosphere. But the Russians weren't willing to let their players go for free.

"InterSport wanted their cut," says Quinn. "Red Army wanted their cut. Boy, all the hands were out in this thing. Fetisov did it all on his own. He said to hell with you guys. Igor tried to do what he thought was the right thing. We were only talking about Igor to start, but they called us back later because they figured there was some money in Krutov."

In the end, the Flames and Canucks would work out the same deals for Makarov, Larionov, and Krutov: $375,000 annually to the players, $375,000 annually to the federation. The Devils would sign Fetisov, Kasatonov, and Sergei Starikov, and the Nordiques would end up with Mylnikov. That fall, all seven players, along with Mogilny and long-time Tikhonov nemesis Helmut Balderis, would make their NHL debuts amid considerable excitement. But, in many respects, the new life in North America didn't prove any easier for the Russian players than the life they'd left behind.

The greatest expectations were in Vancouver, where the Canucks had just extended the Stanley Cup champion Flames to seven games in their opening-round playoff series and Quinn had now landed two-thirds of the best line in hockey. Larionov, the

Canucks knew, wouldn't be a problem. He was worldly. His English was excellent. He viewed the whole experience as a great adventure. Eventually he would adapt. Krutov was another story.

Larionov was in attendance at the start of the Canucks' camp, but Krutov was delayed. When he finally arrived in September, the Canucks put him on the ice at Pacific Coliseum, then brought him in front of the media, where the assembled news-hounds were shocked at what they saw. Krutov had played a lead role in the Soviets' gold at the world championship four months before and he was just two years removed from his bravura per-formance at the 1987 Canada Cup. But there, sitting before the TV cameras, was a lumpen, misshapen slob who was sweating profusely. The Canucks thought they were getting one of the five best players in the world. Instead, they got a player who remains a standing joke in Canucks' lore.

"He was spent," says Bob McCammon, the Canucks' coach that season. "He wanted to play well and he wanted to lose the weight. He'd spend ninety minutes riding the bike but he just couldn't do it. I kind of gave up on him. You couldn't help but feel sorry for him. It was sad."

Krutov, it was quickly revealed, had discovered an unhealthy appetite for fast food and beer. He loved McDonald's. He liked beer even more. One of his former teammates was responsible for driving him to and from practice and one day, he was invited into the Krutov domicile. There, by his bed, the Russian had placed an ice bucket full of beer. He'd also attached a skate lace to the light in the room so he didn't have to get out of bed to turn off the light.

It would have been difficult enough for Krutov to make the adjustment under ordinary circumstances. It was impossible given his conditioning. If that wasn't bad enough, the Canucks played a dump-and-chase style that year and had no one to complement Krutov's and Larionov's puck-possession game. At one point, McCammon sent out heavyweight Craig Coxe to play with the two great Russians. For a while he was referred to as Craig Coxe-ov around the Canucks' dressing room.

"Krutov was a very simple man and there was a certain comfort with his life in the Army and his status within Russian society," Quinn says of Krutov. "I think he was afraid when he came. He seemed confused on the ice as well. He needed help."

Larionov tried. That season he scored seventeen goals and finished with forty-four points, decent production for a first-year NHL player, but not exactly what the Canucks had in mind when they signed him. After one particularly poor outing, Larionov knocked on McCammon's door and apologized for his play. "You should have seen me five years ago," he said. "I was a good player then."

"It was difficult when you're changing your life from the Soviet Union to North America," says Larionov. "Not everyone can do that. It's a different language, a different country and different customs. You look at the superstar soccer players who change countries and the trouble they have. We were twenty-eight, twenty-nine, thirty and we'd established ourselves. Now we were trying to establish ourselves again and open the door for the rest of Russia. It was a big responsibility."

The next season, Krutov returned to Vancouver in roughly the same level of physical fitness and the Canucks sent him home, claiming he'd broken the terms of his contract. The case eventually ended up in an international court of arbitration. Krutov won, but his fall from hockey grace is still astonishing. In the '87 Canada Cup final, he was the third-best player on the ice after Gretzky and Lemieux and the gap wasn't that wide. Two years later, he was a wreck. The Canucks believed part of the problem concerned the "supplements" Krutov had been given when he was in Russia. Larionov intimated that Krutov had been fed steroids on a consistent basis when he played for the national team that helped account for his great strength on the puck. In North America, he had no such advantage.

In 2005, Krutov returned to Vancouver as part of a touring group of old-timers to play an exhibition game. There, with the help of an interpreter, he answered a few questions about his year with the Canucks. He loved the city. He thought the people were friendly. He wished he could have played better. But when the topic turned to his conditioning, he held up a hand, turned and walked away.

Larionov, meanwhile, would play two more seasons with the Canucks, then left for Switzerland when the Russian federation insisted on further payment for his services. He came back and had two successful seasons in San Jose, where he was reunited with Makarov, then moved on to Detroit, where he played eight more seasons, winning three Stanley Cups. The lockout forced his retirement after the 2003–4 season, but before Gretzky took over as coach of the Phoenix Coyotes in 2005–6 his first choice for the job was Larionov.

"He has a sense for the game like no one I've ever seen," says his old pal Vanya.

Makarov, statistically at least, had the best season of the Soviet players who came over in 1989. His first year in Calgary, he scored 24 goals and added 62 assists for 86 points in 80 games and, despite some controversy over his age and experience, was named rookie of the year. Makarov's more lasting contribution to the NHL, in fact, was his role in changing the eligibility requirements for the Calder Cup. After his rookie season, at the age of thirty-one, the maximum rookie age was established at twenty-six.

But the NHL and the Flames wasn't a seamless fit for Makarov. He was essentially brought in to replace Hakan Loob, who returned to Sweden after the Flames' Cup triumph in 1989, and while the numbers were there, Makarov could never replace Loob in the team's locker room. Makarov wanted to play the same puck-possession, speed-and-skill game that had made him a star in Russia, but the Flames, under Terry Crisp, played dump-and-chase. He told friends he was shocked at the Flames' lack of skill. He said he would welcome a trade to Vancouver, where he could be reunited with Larionov and Krutov. You can guess how that went over in Calgary.

"It was hard for him to play at that optimal level three or four times a week like we do in the NHL," Fletcher says of Makarov. "Their whole system was geared to peaking for the world championships and the Olympics and they didn't get a lot of competition.

"He was very stubborn and had his own ideas of how the game should be played. You never knew what you were going to get from shift to shift, but there were nights he was magical."

The Flames and Makarov had some success in the regular season during his four-year career in Calgary, but, after a series of playoff disappointments, he was sent to San Jose, where he was reunited with Larionov. There, first-year coach Kevin Constantine put a five-man unit together with Larionov, Makarov, Swede Johan Garpenlov, and the defensive pairing of Jeff Norton and Sandis Ozolnish, and the group gave the Sharks franchise its first taste of success. Moving into its new rink in San Jose, and after two depressing seasons at the aptly named Cow Palace just outside San Francisco, the Sharks made the playoffs in just their third year of existence in 1993–94 and repeated the feat in 1994–95. They also upset the top-seeded Detroit Red Wings, then the Calgary Flames in the first round and extended Toronto to seven games in a thrilling Western Conference semifinal in 1994. Makarov counted 30 goals and 38 assists that season but suffered through an injury-riddled campaign the following year and played out the string in Switzerland a couple of years later.

In New Jersey, meanwhile, the interesting partnership of Fetisov and Kasatonov was reunited on the Devils' defence. The pair would play together for four seasons and Kasatonov says the bad feelings between the two men eventually evaporated. Kasatonov, the great loyalist, also points out he still lives in the same house in Montclair, New Jersey, he bought his first season with the Devils, and Fetisov, who fought like a tiger to get out of Russia, is now the country's minister of sport where Makarov and Krutov work for him.

"It's funny how things worked out," says Kasatonov.

Fetisov and Larionov also landed in Detroit for the 1995–96 season, and together, they won two Cups playing for the Wings. Scotty Bowman played Larionov and Fetisov with countrymen Fedorov, Slava Kozlov, and Vladimir Konstantinov and they rediscovered the old magic they first found playing for Tikhonov. Konstantinov was paralyzed in a tragic car accident following the Wings' first Cup victory in 1996–97 but, the next year, they repeated.

In the summer of 1997, Fetisov brought the Stanley Cup to Russia with his Detroit teammates. As part of the tour, the Wings were shown Lenin's Tomb. While they gazed at their country's former leader, Kuperman whispered to Kozlov, "If he was still alive, you wouldn't be in the NHL."

Fetisov would show off the Cup at Red Square. He then took it to Red Army, where thousands of players and coaches from all over Russia attended.

Tikhonov was not one of them.

The old coach regarded the mass exodus of his players as desertion and remained resentful through the years. After the first wave of players had left, he called Kuperman into his office and said, "I want to show you something." He then pointed to a file that contained all the articles Kuperman had and said, "I remember."

"I didn't feel too good after that," says Kuperman.

But even the iron Tikhonov would soften over the years. Kasatonov, of course, understood his coach's feelings.

"The team was changing and he didn't understand everything that was happening. Of course, he wanted to hang on to his team. This is a normal reaction for a coach. But how can you blame the coach who's given you a better life, who's given you all these great moments, all these medals, all these victories. I owe him a lot."

And, eventually, Larionov and Fetisov would make their peace with Tikhonov. In December 2006, both men helped organize a benefit game to celebrate the sixtieth anniversary of Russian hockey's birth. The remarkable event was played outdoors on a makeshift rink in Red Square and pitted an eclectic collection of formers NHLers – Ron Duguay, Billy Smith, Esa Tikkanen, Jari Kurri, and Mats Naslund – against a Russian team that featured the great Yakushev and the Green Unit, who were reunited for the first time in seventeen years. Scotty Bowman coached the NHL team. Tikhonov, now seventy-seven and the president of Red Army, coached the Russian team.

"He was quiet and happy," says Larionov. "It wasn't like the old days. I haven't talked to him in seventeen years, but this was part of history. A lot of time has passed. You forget about some things."

Coffey was also part of the NHL team, and Larionov saw his former rival the night before the game, skating around the outdoor rink while he talked to friends back in Toronto on his cellphone. You're never going to believe what I'm doing, he said, I'm skating around Red Square.

As for the game, the KLM line with Fetisov and Kasatonov counted for seven of the ten Russian goals in the 10–10 tie.

"As soon as we stepped on the ice, we felt something," says Larionov. "The puck was moving around. We were scoring goals.

"I was just watching the game on DVD. It was unbelievable to see the different generations of Russian players in the game. It was a great honour and respect for the Russian game. It was a once-in-a-lifetime experience. I feel very privileged."

Larionov said the game's purpose wasn't to raise money for former Russian players so much as it was to raise awareness of the history of the Russian game and the contributions of its players. He said his eight-year-old son, Igor Jr., who was born in North America, knows more about the NHL than Russian hockey, and that concerns him. But what troubles him more deeply is the disconnect between the contemporary Russian game and the great teams and players of the past. Larionov says young Russian players might have heard of him and Fetisov and Krutov, but they have no idea what kind of players they were, of their many accomplishments or the fight they led against the Soviet system.

"These are players that put Russian hockey on the map," says Larionov. "They should know Kharlamov, Yakushev, Firsov, Tarasov.

"There are a lot of players who need help but we have to change the way of thinking. The most important thing is to establish that tradition and history. There's been so much neglect. It's a lot of work."

But Tikhonov remembers. Some time ago, Dave King found himself sitting at a tournament in Sweden with the old coach and his son, Vasily, who'd worked in San Jose for a time as an assistant with the Sharks. The three hockey men carried on a conversation of sorts throughout the game with Vasily acting as an interpreter when King asked the old Russian coach which was the favourite of his teams.

Tikhonov grew silent, seemed to consider the question for a moment, then returned his attention to the game.

"I just thought he didn't want to answer it," says King.

But about fifteen minutes later, Tikhonov, Sr., tugged on his son's sleeve and said something in Russian.

"The 1988 Olympic team," Vasily reported to King. "That was his favourite. They were the best."

That was the team of Larionov, Makarov, Krutov, Kasatonov, and Fetisov. Anyone who saw them wouldn't argue with their coach.

Round-robin Summaries
from the 1987 Canada Cup

QUARTERFINAL ROUND

Calgary, Aug. 28: Canada 4, Czechoslovakia 4

First Period
1. Can, Tocchet (Propp, Gretzky) 5:57
2. Czech, Pasek (Liba, Vlach) 10:22
3. Czech, Horava (Volek, Dolezal) 12:18
4. Can, Hawerchuk (Messier, Bourque) 17:38
Penalties: Liba, Czech 7:58.

Second Period
5. Can, C. Lemieux (M. Lemieux, Dineen) 8:33
6. Czech, Vlk (Horava, Kadlec) 15:19
Penalties: Pasek, Czech 1:25; Jasko, Czech 5:42; M. Lemieux, Can 5:55; Bozik, Czech 15:51.

Third Period
7. Can, Coffey (Gretzky, Lemieux) 2:06 PP
8. Czech,Volek (Hrdina, Stavjana) 7:00 PP
Penalties: Czech bench (served by Lubina) 1:50; Rochefort,
Can 5:03.

Shots on Goal
Canada   13   16   11   – 40
Czech   12   12   12   – 36

Goalies: Fuhr, Canada; Hasek, Czechoslovakia
Outstanding players: Fuhr, Canada; Hasek, Czechoslovakia
Attendance: 8,458

Hartford, Aug. 28: USA 4, Finland 1

First Period
No scoring.
Penalties: Makela, Fin, Housley, USA 1:34; Jutila, Fin 3:09;
Nilan, USA 5:52; Tikkanen, Fin, Carpenter, USA 15:50.

Second Period
1. USA, LaFontaine (A. Broten) 9:17
Penalties: Otto, USA :58; Siren, Fin 4:57; Chelios, USA 11:04;
Housley, USA 13:41; Fraser, USA 18:08.

Third Period
2. USA, LaFontaine (Suter, Housley) 4:57
3. USA, Presley (Suter) 7:31
4. USA, Mullen (Ramsey) 17:49
5. Fin, Jutila (Helminen) 18:29
Penalties: Ruuttu, Fin 8:18; Presley, USA 13:58; Siren, Fin
15:47.

Shots on Goal

USA	11	8	21	− 40
Finland	4	11	8	− 23

Goalies: Vanbiesbrouck, USA; Takko, Finland
Outstanding Players: LaFontaine, USA; Takko, Finland
Attendance: 8,508

Calgary, Aug. 29: Sweden 5, USSR 3

First Period
1. USSR, Kamensky (Bykov, Stelnov) 2:07
2. Swe, Gustafsson (Thelven, Naslund) 5:50
3. Swe, Albelin (Eldebrink, Nilsson) 6:38
4. Swe, Carlsson (Jonsson, Karlsson) 7:37 PP
Penalties: Bergqvist, Swe 4:53; Krutov, USSR 5:42; Lomakin, USSR 11:10; Eklund, Swe 17:24.

Second Period
5. USSR, Krutov 11:49 SH
6. USSR, Khomutov 15:14
7. Swe, Karlsson 16:09
Penalties: Eklund, Swe 3:19; Khmylev, USSR 10:01.

Third Period
8. Swe, Peter Sundstrom (Nilsson) 19:29
Penalties: None.

Shots on Goal

Sweden	7	9	4	− 20
USSR	4	5	5	− 14

Goalies: Lindmark, Sweden; Belosheikin, USSR
Outstanding Players: Albelin, Sweden; Khomutov, USSR
Attendance: 3,055

Hamilton, Aug. 30: Canada 4, Finland 1

First Period
1. Can, Hawerchuk (Dineen, Propp) 3:12
2. Can, Tocchet 4:50
Penalties: Skriko, Fin 1:11; Makela, Fin (misconduct) 7:22;
Rochefort, Can 11:03; Tocchet, Can 13:51.

Second Period
3. Can, Dineen (Murphy) 2:49
4. Fin, Ruuttu (Makela, Virta) 7:22 PP
5. Can, Messier (C. Lemieux, Bourque) 13:15
Penalties: Gilmour, Can 5:37; Jarvi, Fin 7:56; Ruuttu, Fin 15:54;
Bourque, Can 19:21.

Third Period
No scoring.
Penalties: Rochefort, Can, Kurri, Fin :06; Bourque, Can 14:06.

Shots on Goal
Canada   21   17   16   — 54
Finland   12   13   15   — 40

Goalies: Fuhr, Canada; Takko, Finland
Outstanding Players: Dineen, Canada; Takko, Finland
Attendance: 9,624

Regina, Aug. 31: USSR 4, Czechoslovakia 0

First Period
1. USSR, Krutov (Makarov, Stelnov) 15:25
2. USSR, Semak (Priakhin, Kravchuk) 18:17
Penalties: Kasatonov, USSR, Pasek, Czech 3:33; Kasatonov,
USSR 7:26; Larionov, USSR 11:38; Horava, Czech 12:08.

Second Period
3. USSR, Stelnov (Kravchuk) 6:27
Penalties: Pasek, Czech 4:21; Stelnov, USSR 6:54; Kamensky,
USSR 13:09; Pasek, Czech 13:18; Kadlec, Czech (minor,
misconduct) 18:54.

Third Period
4. USSR, Semenov (Lomakin, Fedotov) 6:03
Penalties: Rosol, Czech 3:38; Semak, USSR 6:58; Priakin,
USSR 9:54; Pasek, Czech 15:45; Fetisov, USSR (major) 19:29.

Shots on Goal
USSR   11   10   6   − 27
Czech   10   4   9   − 23

Goalies: Mylnikov, USSR; Hasek, Czech
Outstanding Players: Kravchuk, USSR; Rosol, Czech
Attendance: 5,477

Hamilton, Aug. 31: USA 5, Sweden 2

First Period
1. USA, Carpenter (Olczyk, Otto) 3:38
Penalties: Gustafsson, Swe :15; Presley, USA 5:00; Presley, USA
11:38; Brooke, USA 15:23; Thelven, Swe 17:11.

Second Period
2. USA, Olczyk (Otto, Carpenter) 2:54
3. USA, Nilan (Fraser, Housley) 6:15
4. USA, Brooke (Langway) 12:51
5. Swe, Gustafsson (Naslund, Eldebrink) 15:55
Penalties: Roupe, Swe 7:15; A. Broten, USA 12:57.

Third Period
6. USA, Mullen (A. Broten, Johnson) 2:13
7. Swe, Naslund (Eldebrink, Nilsson) 7:34 PP
Penalties: Langway, USA 7:01; Presley, USA 12:45.

Shots on Goal
USA   6   17   7   — 30
Sweden   7   8   13   — 28

Goalies: Vanbiesbrouck, USA; Lindmark, Sweden
Outstanding Players: Vanbiesbrouck, USA; Naslund, Sweden
Attendance: 4,474

Halifax, Sept. 2: USSR 7, Finland 4

First Period
1. USSR, Kamensky (Khomutov, Kravchuk) 2:02 PP
2. USSR, Lomakin (Semenov) 2:51
3. Fin, Numminen (Kurri, Ruuttu) 3:59
4. USSR, Makarov (Krutov, Bykov) 5:02
5. Fin, Summanen (Helminen) 13:14
6. Fin, Seppo (Ojanen, Kyllonen) 14:05
Penalties: Jutila, Fin 1:03; Siren, Fin 8:02; Stelnov, USSR 15:22.

Second Period
7. USSR, Lomakin (Svetlov, Pervukhin) 2:03
8. USSR, Makarov (Stelnov, Larionov) 3:45
9. USSR, Makarov (Larionov, Khmylev) 19:24
Penalties: Ruuttu, Fin, Kasatonov, USSR (double minors) 3:18;
Semak, USSR 16:35.

Third Period
10. USSR, Kamensky (Kravchuk, Bykov) 2:28
11. Fin, Makela (Helminen, Summanen) 15:47
Penalties: None.

Shots on Goal
USSR   15   16   6   − 37
Finland   7   9   6   − 22

Goalies: Mylnikov, USSR; Takko, Finland
Outstanding Players: Makarov, USSR; Summanen, Finland
Attendance: 3,262

Hamilton, Sept. 2: Canada 3, USA 2

First Period
1. USA, LaFontaine 10:40
Penalties: Carpenter, USA :43; Langway, USA, Tocchet,
Can 11:26; Otto, USA 17:21.

Second Period
2. Can, M. Lemieux (Hartsburg) 5:23
3. Can, M. Lemieux (Gretzky) 19:57 PP
Penalties: Presley, USA, Hartsburg, Can 7:30; Suter, USA 9:56;
Tocchet, Can, 12:55; M. Lemieux, Can, Fraser, USA, Nilan,
USA (misconduct) 16:29; USA bench minor (served by
Olczyk) 18:48.

Third Period
4. Can, M. Lemieux (Gretzky, Messier) 5:51
5. USA, Millen (Suter, Chelios) 6:47
Penalties: Langway, USA, Hartsburg, Can 1:49; Murphy, Can
11:30; Brooke, USA 17:44.

Shots on Goal
Canada   11   16   13   − 40
USA   13   10   7   − 30

Goalies: Vanbiesbrouck, USA; Fuhr, Canada
Outstanding Players: M. Lemieux, Canada; Otto, USA
Attendance: 17,026

Regina, Sept. 2: Sweden 4, Czechoslovakia 0

First Period
1. Swe, Bergqvist (Sodergren) 14:30
Penalties: Liba, Czech, Rundqvist, Swe :58; Bergqvist, Swe
10:55; Rundqvist, Swe 15:51; Dolezal, Czech, Sundstrom,
Swe 17:17.

Second Period
2. Swe, Eldebrink (M. Andersson) 13:11
Penalties: P. Andersson, Swe 2:33; Benak, Czech 11:00; Eklund,
Swe 16:23; Eldebrink, Swe 17:30; Rosol, Czech 18:17.

Third Period
3. Swe, Pettersson (Eklund, Thelven) 9:05
4. Swe, Eklund (Samuelsson, M. Andersson) 17:40 PP
Penalties: Sejba, Czech 6:57; Lubina, Czech 15:43; Rundqvist,
Swe 18:51; Samuelsson, Swe, Volek, Czech 19:49.

Shots on Goal

Sweden   9   8   9   − 26
Czech   12   13   3   − 28

Goalies: Lindmark, Sweden; Hasek, Czechoslovakia
Outstanding Players: Lindmark, Sweden; Vlach, Czechoslovakia
Attendance: 5,126

Hartford, Sept. 4: USSR 5, USA 1

First Period
1. USSR, Kamensky (Bykov) 4:30 PP
2. USSR, Makarov (Kasatonov, Krutov) 16:16 PP
Penalties: Hatcher, USA 4:14; Suter USA (major) 16:00

Second Period
3. USA, Mullen (Chelios) 10:22
4. USSR, Svetlov (Lomakin) 18:30
Penalties: Fetisov, USSR, Nilan, USA 19:04.

Third Period
5. USSR, Krutov (Kasatonov, Makarov) SH
6. USSR, Semenov (Svetlov) 19:07
Penalties: Pervukhin USSR 8:36; Kamensky USSR 13:27

Shots on Goal

USSR   12   7   8   − 27
USA   6   6   8   − 20

Goalies: Mylnikov, USSR; Barrasso, USA
Outstanding Players: Svetlov, USSR; Mullen, USA
Attendance: 14,838

Sept. 4, Sydney: Czechoslovakia 5, Finland 2

First Period
1. Czech, Pasek (Cajka, Liba) 4:55
2. Czech, Sebja (Pasek, Horava) 9:40 PP
Penalties: Tikkanen, Fin 6:15; Ruotsalainen, Fin, Jutila, Fin,
Dolezal, Czech 8:45; Benak, Czech 15:09

Second Period
3. Czech, Benak (Lubina, Bozik) 2:22
4. Czech, Ruzicka (6:57)
Penalties: Horava, Czech 18:52.

Third Period
5. Czech, Vlk (Cajka) 7:29
6. Fin, Hagman (Kyllonen, Tikkanen) 13:54
7. Fin, Kurri (Skriko) 16:58
Penalties: Liba, Czech 10:45; Ruuttu, Fin, Pasek, Czech 16:39.

Shots on Goal
Czech   13   14   8   − 35
Finland   5   11   6   − 22

Goalies: Hasek, Czechoslovakia; Takko, Myllys, Finland
Outstanding Players: Pasek, Czechoslovakia; Jutila, Finland
Attendance: 3,000

Sept. 4, Montreal: Canada 5, Sweden 3

First Period
1. Can, Gretzky (Bourque, Coffey) 1:55 PP
2. Swe, Gustafsson (Roupe) 10:01

3. Swe, Pettersson (Albelin, Andersson) 11:26
4. Can, M. Lemieux (Gretzky, Coffey) 17:10 PP
Penalties: Jonsson, Swe 1:17; Roupe, Swe, Gartner, Can 12:30;
Elderbrink, Swe 16:41.

Second Period
5. Can, Gartner 18:23
Penalties: C. Lemieux, Can 2:50; Rochefort, Can 6:51;
Thelven, Swe 7:00; Anderson, Can 7:48; Gretzky, Can 13:19.

Third Period
6. Swe, M. Andersson (Eklund) 2:12
7. Can, M. Lemieux (Gretzky) 5:40
8. Can, Goulet (Gretzky, Patrick) 11:20
Penalties: Patrick, Can 4:07; Thelven, Swe 4:52.

Shots on Goal
Canada   11   7   14   — 32
Sweden   5   10   7   — 22

Goalies: Fuhr, Canada; Lindmark, Sweden
Outstanding Players: Gretzky, Canada; Lindmark, Sweden
Attendance: 12,360

Sept. 6, Sydney: Sweden 3, Finland 1

First Period
1. Swe, Jonsson (M. Andersson, Thelven) 10:38 PP
Penalties: Samuelsson, Swe 2:45; Ruuttu, Fin 6:48; Numminen,
Fin 10:21; Thelven, Swe 13:19.

Second Period
2. Swe, Albelin (Nilsson, Rundqvist) 18:04
Penalties: Tikkanen, Fin, Rundqvist, Swe 10:50.

Third Period
3. Swe, Roupe 8:53
4. Fin, Ruuttu 10:17
Penalties: Thelven, Swe 13:40.

Shots on Goal
Sweden   10   8   3   – 21
Finland   6   8   9   – 23

Goalies: Lindmark, Sweden; Takko, Finland
Outstanding Players: Nilsson, Sweden; Takko, Finland
Attendance: 4,500

Sept. 6, Sydney: Czechoslovakia 3, USA 1

First Period
1. Czech, Ruzicka (Rosol) 13:38
Penalties: Ramsey, USA :53; Presley, USA 4:10; Kucera, Czech
6:30.

Second Period
2. USA, Nilan 2:29
3. Czech, Pasek (Benak, Bozik) 14:12
Penalties: Stavjana, Czech 6:08; Vlk, Czech 8:15; Suter, USA
13:05; Otto, USA 18:23.

Third Period
4. Czech, Hrdina (Cajka) 16:04 SH
Penalties: Benak, Czech 2:55; Olczyk, USA 7:28; Scerban,
Czech 14:12; Lubina, Czech 18:23.

Shots on Goal
Czech   8   9   8   – 25
USA   5   14   18   – 37
Goalies: Hasek, Czechoslovakia;Vanbiesbrouck, USA
Outstanding Players: Hasek, Czechoslovakia; Housley, USA
Attendance: 4,500

Sept. 6, Hamilton: Canada 3, USSR 3

First Period
1. Can, Anderson (M. Lemieux) 5:37
Penalties: Sutter, Can, Kamensky, USSR 11:52; Lomakin
USSR 12:44.

Second Period
2. USSR, Svetlov (Semenov, Lomakin) 1:32
3. USSR, Krutov (Makarov, Stelnov) 3:27
4. USSR, Svetlov (Fetisov, Semenov) 8:15 SH
5. Can, Bourque (Gretzky, Messier) 11:16 PP
Penalties: Makarov, USSR 6:45; Pervukhin, USSR 10:51; C.
Lemieux, Can, Lomakin, USSR 19:50.

Third Period
6. Can, Gretzky (Anderson, Messier) 17:33
Penalties: Lomakin, USSR 11:15; USSR bench (served by
Kamensky) 13:40

Shots on Goal
Canada   7   13   10   – 30
USSR   16   9   11   – 36

Goalies: Fuhr, Canada; Belosheikin, USSR
Outstanding Players: Messier, Canada; Svetlov, USSR
Attendance: 17,056

SEMIFINAL ROUND

Sept. 8, Hamilton: USSR 4, Sweden 2

First Period
1. USSR, Krutov (Makarov, Kasatonov) 1:09 PP
Penalties: Gustaffson, Swe :39; Sodergren, Swe 5:22; Priakhin,
USSR 11:57; Makarov, USSR 15:52; Larionov, USSR 19:01.

Second Period
2. USSR, Bykov (Krutov) 7:29
3. USSR, Larionov (Makarov, Fetisov) 8:37 PP
4. Swe, Bergqvist (Sodergren, P. Andersson) 14:39
Penalties: Naslund, Swe 8:25; Fetisov, USSR 11:34; Rundqvist,
Swe 17:26.

Third Period
5. USSR, Makarov (Fetisov, Krutov) 7:42
6. Swe, P. Andersson (M. Andersson, Rundqvist) 13:47 PP
Penalties: Albelin, Swe, Semak, USSR 2:42; Gusarov, USSR
13:28.

Shots on Goal

USSR	7	7	10	− 24
Sweden	14	6	6	− 26

Goalies: Mylnikov, USSR; Lindmark, Sweden
Outstanding Players: Krutov, USSR; P. Andersson, Sweden
Attendance: 7,051

Sept. 9, Montreal: Canada 5, Czechoslovakia 3

First Period
1. Czech, Pasek (Liba, Sejba) 8:06
2. Czech, Benak (Liba, Sejba) 13:41
Penalties: Jasko, Czech 4:26; Gartner, Can 9:25; Messier, Can 16:26.

Second Period
3. Can, Hawerchuk (Murphy, Goulet) 10:43
4. Can, M. Lemieux (Goulet) 11:25
5. Can, M. Lemieux (Bourque, Gretzky) 13:08 PP
Penalties: Anderson, Can 5:11; Bozik, Czech, Propp, Can 7:49; Lubina, Czech 12:34.

Third Period
6. Can, Goulet (Gretzky, Sutter) 8:16
7. Czech, Volek (Hrdina, Benak) 15:26
8. Can, Propp (M. Lemieux, Sutter) 17:56
Penalties: None.

Shots on Goal

Canada	13	11	13	− 37
Czech	9	5	10	− 24

Goalies: Fuhr, Canada; Hasek, Czechoslovakia
Outstanding Players: M. Lemieux, Canada; Liba, Czechoslovakia
Attendance: 10,262

FINAL ROUND

Sept. 11, Montreal: USSR 6, Canada 5

First Period
1. Can, Gartner (M. Lemieux, Rochefort) 1:49
2. USSR, Kasatonov (Fetisov, Semenov) 9:34 PP
3. USSR, Krutov (Fetisov, Makarov) 13:53 PP
4. USSR, Makarov (Krutov) 17:44 SH
Penalties: Gusarov, USSR 3:19; Sutter, Can 9:07; Hartsburg, Can 13:06; Lomakin, USSR 17:09.

Second Period
5. USSR, Kamensky (Khomutov, Gusarov) 2:10
6. Can, Bourque (Gretzky, M. Lemieux) 19:18 PP
Penalties: Murphy, Can 2:27; Makarov, USSR 3:10; Priakhin USSR 3:27; Tocchet, Can 6:39; Fedotov, USSR 14:23; Krutov, USSR 15:24; Bourque, Can 15:34; Fedotov, USSR 18:06.

Third Period
7. Can, Gilmour (Gartner, Hartsburg) 1:35
8. Can, Anderson (Messier, Murphy) 14:39
9. Can, Gretzky (Bourque) 17:01
10. USSR, Khomutov (Bykov) 17:33
Penalties: Messier, Can 4:23; USSR bench (served by Kamensky) 8:37.

Overtime
11. USSR, Semak (Semonov, Lomakin) 5:33.
Penalties: None.

Shots on Goal

Canada	11	9	13	0	− 33
USSR	12	10	16	5	− 43

Goalies: Fuhr, Canada; Mylnikov, USSR
Outstanding Players: Gartner, Canada; Krutov, USSR
Attendance: 14,558

Sept. 13, Hamilton: Canada 6, USSR 5

First Period
1. Can, Rochefort (Messier, Hawerchuk) :43
2. USSR, Khomutov (Bykov) 1:27
3. Can, Gilmour (Rochefort, Gretzky) 3:48
4. Can, Coffey (Gretzky, Gartner) 12:41
Penalties: Gilmour, Can 1:42; Semenov, USSR 4:54; M.
Lemieux, Can, Nemchinov, USSR 8:49; Messier, Can 9:50;
Crossman, Can, Nemchinov, USSR 11:21; Gartner, Can 19:29.

Second Period
5. USSR, Fetisov (Krutov, Kasatonov) 12:11 PP
6. USSR, Krutov (Makarov) 14:17 SH
7. Can, M. Lemieux (Gretzky) 16:32
Penalties: Stelnov, USSR 7:04; Crossman, Can 11:26;
Nemchinov, USSR 14:04.

Third Period
8. USSR, Bykov (Khomutov, Kamensky) 4:45
9. Can, M. Lemieux (Gretzky, Coffey) 14:17 PP
10. USSR, Kamensky (Bykov, Pervukhin) 18:56
Penalties: Gusarov, USSR 9:52.

First Overtime
Penalties: None.

Second Overtime
11. Can, M. Lemieux (Gretzky, Murphy) 10:07
Penalties: None.

Shots on Goal

Canada	17	13	9	9	13	− 61
USSR	13	9	9	12	7	− 50

Goalies: Fuhr, Canada; Belosheikin, USSR
Outstanding Players: Gretzky, Canada; Krutov, USSR
Attendance: 17,026

Sept. 15, Hamilton: Canada 6, USSR 5

First Period
1. USSR, Makarov (Krutov) :26
2. USSR, Gusarov 7:04
3. USSR, Fetisov (Makarov) 8:00
4. Can, Tocchet (Goulet, Murphy) 9:50
5. Can, Propp (Tocchet, Sutter) 15:23
6. USSR, Khomutov 19:32
Penalties: Bykov, USSR 4:59; Igor Kravchuk, USSR 9:10;
Sutter, Can 10:16; Makarov, USSR 17:11.

Second Period
7. Can, Murphy (Gretzky, M. Lemieux) 9:20 PP
8. Can, Sutter (Hawerchuk, Crossman) 11:06
9. Can, Hawerchuk (Murphy, Propp) 15:32
Penalties: Bykov, USSR 8:24; M. Lemieux, Can 11:34;
Larionov, USSR 12:37; Bourque, Can, 16:05; Bourque,
Can 18:51.

Third Period
10. USSR, Semak (Lomakin) 12:21
11. Can, M. Lemieux (Gretzky) 18:34
Penalties: None.

Shots on Goal

Canada	19	12	15	− 46
USSR	9	8	6	− 23

Goalies: Fuhr, Canada; Mylnikov, USSR

Outstanding Players: Hawerchuk, Canada; Fetisov, USSR

Attendance: 17,026

Tournament Statistics

Categories reading across are: games, goals, assists, points, penalty minutes, plus-minus.

CANADA

Wayne Gretzky	9	3	18	21	2	minus 2
Mario Lemieux	9	11	7	18	8	plus 5
Ray Bourque	9	2	6	8	10	plus 3
Larry Murphy	8	1	6	7	4	plus 8
Mark Messier	9	1	6	7	6	plus 2
Dale Hawerchuk	9	4	2	6	0	plus 4
Paul Coffey	9	2	4	6	0	plus 1
Rick Tocchet	7	3	2	5	8	0
Michel Goulet	8	2	3	5	0	minus 1
Mike Gartner	9	2	2	4	0	plus 1
Brian Propp	9	2	2	4	0	plus 4

Brent Sutter	9	1	3	4	6	minus 2
Glenn Anderson	7	2	1	3	0	minus 1
Kevin Dineen	3	1	2	3	0	plus 3
Normand Rochefort	9	1	2	3	8	plus 3
Doug Gilmour	8	2	0	2	4	plus 1
Claude Lemieux	6	1	1	2	2	0
Craig Hartsburg	9	0	2	2	6	0
James Patrick	6	0	1	1	2	plus 1
Doug Crossman	8	0	1	1	4	minus 4

Goalies (categories across are: games, minutes played, wins, losses, ties, GAA and save percentage)

Grant Fuhr	9	575	6	1	2	3.34	.893

USSR

Sergei Makarov	9	7	8	15	8	plus 1
Vladimir Krutov	9	7	7	14	4	minus 4
Vyacheslav Bykov	9	2	7	9	4	plus 2
Valeri Kamensky	9	6	1	7	2	plus 2
Andrei Khomutov	9	4	3	7	0	plus 1
Viacheslav Fetisov	9	2	5	7	9	minus 6
Anatoli Semenov	9	2	5	7	2	plus 7
Andrei Lomakin	9	2	4	6	10	plus 4
Sergei Svetlov	6	3	2	5	0	plus 6
Igor Stelnov	9	1	4	5	6	plus 1
Alexei Kasatonov	9	1	4	5	4	minus 5
Igor Kravchuk	5	0	4	4	2	plus 5
Alexander Semak	7	3	0	3	10	plus 2
Igor Larionov	9	1	2	3	6	minus 3
Vasily Pervukhin	8	0	2	2	4	plus 5
Sergei Priakhin	9	0	2	2	6	plus 1

Yuri Khmylev	9	0	1	1	2	0
Anatoli Fedotov	8	0	1	1	4	plus 5
Sergei Nemchinov	5	0	0	0	6	minus 2

Goalies

Sergei Mylnikov	6	210	5	1	0	2.96	.894
Evgeny Belosheikin	3	210	0	2	1	4.00	.880

CZECHOSLOVAKIA

Dusan Pasek	6	4	15	12	0	
Jaroslav Benak	6	2	2	4	6	minus 1
David Volek	6	2	2	4	2	plus 1
Igor Liba	6	0	4	4	6	minus 1
Jiri Sejba	5	1	2	3	2	plus 1
Miloslav Horava	6	1	2	3	4	plus 3
Jiri Hrdina	6	1	2	3	0	0
Ludek Cajka	3	0	3	3	0	plus 5
Petr Vlk	5	2	0	2	2	minus 4
Vladimir Ruzicka	6	2	0	2	0	minus 2
Drahomir Kadlec	3	0	1	1	12	plus 1
Mojmir Bozik	6	0	1	1	4	minus 2
Antonin Stavjana	6	0	1	1	2	minus 8
Ladislav Lubina	6	0	1	1	6	minus 1
Rostislav Vlach	6	0	1	1	0	minus 3
Jiri Dolezal	6	0	1	1	4	minus 1
Jan Jasko	2	0	0	0	4	minus 1
Jiri Kucera	6	0	0	0	2	minus 4
Bedrich Scerban	6	0	0	0	2	minus 9
Petr Rosol	6	0	0	0	4	minus 3

Goalies

Dominik Hasek	6	360	2	3	1	3.33	.894

SWEDEN

Mikael Andersson	5	1	5	6	0	plus 4
Anders Eldebrink	6	1	3	4	4	plus 4
Kent Nilsson	6	0	4	4	0	plus 3
Bengt-Ake Gustafsson	6	3	0	3	4	minus 1
Tommy Albelin	6	2	1	3	2	plus 3
Mats Naslund	6	1	2	3	2	minus 1
Thomas Eklund	6	1	2	3	6	plus 1
Michael Thelven	6	0	3	3	10	plus 2
Lars Gunnar Petersson	5	0	2	2	0	plus 1
Jonas Bergqvist	6	0	2	2	4	minus 4
Lars Karlsson	4	1	1	2	0	minus 4
Magnus Roupe	5	1	1	2	4	minus 1
Peter Andersson	5	1	1	2	2	plus 1
Tomas Jonsson	6	1	1	2	2	minus 4
Tomas Rundqvist	6	0	2	2	10	plus 3
Hakan Sodergren	6	0	2	2	2	minus 2
Peter Sundstrom	6	1	0	1	2	plus 2
Anders Carlsson	6	1	0	1	0	minus 3
Tommy Samuelsson	3	0	1	1	4	0
Peter Eriksson	3	0	0	0	0	0

Goalies

Peter Lindmark	6	360	3	3	0	3.00	.882

USA

Joe Mullen	5	3	0	3	0	plus 1
Pat LaFontaine	5	3	0	3	0	plus 2
Bobby Carpenter	5	1	2	3	4	plus 4
Gary Suter	5	0	3	3	9	plus 3
Chris Nilan	5	0	2	2	14	plus 1

Eddie Olczyk	5	1	1	2	2	plus 2
Aaron Broten	5	0	2	2	2	plus 2
Chris Chelios	5	0	2	2	2	plus 3
Joel Otto	5	0	2	2	4	plus 3
Phil Housley	5	0	2	2	4	plus 3
Corey Millen	1	1	0	1	0	plus 1
Bob Brooke	5	1	0	1	4	plus 2
Wayne Presley	5	1	0	1	12	plus 1
Rod Langway	5	0	1	1	6	plus 1
Curt Fraser	5	0	1	1	4	plus 2
Mark Johnson	5	0	1	1	0	0
Kevin Hatcher	5	0	0	0	4	plus 1
Kelly Miller	5	0	0	0	0	0

Goalies

John Vanbiesbrouck	4	240	2	2	0	2.25	.922
Tom Barrasso	1	60	0	1	0	5.00	.815

FINLAND

Christian Ruuttu	5	2	1	3	10	minus 1
Raimo Helminen	5	0	3	3	0	minus 6
Jari Kurri	5	1	1	2	4	minus 4
Raimo Summanen	5	1	1	2	0	minus 6
Mikko Makela	5	1	1	2	12	minus 6
Markkus Kyllonen	5	0	2	2	0	minus 1
Teppo Numminen	4	1	0	1	2	minus 1
Jukka Seppo	4	1	0	1	0	minus 1
Matti Hagman	5	1	0	1	0	minus 4
Timo Jutila	5	1	0	1	6	minus 6
Petri Skriko	5	0	1	1	2	minus 3
Janne Ojanen	5	0	1	1	0	0
Hannu Virta	5	0	1	1	0	minus 4

Esa Tikkanen	5	0	1	1	6	minus 3
Iiro Jarvi	4	0	0	0	2	minus 1
Ville Siren	5	0	0	0	6	minus 1
Jari Gronstrand	4	0	0	0	0	minus 6
Jouka Narvanmaa	1	0	0	0	0	minus 1
Timo Blomqvist	4	0	0	0	0	minus 5
Reijo Ruotsalanein	4	0	0	0	2	minus 2

Goalies

Kari Takko	5	280	0	5	0	4.71	.877
Jarmo Myllys	1	20	0	0	0	3.00	.875

Tournament MVP: Wayne Gretzky, Canada

ALL-STAR TEAM

Goaltender:	Grant Fuhr, Canada
Defence:	Ray Bourque, Canada;
	Viacheslav Fetisov, USSR
Forwards:	Wayne Gretzky, Canada;
	Mario Lemieux, Canada;
	Vladimir Krutov, USSR

INDEX

Tikhonov, Viktor, 39, 40, 41, 43–44,
47, 56, 58, 61, 62, 207, 208; and
Canada Cup (1987), 72, 103, 106,
113, 141, 148–49, 159–60, 168,
170, 172; and players, 42, 48, 50,
51–53, 57, 142, 196–98, 200, 206
Tikkanen, Esa, 207
Tocchet, Rick, 3, 11, 15, 20, 22,
23–24, 31, 33–34, 68, 69, 164;
Game 1, 87-88, 96, 104, 109;
Game 3, 147–48, 150, 151,
153–54, 155–56, 157, 167
Tonelli, John, 13, 14, 33
Tremblay, Vincent, 124
Tretiak, Alexander, 52
Tretiak, Vladislav, 55, 60, 142
Trottier, Bryan, 13, 14
Tuele, Bill, 35, 146
Turner, John, 196

Ungerman, Howard, 79
Ungerman, Irving, 190
USA team, 63, 67, 71

Van Dorp, Wayne, 182
Van Hellemond, Andy, 110
Vanbiesbrouck, John, 67
Vancouver Canucks, 201, 202
Vernon, Mike, 15
Volek, David, 83

Warner, Dan, 187
Watt, Tom, 17, 29, 101, 159, 161
Watters, Bill, 77–78
WHA, 80
Wilson, Doug, 12, 13
Wilson, Murray, 85
Winnipeg Jets, 160, 161
Winter, Rich, 74, 82–83, 84, 187,
191, 193, 195
Wirtz, Bill, 84, 192

Yakushev, Alexander, 55, 207
Yzerman, Steve, 16, 28, 29

Zezel, Peter, 20
Zhluktov, Viktor, 47
Ziegler, John, 85, 193